COREY • BECHKO • ARAGON • SEGALA

THE EXPANSE ™

Published by

BOOM!
STUDIOS

SERIES DESIGNER
SCOTT NEWMAN

COLLECTION DESIGNER
CHELSEA ROBERTS

EDITOR
JONATHAN MANNING

SENIOR EDITOR
ERIC HARBURN

ONLY ON

THE EXPANSE, August 2021. Published by BOOM! Studios, a division of Boom Entertainment, Inc., 5670 Wilshire Boulevard, Suite 400, Los Angeles, CA 90036-5679. The Expanse is ™ & © Expanding Universe Productions, LLC. All rights reserved. Originally published in single magazine form as THE EXPANSE No. 1-4. ™ & © 2020 Expanding Universe Productions, LLC. All rights reserved. BOOM! Studios™ and the BOOM! Studios logo are trademarks of Boom Entertainment, Inc., registered in various countries and categories. All characters, events, and institutions depicted herein are fictional. Any similarity between any of the names, characters, persons, events, and/or institutions in this publication to actual names, characters, and persons, whether living or dead, events, and/or institutions is unintended and purely coincidental. BOOM! Studios does not read or accept unsolicited submissions of ideas, stories, or artwork.

BOOM! Studios, 5670 Wilshire Boulevard, Suite 400, Los Angeles, CA, 90036-5679. Printed in China. First Printing.

ISBN: 978-1-68415-691-7, eISBN: 978-1-64668-235-5

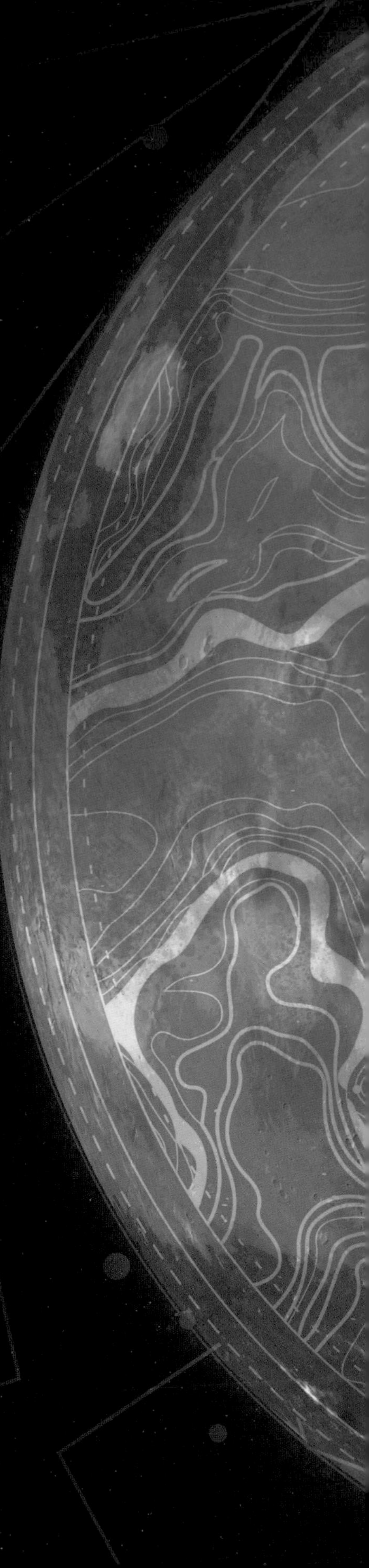

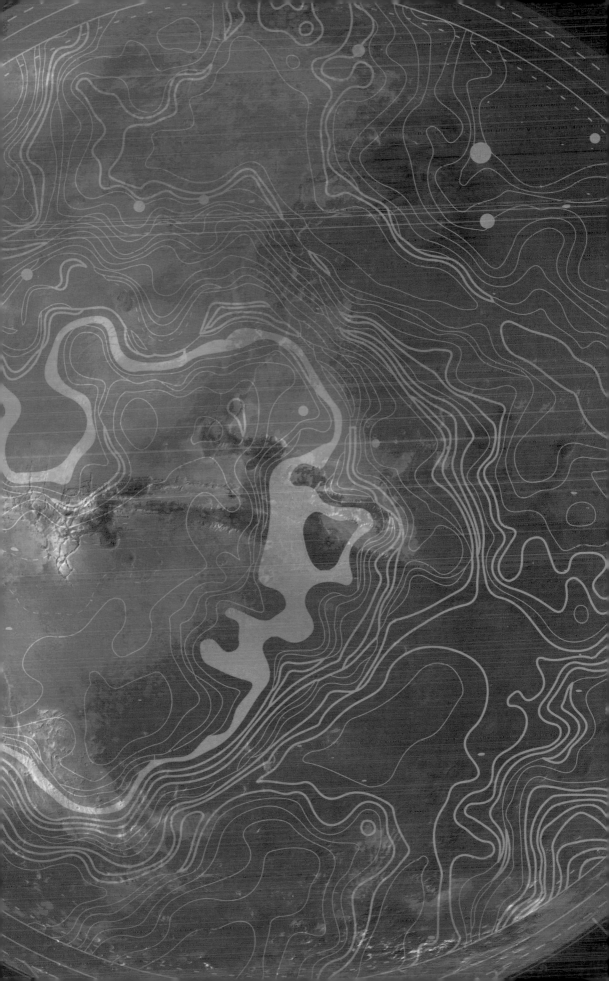

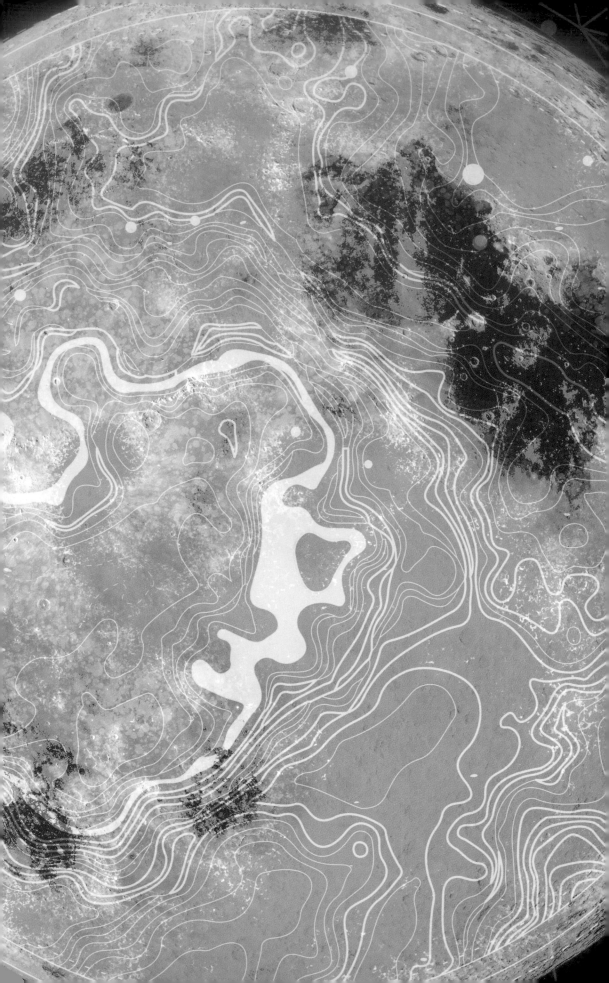

THE EXPANSE

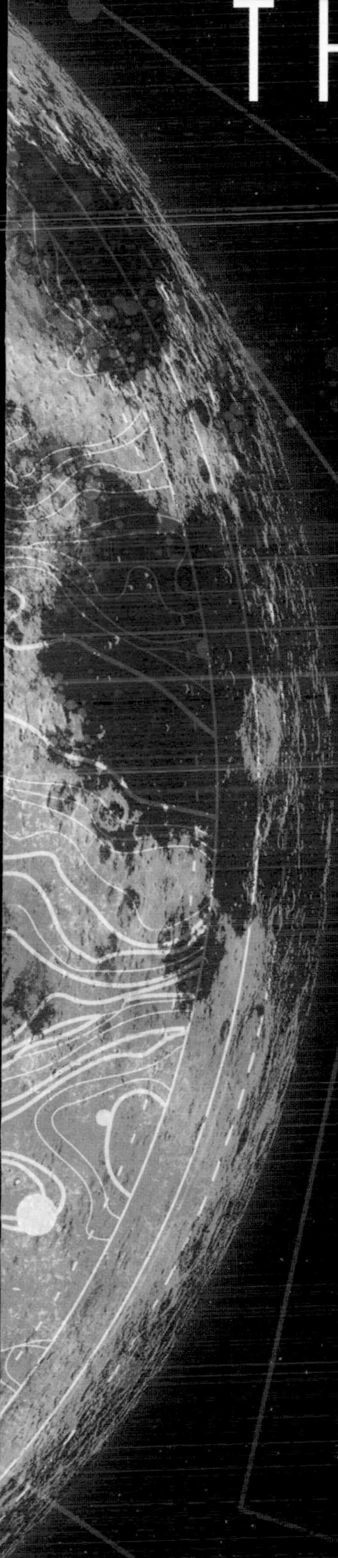

BASED ON THE BOOKS BY
JAMES S.A. COREY

WRITTEN BY
CORINNA BECHKO

ILLUSTRATED BY
ALEJANDRO ARAGON

COLORED BY
FRANCESCO SEGALA

LETTERED BY
ED DUKESHIRE

COVER BY
W. SCOTT FORBES

DEVELOPED BY
NAREN SHANKAR, DANIEL ABRAHAM, TY FRANCK

SPECIAL THANKS
ANDREW KOSOVE, BRODERICK JOHNSON, BEN ROBERTS, BEN COOK

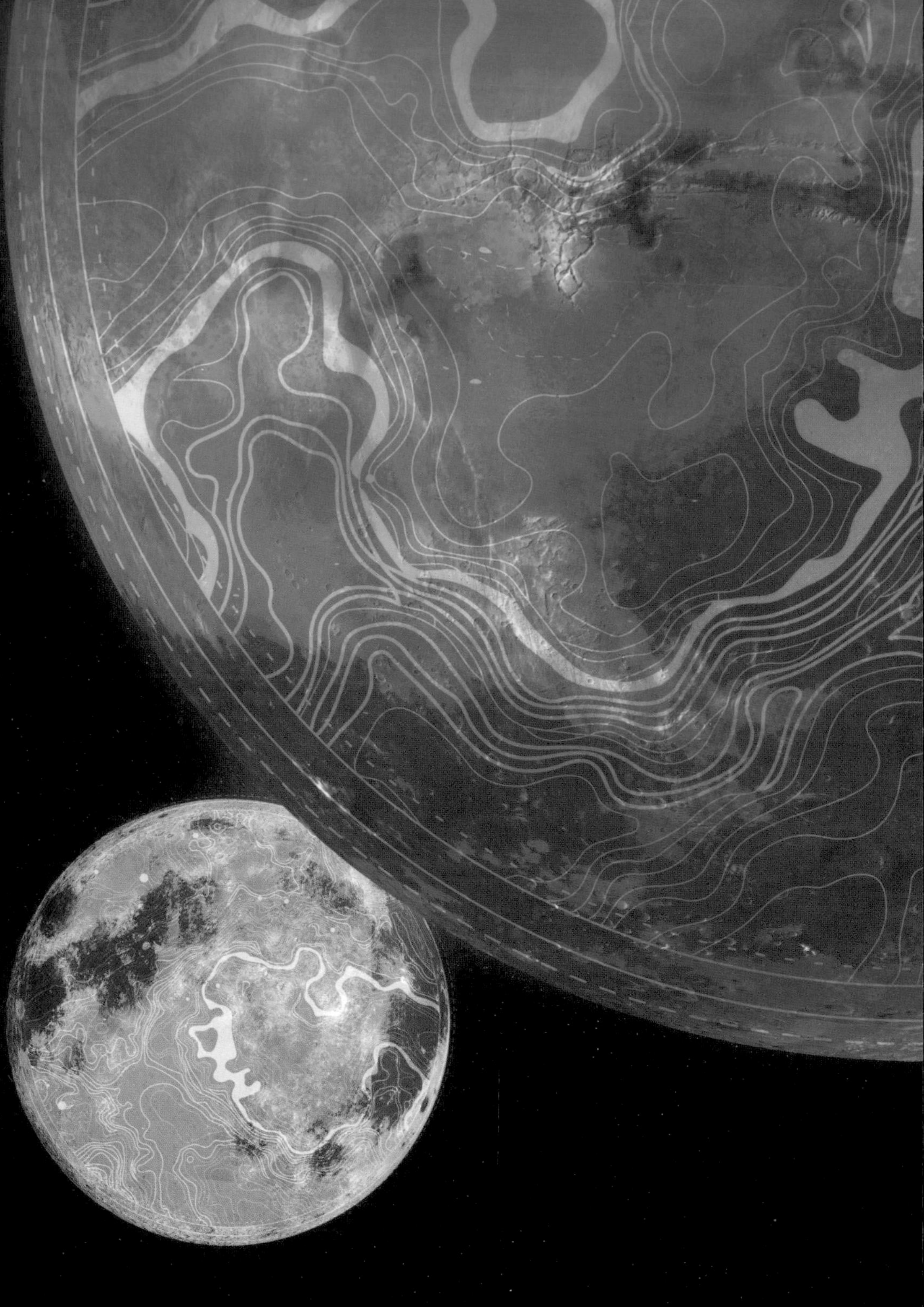

CHAPTER ONE

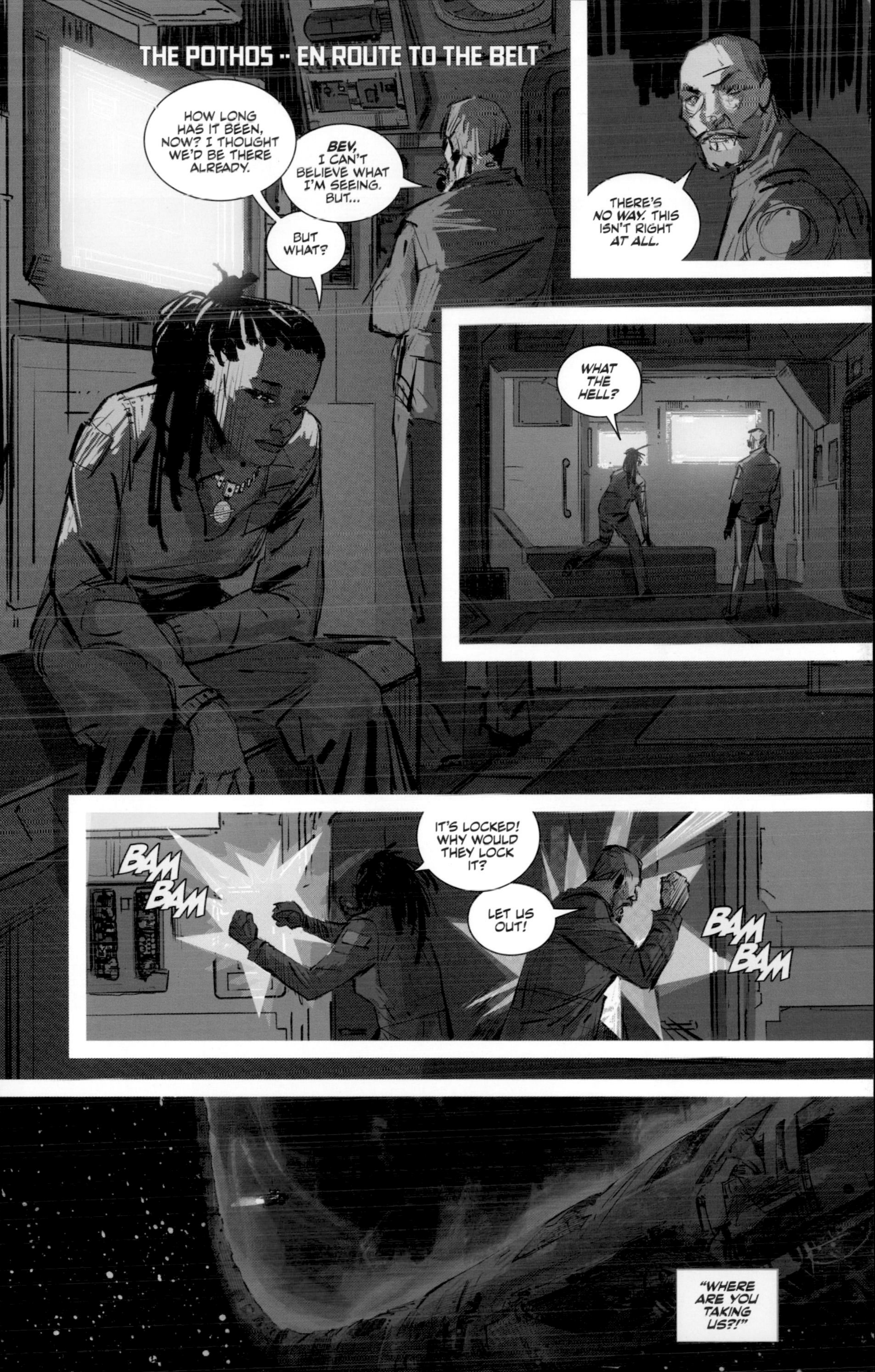
THE POTHOS -- EN ROUTE TO THE BELT
HOW LONG HAS IT BEEN, NOW? I THOUGHT WE'D BE THERE ALREADY.
BEV, I CAN'T BELIEVE WHAT I'M SEEING. BUT...
BUT WHAT?
THERE'S NO WAY. THIS ISN'T RIGHT AT ALL.
WHAT THE HELL?
BAM BAM
IT'S LOCKED! WHY WOULD THEY LOCK IT?
LET US OUT!
BAM BAM
"WHERE ARE YOU TAKING US?!"

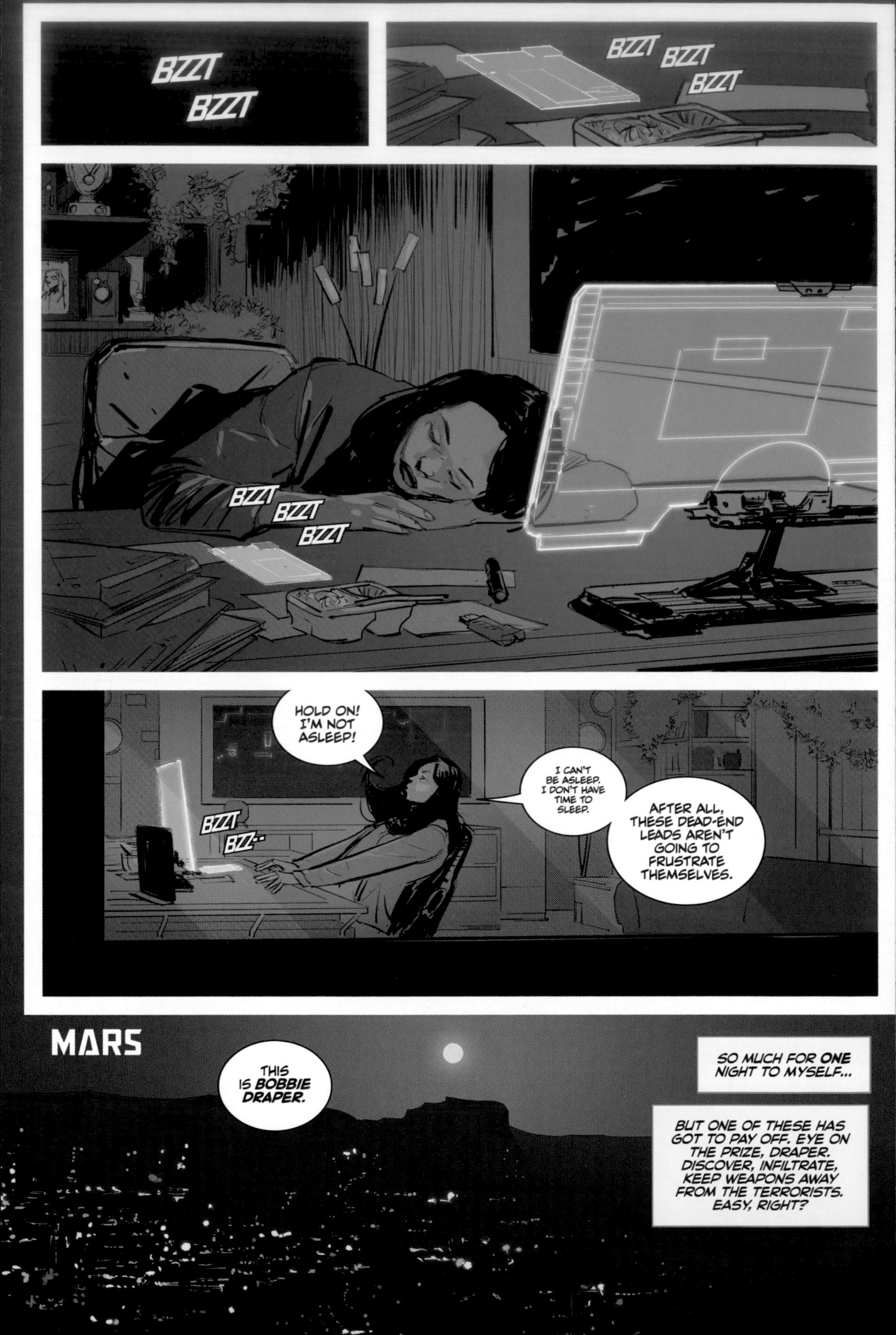
BZZT
BZZT
BZZT
BZZT
BZZT
BZZT
BZZT
BZZT
HOLD ON! I'M NOT ASLEEP!
BZZT
BZZ--
I CAN'T BE ASLEEP. I DON'T HAVE TIME TO SLEEP.
AFTER ALL, THESE DEAD-END LEADS AREN'T GOING TO FRUSTRATE THEMSELVES.
MARS
THIS IS BOBBIE DRAPER.
SO MUCH FOR ONE NIGHT TO MYSELF...
BUT ONE OF THESE HAS GOT TO PAY OFF. EYE ON THE PRIZE, DRAPER. DISCOVER, INFILTRATE, KEEP WEAPONS AWAY FROM THE TERRORISTS. EASY, RIGHT?

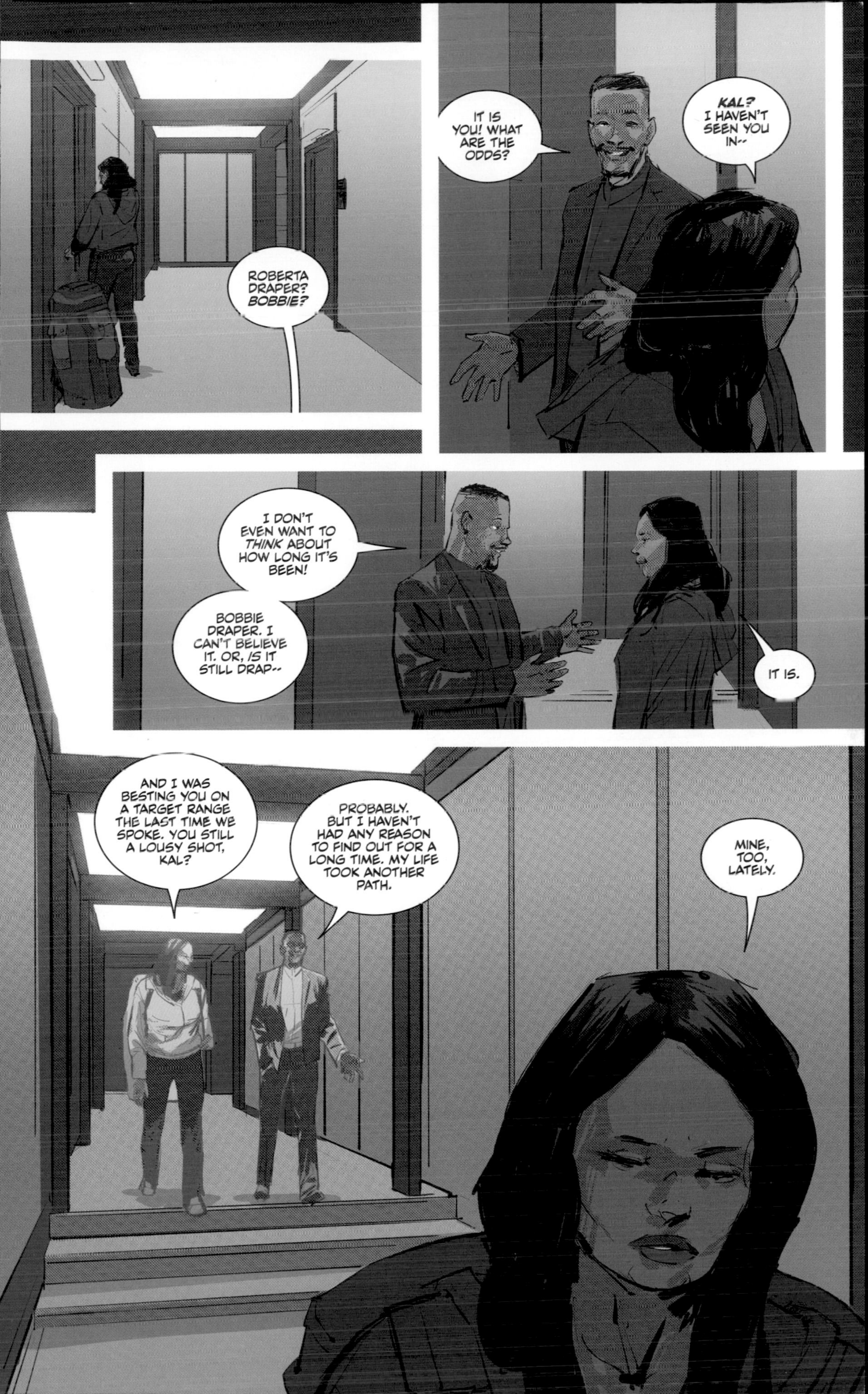
ROBERTA DRAPER? BOBBIE?
IT IS YOU! WHAT ARE THE ODDS?
KAL? I HAVEN'T SEEN YOU IN--
I DON'T EVEN WANT TO THINK ABOUT HOW LONG IT'S BEEN!
BOBBIE DRAPER. I CAN'T BELIEVE IT. OR, IS IT STILL DRAP--
IT IS.
AND I WAS BESTING YOU ON A TARGET RANGE THE LAST TIME WE SPOKE. YOU STILL A LOUSY SHOT, KAL?
PROBABLY. BUT I HAVEN'T HAD ANY REASON TO FIND OUT FOR A LONG TIME. MY LIFE TOOK ANOTHER PATH.
MINE, TOO, LATELY.

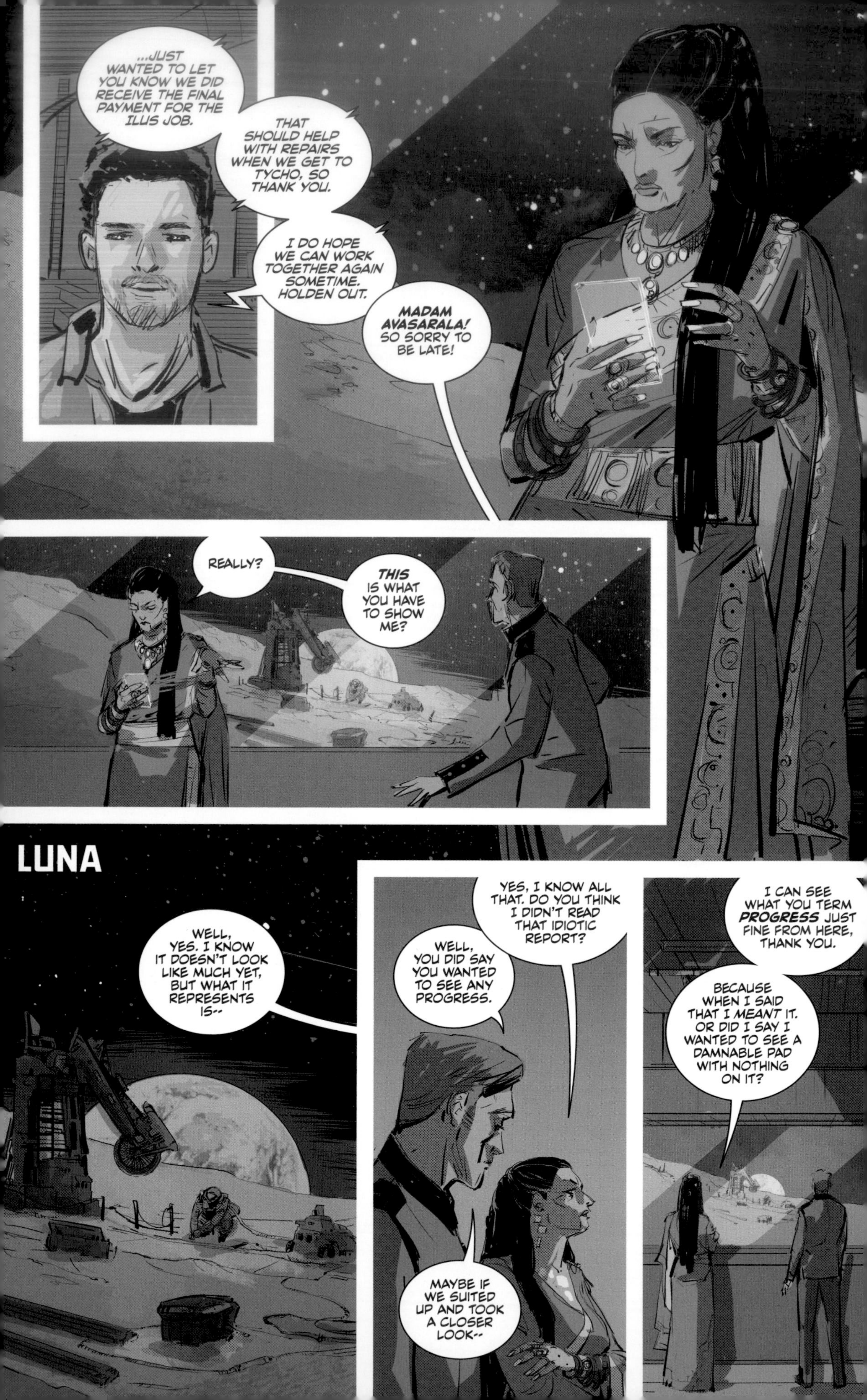
...JUST WANTED TO LET YOU KNOW WE DID RECEIVE THE FINAL PAYMENT FOR THE ILUS JOB.
THAT SHOULD HELP WITH REPAIRS WHEN WE GET TO TYCHO, SO THANK YOU.
I DO HOPE WE CAN WORK TOGETHER AGAIN SOMETIME. HOLDEN OUT.
MADAM AVASARALA! SO SORRY TO BE LATE!
REALLY?
THIS IS WHAT YOU HAVE TO SHOW ME?
LUNA
WELL, YES. I KNOW IT DOESN'T LOOK LIKE MUCH YET, BUT WHAT IT REPRESENTS IS--
YES, I KNOW ALL THAT. DO YOU THINK I DIDN'T READ THAT IDIOTIC REPORT?
WELL, YOU DID SAY YOU WANTED TO SEE ANY PROGRESS.
MAYBE IF WE SUITED UP AND TOOK A CLOSER LOOK--
I CAN SEE WHAT YOU TERM PROGRESS JUST FINE FROM HERE, THANK YOU.
BECAUSE WHEN I SAID THAT I MEANT IT. OR DID I SAY I WANTED TO SEE A DAMNABLE PAD WITH NOTHING ON IT?

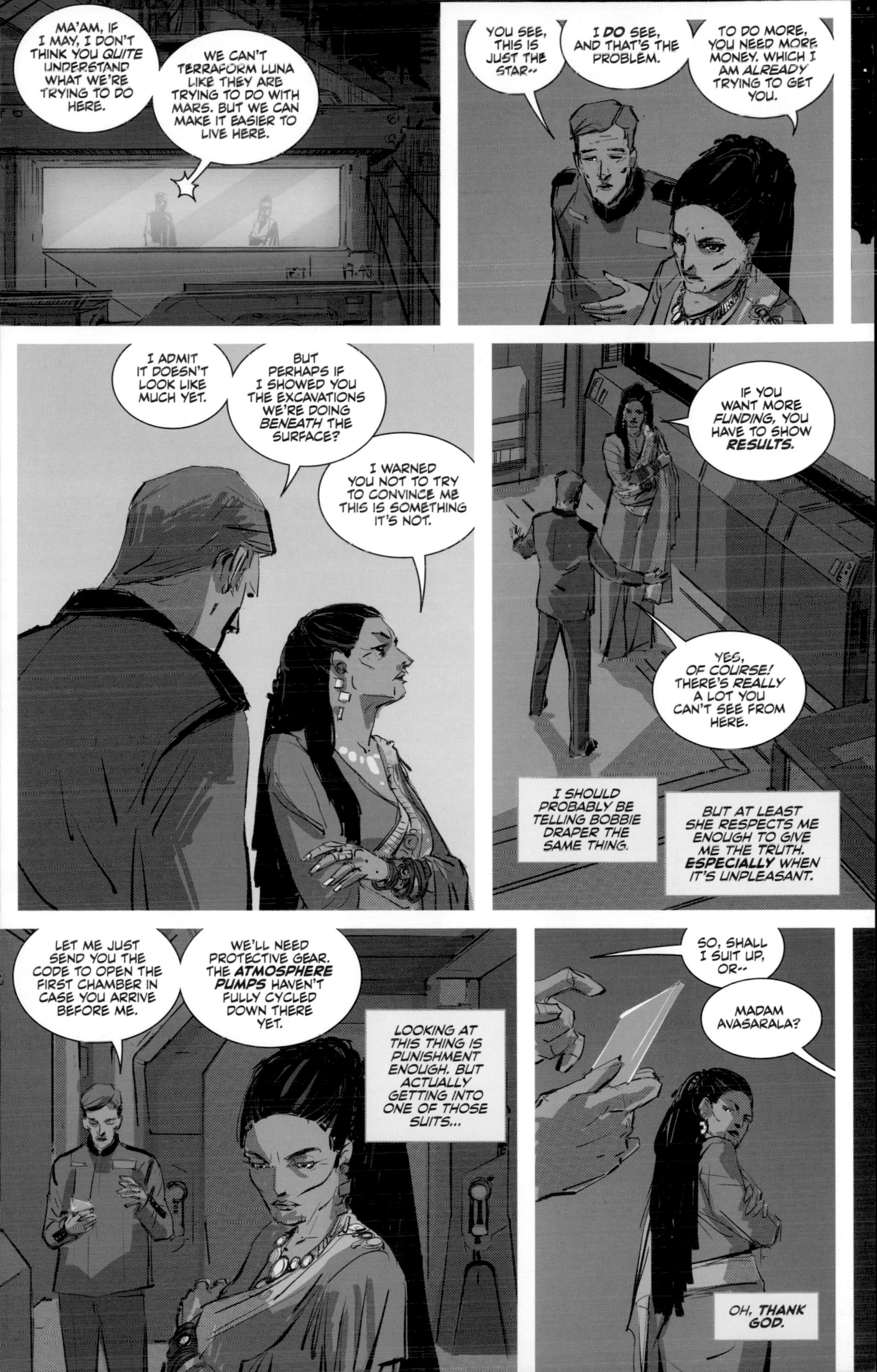
MA'AM, IF I MAY, I DON'T THINK YOU *QUITE* UNDERSTAND WHAT WE'RE TRYING TO DO HERE.
WE CAN'T TERRAFORM LUNA LIKE THEY ARE TRYING TO DO WITH MARS. BUT WE CAN MAKE IT EASIER TO LIVE HERE.
YOU SEE, THIS IS JUST THE STAR--
I *DO* SEE, AND THAT'S THE PROBLEM.
TO DO MORE, YOU NEED MORE MONEY. WHICH I AM *ALREADY* TRYING TO GET YOU.
I ADMIT IT DOESN'T LOOK LIKE MUCH YET.
BUT PERHAPS IF I SHOWED YOU THE EXCAVATIONS WE'RE DOING *BENEATH* THE SURFACE?
I WARNED YOU NOT TO TRY TO CONVINCE ME THIS IS SOMETHING IT'S NOT.
IF YOU WANT MORE *FUNDING*, YOU HAVE TO SHOW ***RESULTS.***
YES, OF COURSE! THERE'S *REALLY* A LOT YOU CAN'T SEE FROM HERE.
I SHOULD PROBABLY BE TELLING BOBBIE DRAPER THE SAME THING.
BUT AT LEAST SHE RESPECTS ME ENOUGH TO GIVE ME THE TRUTH. ***ESPECIALLY*** *WHEN IT'S UNPLEASANT.*
LET ME JUST SEND YOU THE CODE TO OPEN THE FIRST CHAMBER IN CASE YOU ARRIVE BEFORE ME.
WE'LL NEED PROTECTIVE GEAR. THE ***ATMOSPHERE PUMPS*** HAVEN'T FULLY CYCLED DOWN THERE YET.
LOOKING AT THIS THING IS PUNISHMENT ENOUGH. BUT ACTUALLY GETTING INTO ONE OF THOSE SUITS...
SO, SHALL I SUIT UP, OR--
MADAM AVASARALA?
OH, ***THANK GOD.***

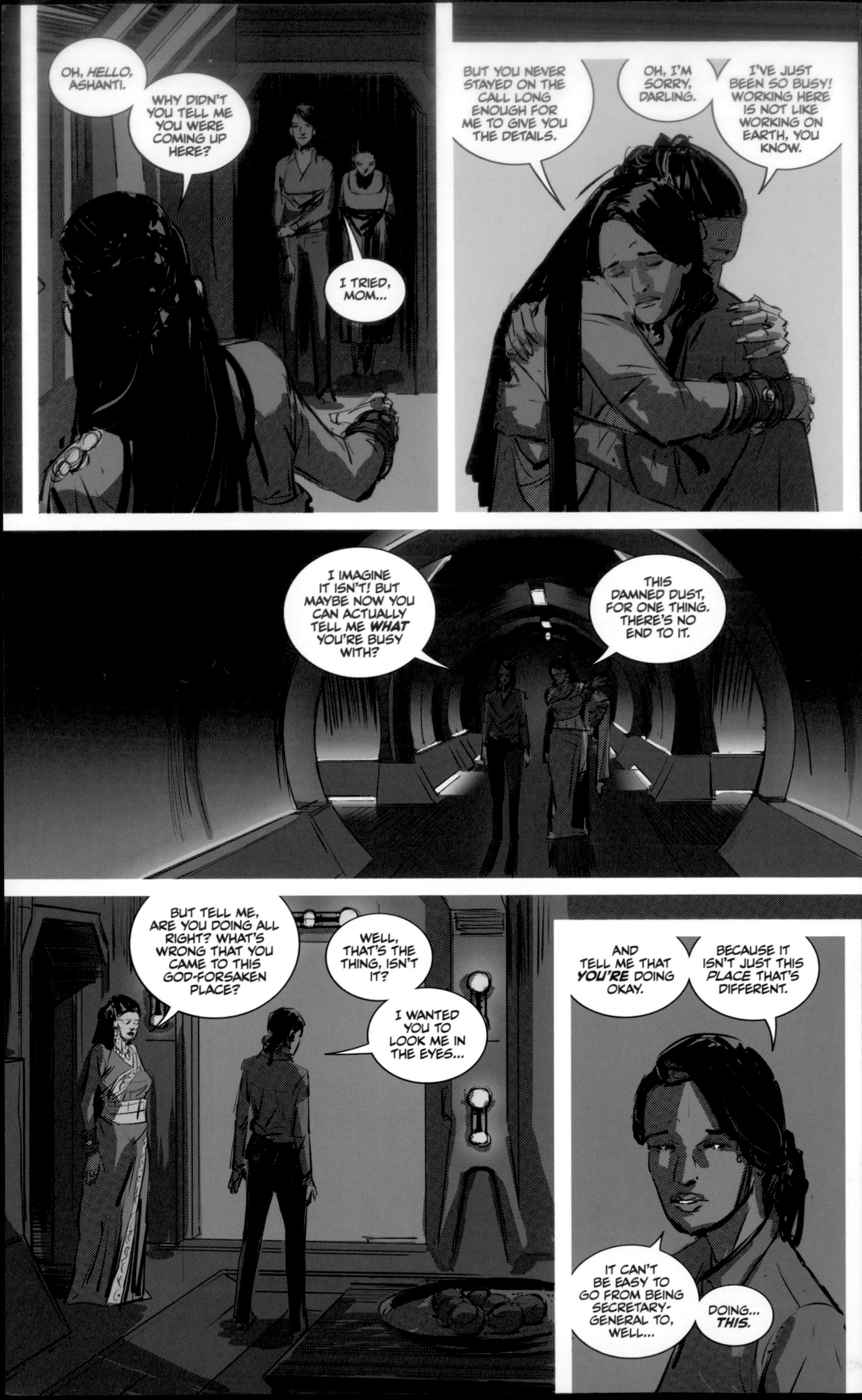
OH, *HELLO*, ASHANTI.
WHY DIDN'T YOU TELL ME YOU WERE COMING UP HERE?
I TRIED, MOM...
BUT YOU NEVER STAYED ON THE CALL LONG ENOUGH FOR ME TO GIVE YOU THE DETAILS.
OH, I'M SORRY, DARLING.
I'VE JUST BEEN SO BUSY! WORKING HERE IS NOT LIKE WORKING ON EARTH, YOU KNOW.
I IMAGINE IT ISN'T! BUT MAYBE NOW YOU CAN ACTUALLY TELL ME ***WHAT*** YOU'RE BUSY WITH?
THIS DAMNED DUST, FOR ONE THING. THERE'S NO END TO IT.
BUT TELL ME, ARE YOU DOING ALL RIGHT? WHAT'S WRONG THAT YOU CAME TO THIS GOD-FORSAKEN PLACE?
WELL, THAT'S THE THING, ISN'T IT?
I WANTED YOU TO LOOK ME IN THE EYES...
AND TELL ME THAT ***YOU'RE*** DOING OKAY.
BECAUSE IT ISN'T JUST THIS *PLACE* THAT'S DIFFERENT.
IT CAN'T BE EASY TO GO FROM BEING SECRETARY-GENERAL TO, WELL...
DOING... ***THIS.***

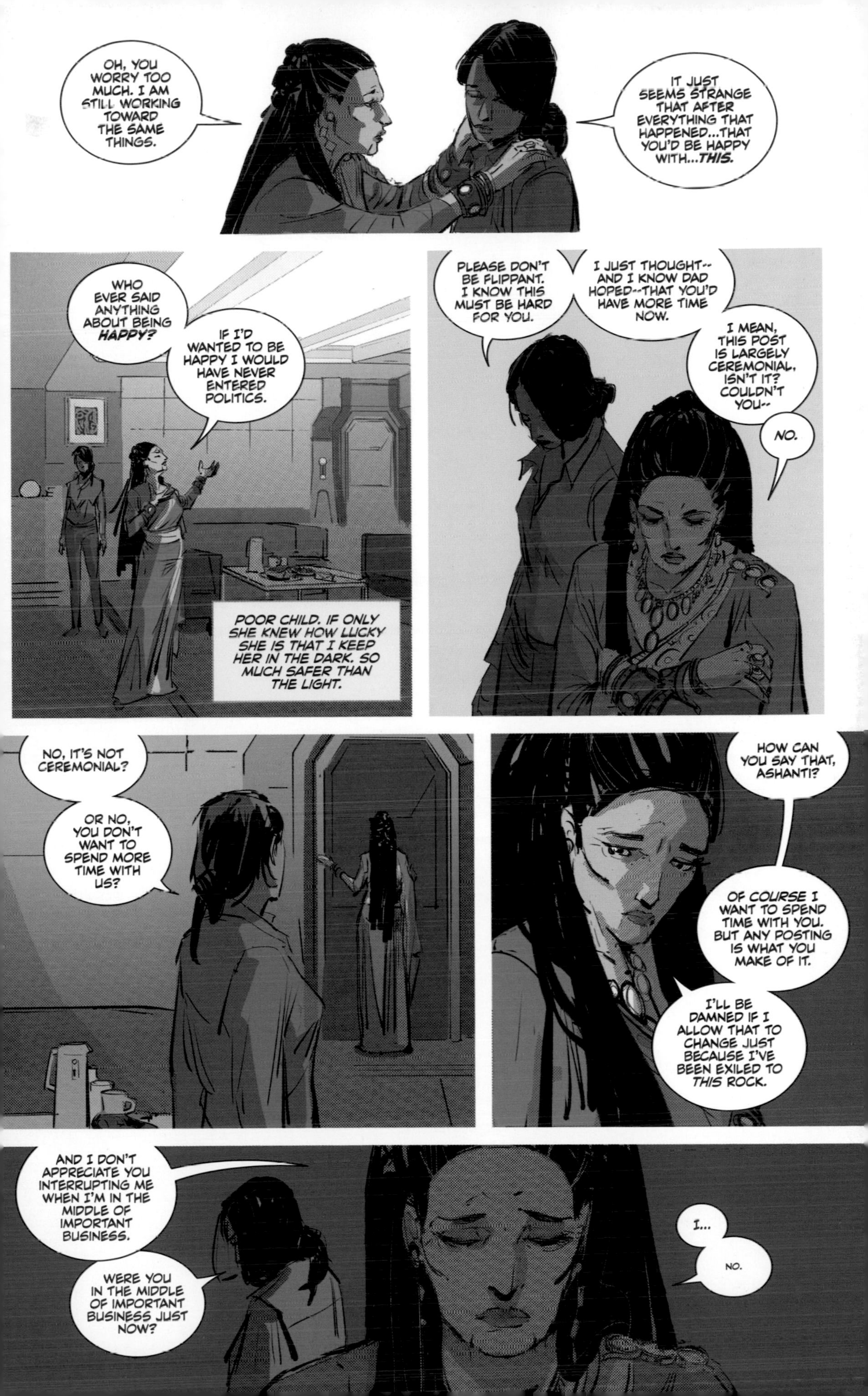
OH, YOU WORRY TOO MUCH. I AM STILL WORKING TOWARD THE SAME THINGS.
IT JUST SEEMS STRANGE THAT AFTER EVERYTHING THAT HAPPENED...THAT YOU'D BE HAPPY WITH...*THIS.*
WHO EVER SAID ANYTHING ABOUT BEING *HAPPY?*
IF I'D WANTED TO BE HAPPY I WOULD HAVE NEVER ENTERED POLITICS.
POOR CHILD. IF ONLY SHE KNEW HOW LUCKY SHE IS THAT I KEEP HER IN THE DARK. SO MUCH SAFER THAN THE LIGHT.
PLEASE DON'T BE FLIPPANT. I KNOW THIS MUST BE HARD FOR YOU.
I JUST THOUGHT--AND I KNOW DAD HOPED--THAT YOU'D HAVE MORE TIME NOW.
I MEAN, THIS POST IS LARGELY CEREMONIAL, ISN'T IT? COULDN'T YOU--
NO.
NO, IT'S NOT CEREMONIAL?
OR NO, YOU DON'T WANT TO SPEND MORE TIME WITH US?
HOW CAN YOU SAY THAT, ASHANTI?
OF *COURSE* I WANT TO SPEND TIME WITH YOU. BUT ANY POSTING IS WHAT YOU MAKE OF IT.
I'LL BE DAMNED IF I ALLOW THAT TO CHANGE JUST BECAUSE I'VE BEEN EXILED TO *THIS* ROCK.
AND I DON'T APPRECIATE YOU INTERRUPTING ME WHEN I'M IN THE MIDDLE OF IMPORTANT BUSINESS.
WERE YOU IN THE MIDDLE OF IMPORTANT BUSINESS JUST NOW?
I...
NO.

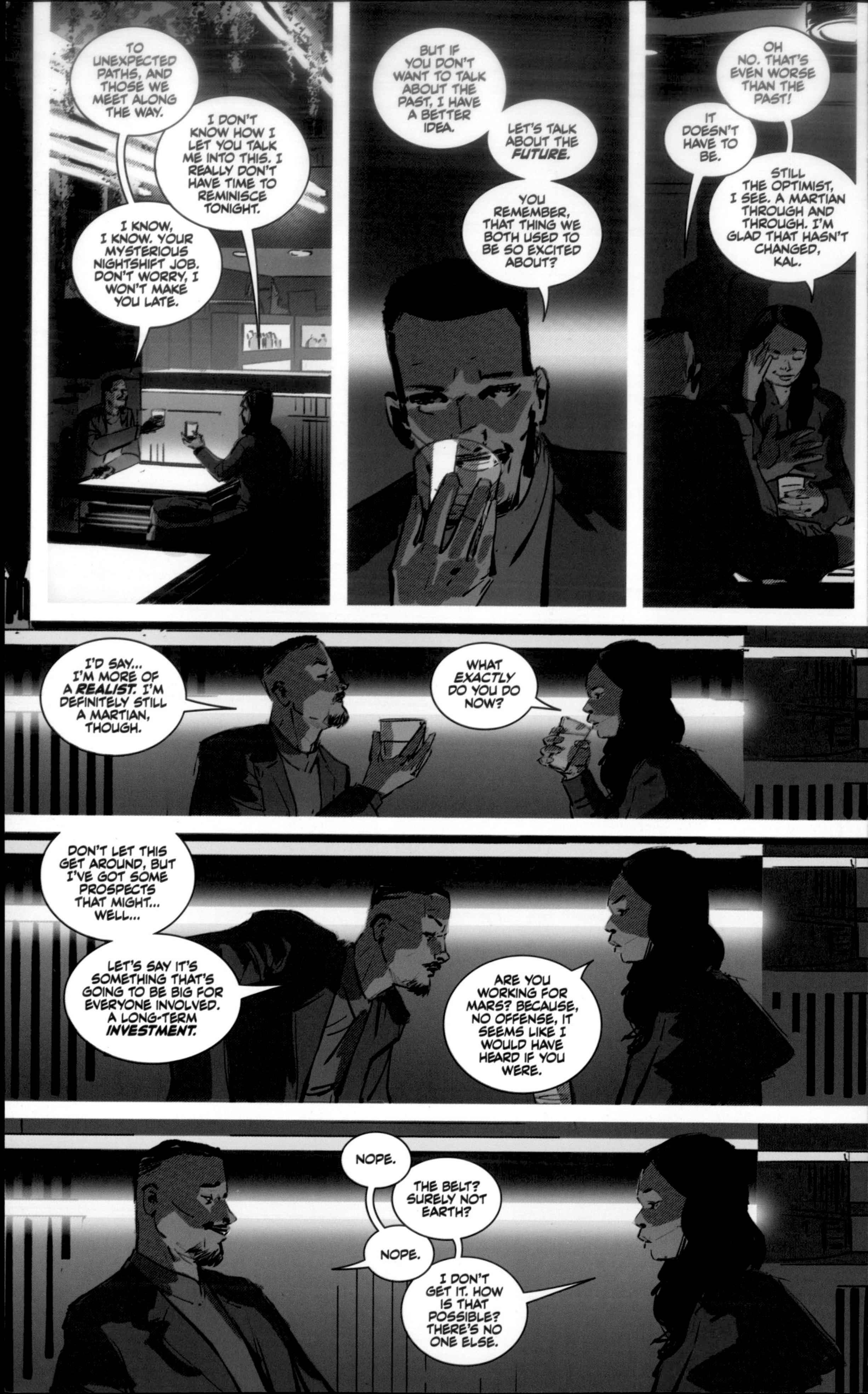
TO UNEXPECTED PATHS, AND THOSE WE MEET ALONG THE WAY.
I DON'T KNOW HOW I LET YOU TALK ME INTO THIS. I REALLY DON'T HAVE TIME TO REMINISCE TONIGHT.
I KNOW, I KNOW. YOUR MYSTERIOUS NIGHTSHIFT JOB. DON'T WORRY, I WON'T MAKE YOU LATE.
BUT IF YOU DON'T WANT TO TALK ABOUT THE PAST, I HAVE A BETTER IDEA.
LET'S TALK ABOUT THE *FUTURE.*
YOU REMEMBER, THAT THING WE BOTH USED TO BE SO EXCITED ABOUT?
OH NO. THAT'S EVEN WORSE THAN THE PAST!
IT DOESN'T HAVE TO BE.
STILL THE OPTIMIST, I SEE. A MARTIAN THROUGH AND THROUGH. I'M GLAD THAT HASN'T CHANGED, KAL.
I'D SAY... I'M MORE OF A **REALIST.** I'M DEFINITELY STILL A MARTIAN, THOUGH.
WHAT *EXACTLY* DO YOU DO NOW?
DON'T LET THIS GET AROUND, BUT I'VE GOT SOME PROSPECTS THAT MIGHT... WELL...
LET'S SAY IT'S SOMETHING THAT'S GOING TO BE BIG FOR EVERYONE INVOLVED. A LONG-TERM ***INVESTMENT.***
ARE YOU WORKING FOR MARS? BECAUSE, NO OFFENSE, IT SEEMS LIKE I WOULD HAVE HEARD IF YOU WERE.
NOPE.
THE BELT? SURELY NOT EARTH?
NOPE.
I DON'T GET IT. HOW IS THAT POSSIBLE? THERE'S NO ONE ELSE.

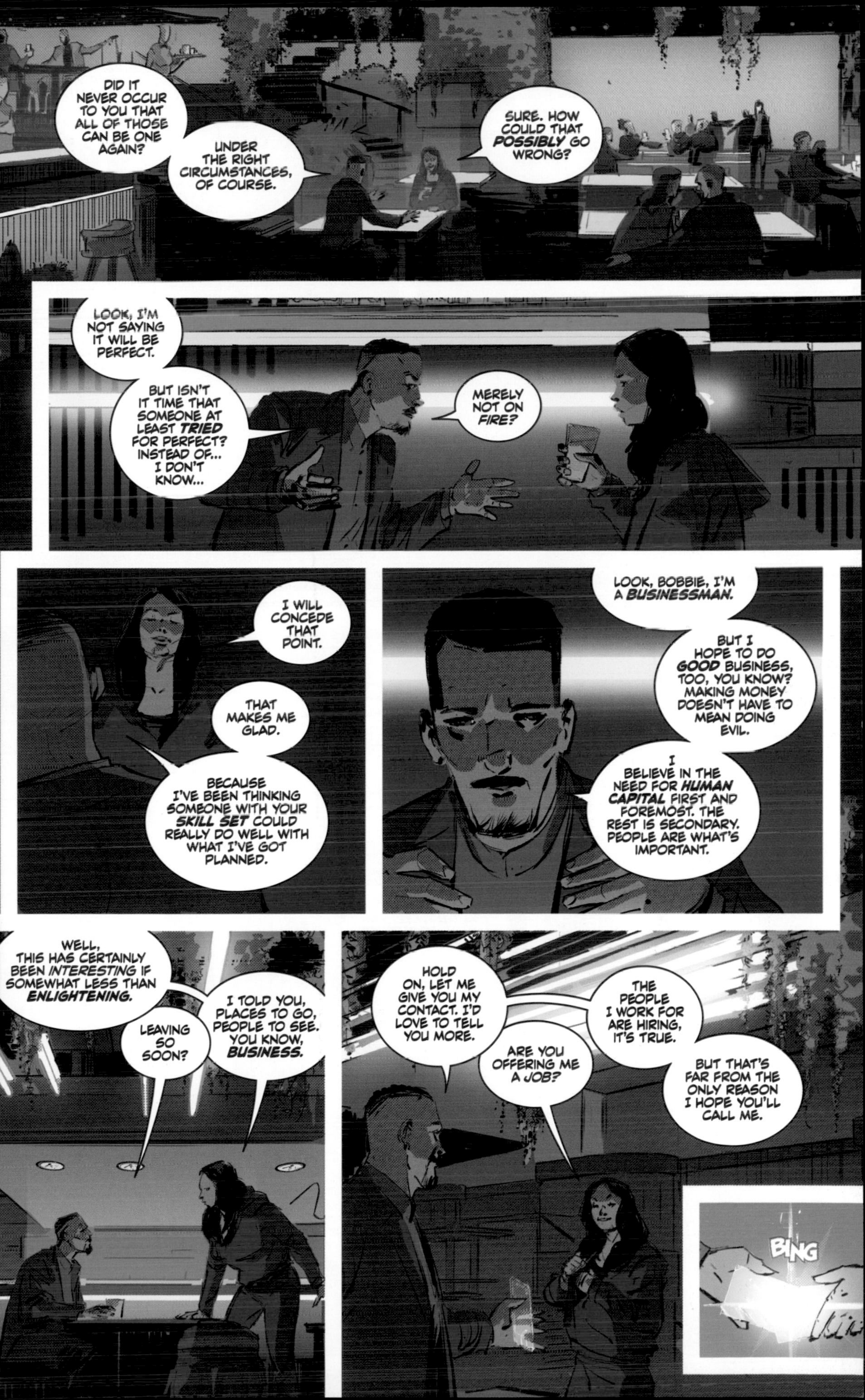
DID IT NEVER OCCUR TO YOU THAT ALL OF THOSE CAN BE ONE AGAIN?
UNDER THE RIGHT CIRCUMSTANCES, OF COURSE.
SURE. HOW COULD THAT POSSIBLY GO WRONG?
LOOK, I'M NOT SAYING IT WILL BE PERFECT.
BUT ISN'T IT TIME THAT SOMEONE AT LEAST TRIED FOR PERFECT? INSTEAD OF... I DON'T KNOW...
MERELY NOT ON FIRE?
I WILL CONCEDE THAT POINT.
THAT MAKES ME GLAD.
BECAUSE I'VE BEEN THINKING SOMEONE WITH YOUR SKILL SET COULD REALLY DO WELL WITH WHAT I'VE GOT PLANNED.
LOOK, BOBBIE, I'M A BUSINESSMAN.
BUT I HOPE TO DO GOOD BUSINESS, TOO, YOU KNOW? MAKING MONEY DOESN'T HAVE TO MEAN DOING EVIL.
I BELIEVE IN THE NEED FOR HUMAN CAPITAL FIRST AND FOREMOST. THE REST IS SECONDARY. PEOPLE ARE WHAT'S IMPORTANT.
WELL, THIS HAS CERTAINLY BEEN INTERESTING IF SOMEWHAT LESS THAN ENLIGHTENING.
LEAVING SO SOON?
I TOLD YOU, PLACES TO GO, PEOPLE TO SEE. YOU KNOW, BUSINESS.
HOLD ON, LET ME GIVE YOU MY CONTACT. I'D LOVE TO TELL YOU MORE.
ARE YOU OFFERING ME A JOB?
THE PEOPLE I WORK FOR ARE HIRING, IT'S TRUE.
BUT THAT'S FAR FROM THE ONLY REASON I HOPE YOU'LL CALL ME.
BING

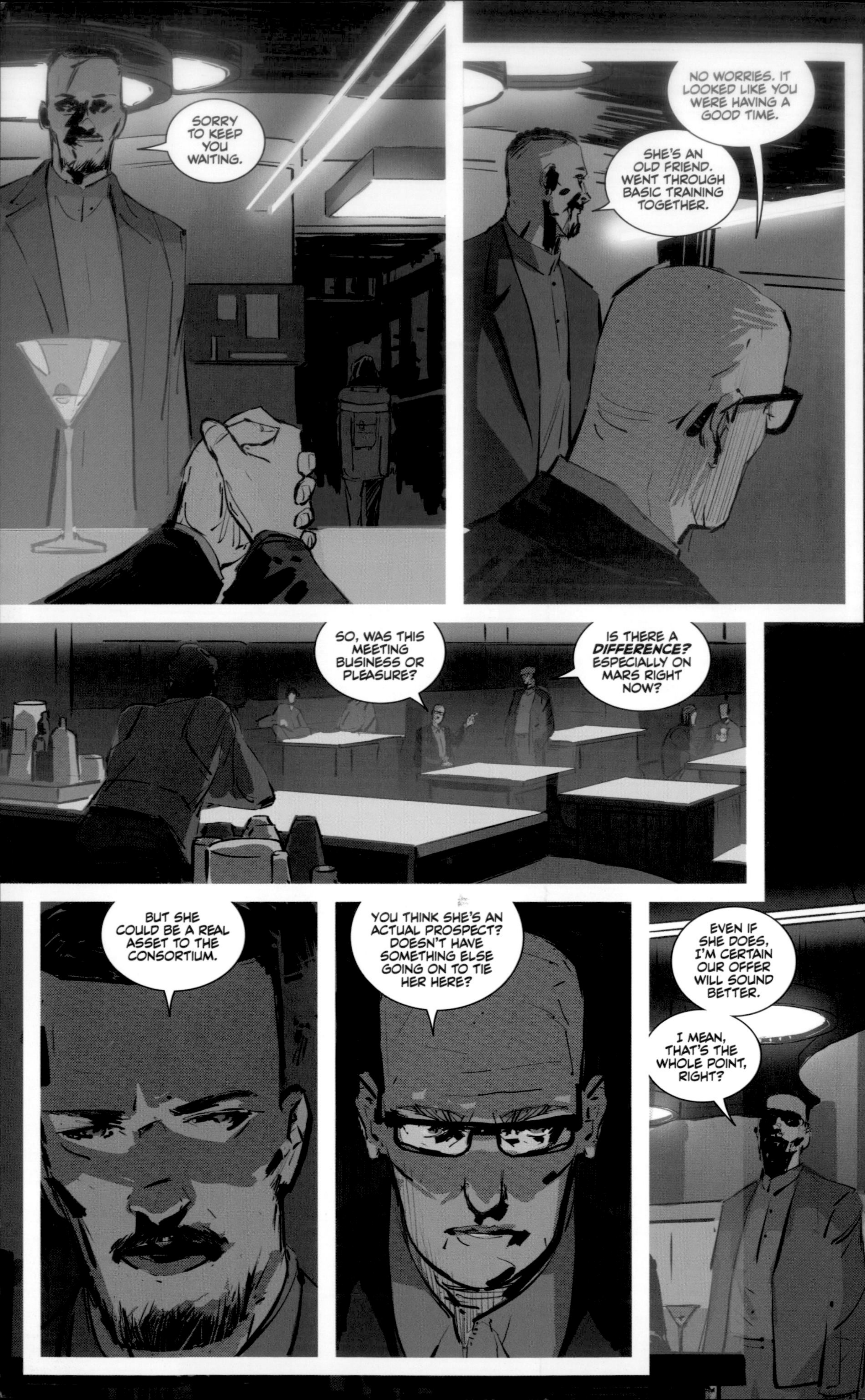
SORRY TO KEEP YOU WAITING.
NO WORRIES. IT LOOKED LIKE YOU WERE HAVING A GOOD TIME.
SHE'S AN OLD FRIEND. WENT THROUGH BASIC TRAINING TOGETHER.
SO, WAS THIS MEETING BUSINESS OR PLEASURE?
IS THERE A *DIFFERENCE?* ESPECIALLY ON MARS RIGHT NOW?
BUT SHE COULD BE A REAL ASSET TO THE CONSORTIUM.
YOU THINK SHE'S AN ACTUAL PROSPECT? DOESN'T HAVE SOMETHING ELSE GOING ON TO TIE HER HERE?
EVEN IF SHE DOES, I'M CERTAIN OUR OFFER WILL SOUND BETTER.
I MEAN, THAT'S THE WHOLE POINT, RIGHT?

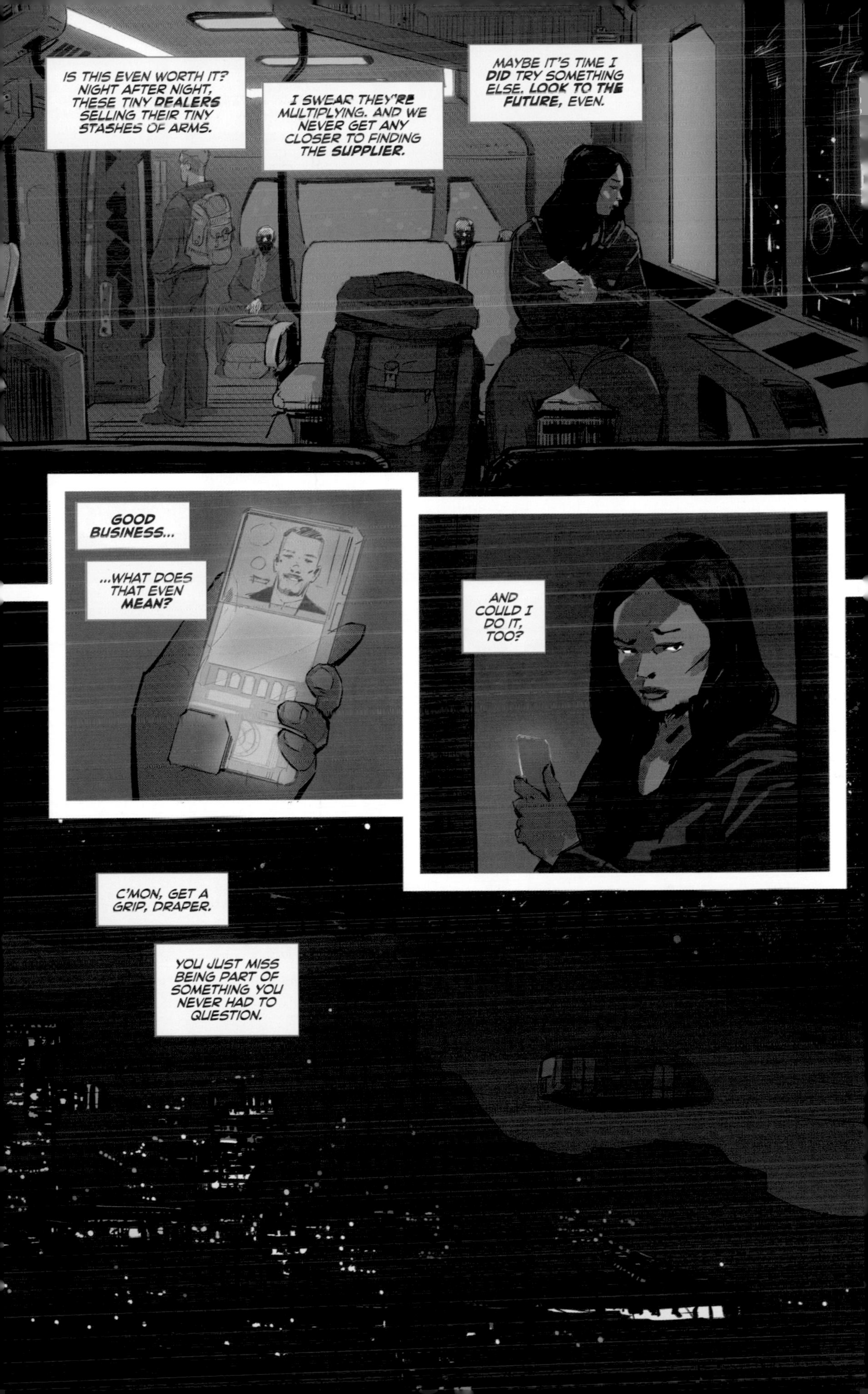
IS THIS EVEN WORTH IT? NIGHT AFTER NIGHT, THESE TINY DEALERS SELLING THEIR TINY STASHES OF ARMS.
I SWEAR THEY'RE MULTIPLYING. AND WE NEVER GET ANY CLOSER TO FINDING THE SUPPLIER.
MAYBE IT'S TIME I DID TRY SOMETHING ELSE. LOOK TO THE FUTURE, EVEN.
GOOD BUSINESS...
...WHAT DOES THAT EVEN MEAN?
AND COULD I DO IT, TOO?
C'MON, GET A GRIP, DRAPER.
YOU JUST MISS BEING PART OF SOMETHING YOU NEVER HAD TO QUESTION.

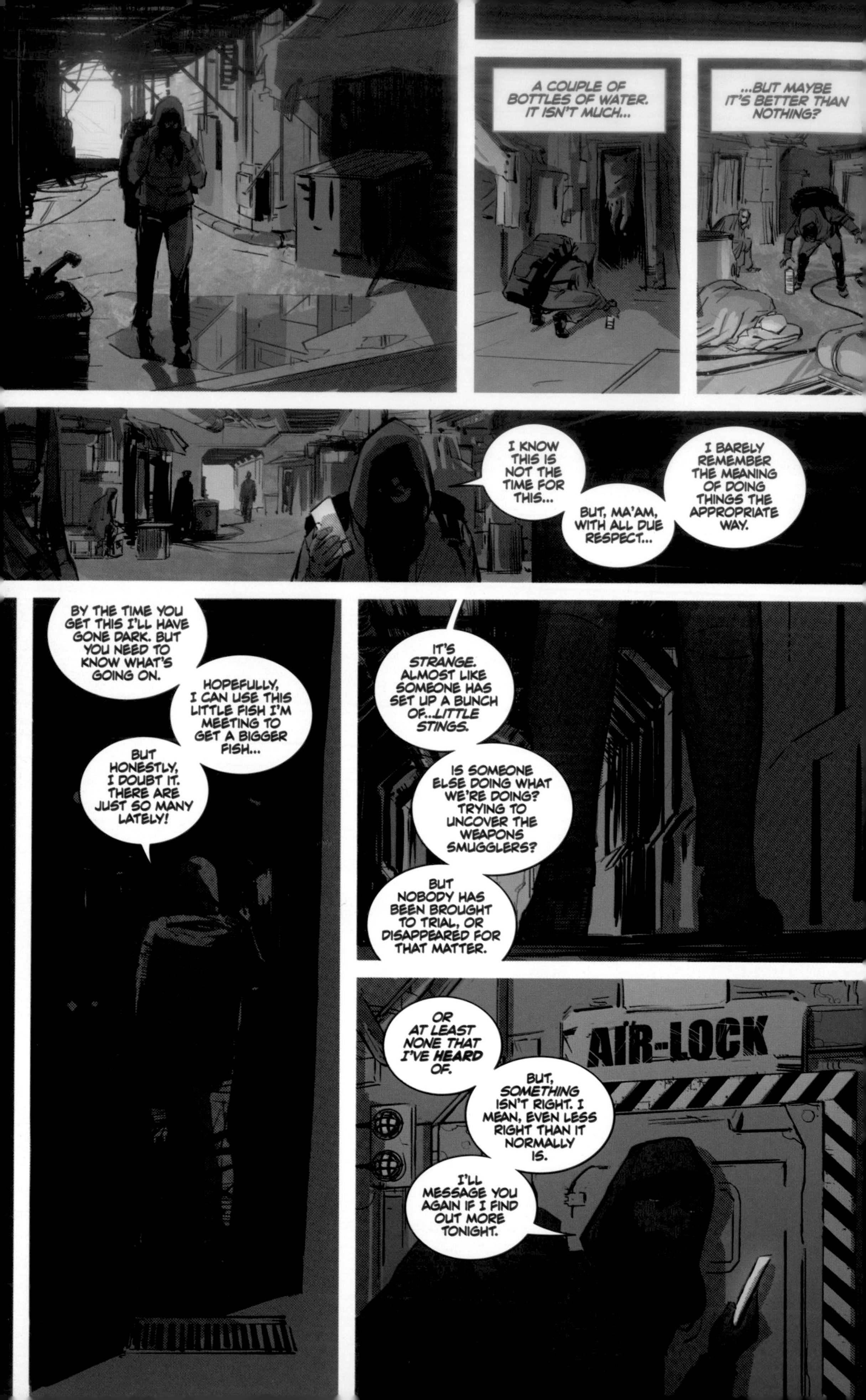
A COUPLE OF BOTTLES OF WATER. IT ISN'T MUCH...
...BUT MAYBE IT'S BETTER THAN NOTHING?
I KNOW THIS IS NOT THE TIME FOR THIS...
BUT, MA'AM, WITH ALL DUE RESPECT...
I BARELY REMEMBER THE MEANING OF DOING THINGS THE APPROPRIATE WAY.
BY THE TIME YOU GET THIS I'LL HAVE GONE DARK. BUT YOU NEED TO KNOW WHAT'S GOING ON.
HOPEFULLY, I CAN USE THIS LITTLE FISH I'M MEETING TO GET A BIGGER FISH...
BUT HONESTLY, I DOUBT IT. THERE ARE JUST SO MANY LATELY!
IT'S STRANGE. ALMOST LIKE SOMEONE HAS SET UP A BUNCH OF...LITTLE STINGS.
IS SOMEONE ELSE DOING WHAT WE'RE DOING? TRYING TO UNCOVER THE WEAPONS SMUGGLERS?
BUT NOBODY HAS BEEN BROUGHT TO TRIAL, OR DISAPPEARED FOR THAT MATTER.
OR AT LEAST NONE THAT I'VE HEARD OF.
AIR-LOCK
BUT, SOMETHING ISN'T RIGHT. I MEAN, EVEN LESS RIGHT THAN IT NORMALLY IS.
I'LL MESSAGE YOU AGAIN IF I FIND OUT MORE TONIGHT.

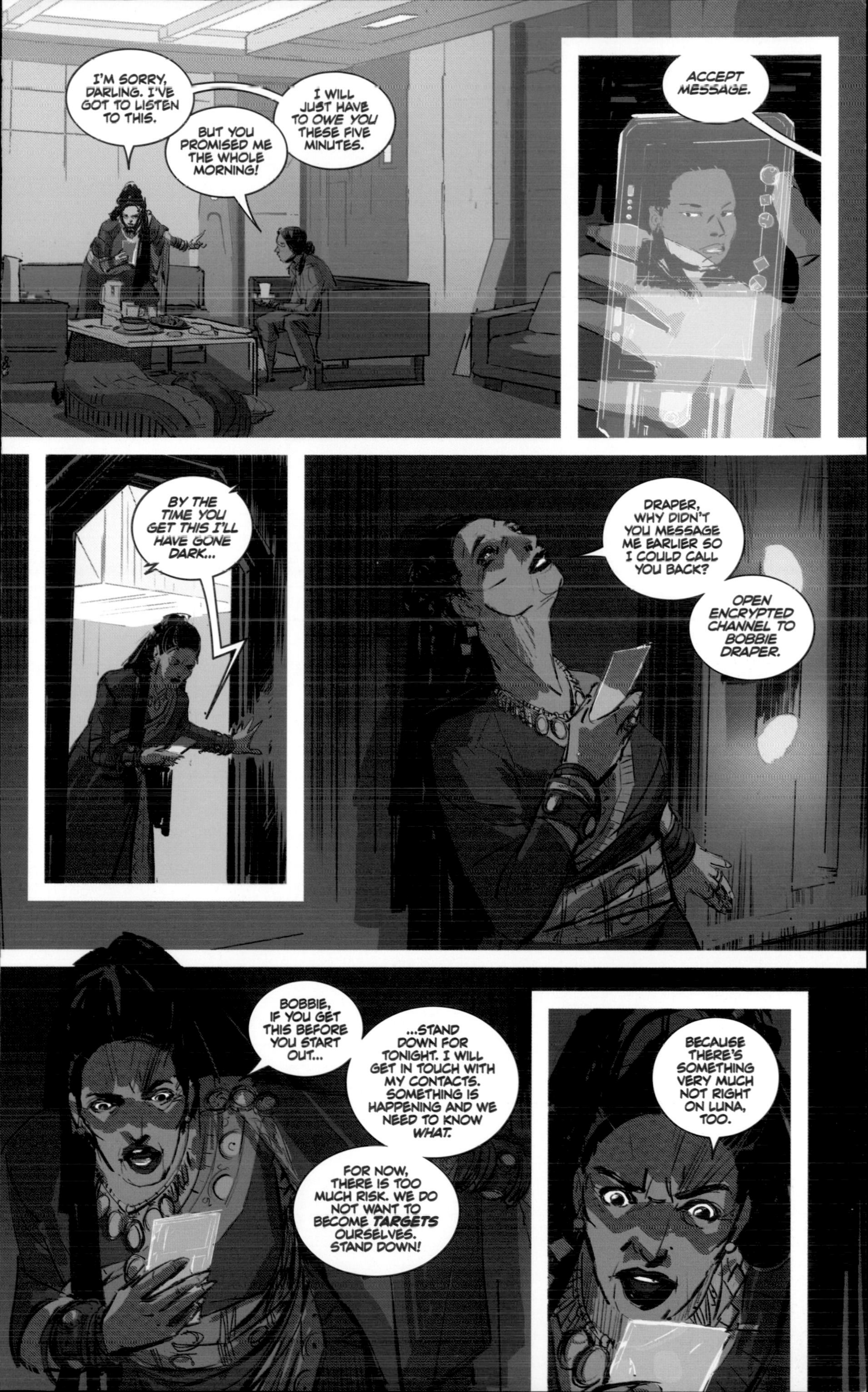
I'M SORRY, DARLING. I'VE GOT TO LISTEN TO THIS.
BUT YOU PROMISED ME THE WHOLE MORNING!
I WILL JUST HAVE TO OWE YOU THESE FIVE MINUTES.
ACCEPT MESSAGE.
BY THE TIME YOU GET THIS I'LL HAVE GONE DARK...
DRAPER, WHY DIDN'T YOU MESSAGE ME EARLIER SO I COULD CALL YOU BACK?
OPEN ENCRYPTED CHANNEL TO BOBBIE DRAPER.
BOBBIE, IF YOU GET THIS BEFORE YOU START OUT...
...STAND DOWN FOR TONIGHT. I WILL GET IN TOUCH WITH MY CONTACTS. SOMETHING IS HAPPENING AND WE NEED TO KNOW WHAT.
FOR NOW, THERE IS TOO MUCH RISK. WE DO NOT WANT TO BECOME TARGETS OURSELVES. STAND DOWN!
BECAUSE THERE'S SOMETHING VERY MUCH NOT RIGHT ON LUNA, TOO.

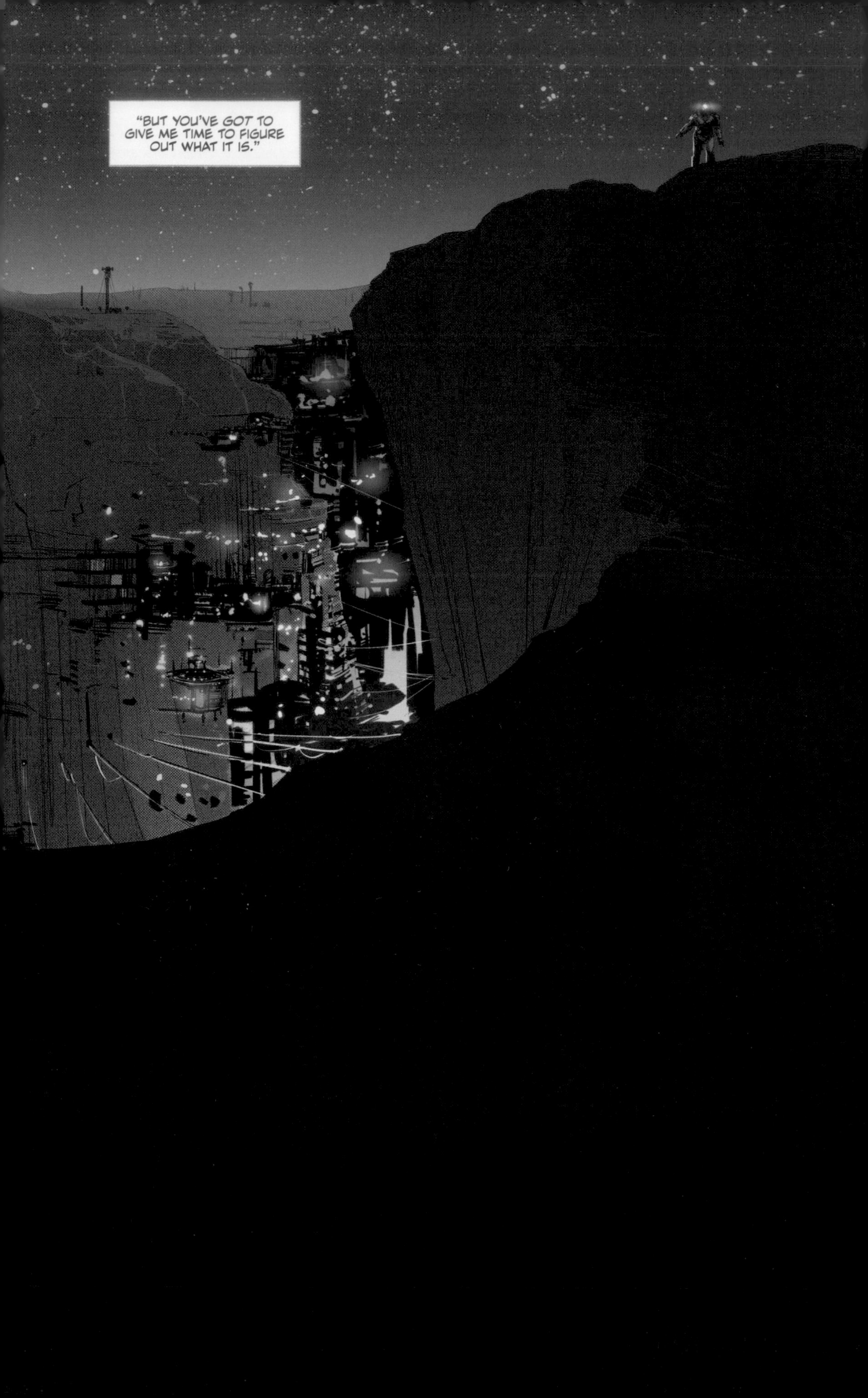
"BUT YOU'VE GOT TO GIVE ME TIME TO FIGURE OUT WHAT IT IS."

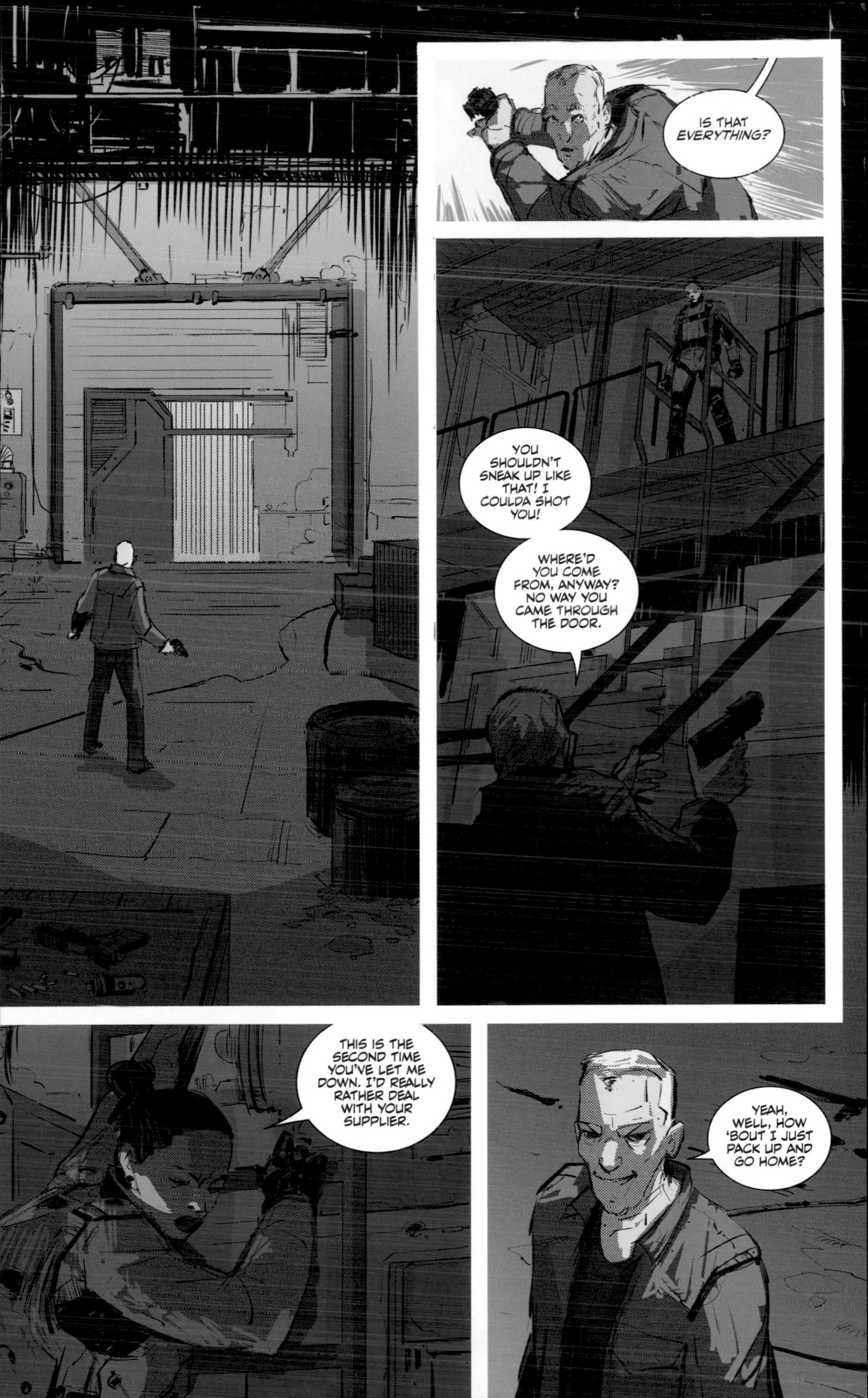
IS THAT EVERYTHING?
YOU SHOULDN'T SNEAK UP LIKE THAT! I COULDA SHOT YOU!
WHERE'D YOU COME FROM, ANYWAY? NO WAY YOU CAME THROUGH THE DOOR.
THIS IS THE SECOND TIME YOU'VE LET ME DOWN. I'D REALLY RATHER DEAL WITH YOUR SUPPLIER.
YEAH, WELL, HOW 'BOUT I JUST PACK UP AND GO HOME?

LOOK, NO ONE IS GETTING WHAT THEY WANT OUT OF THIS TONIGHT, RIGHT?

TELL YOU WHAT, I'LL GIVE YOU WHAT WE AGREED TO...

...AND I'LL GIVE YOU A BONUS AFTER YOU PUT ME IN TOUCH.

NO CAN DO, LADY.

YOU'RE TOO LATE.

I ALREADY MADE THAT DEAL WITH SOMEONE ELSE.

YOU WHAT?

OUR AGREEMENT WAS NO OTHER PARTIES. THIS IS OFF. YOU CAN KEEP THIS PITIFUL COLLECTION.

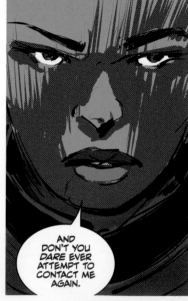

AND DON'T YOU DARE EVER ATTEMPT TO CONTACT ME AGAIN.

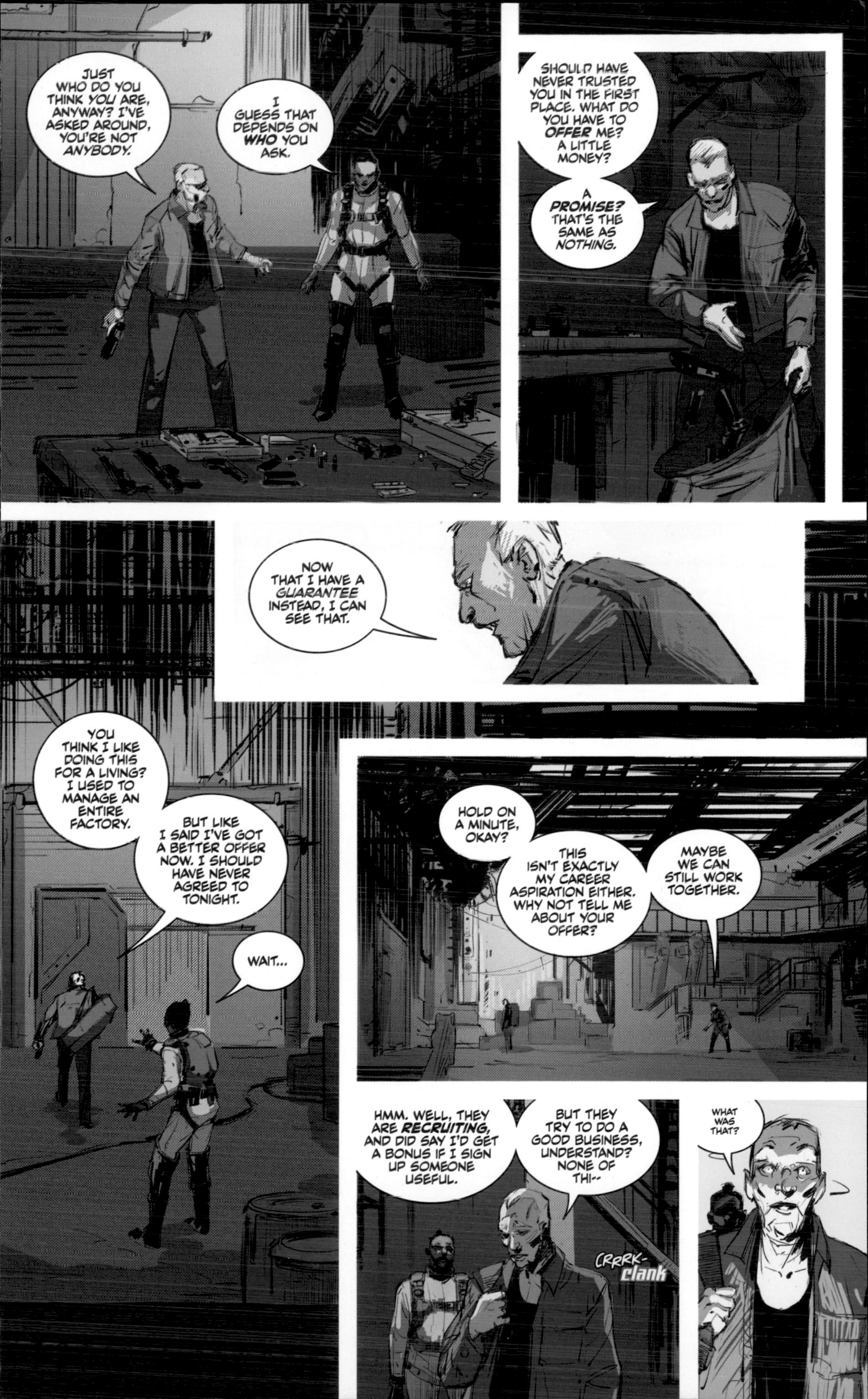
JUST WHO DO YOU THINK YOU ARE, ANYWAY? I'VE ASKED AROUND, YOU'RE NOT ANYBODY.
I GUESS THAT DEPENDS ON WHO YOU ASK.
SHOULD HAVE NEVER TRUSTED YOU IN THE FIRST PLACE. WHAT DO YOU HAVE TO OFFER ME? A LITTLE MONEY?
A PROMISE? THAT'S THE SAME AS NOTHING.
NOW THAT I HAVE A GUARANTEE INSTEAD, I CAN SEE THAT.
YOU THINK I LIKE DOING THIS FOR A LIVING? I USED TO MANAGE AN ENTIRE FACTORY.
BUT LIKE I SAID I'VE GOT A BETTER OFFER NOW. I SHOULD HAVE NEVER AGREED TO TONIGHT.
WAIT...
HOLD ON A MINUTE, OKAY?
THIS ISN'T EXACTLY MY CAREER ASPIRATION EITHER. WHY NOT TELL ME ABOUT YOUR OFFER?
MAYBE WE CAN STILL WORK TOGETHER.
HMM. WELL, THEY ARE RECRUITING, AND DID SAY I'D GET A BONUS IF I SIGN UP SOMEONE USEFUL.
BUT THEY TRY TO DO A GOOD BUSINESS, UNDERSTAND? NONE OF THI--
CRRRK-
clank
WHAT WAS THAT?

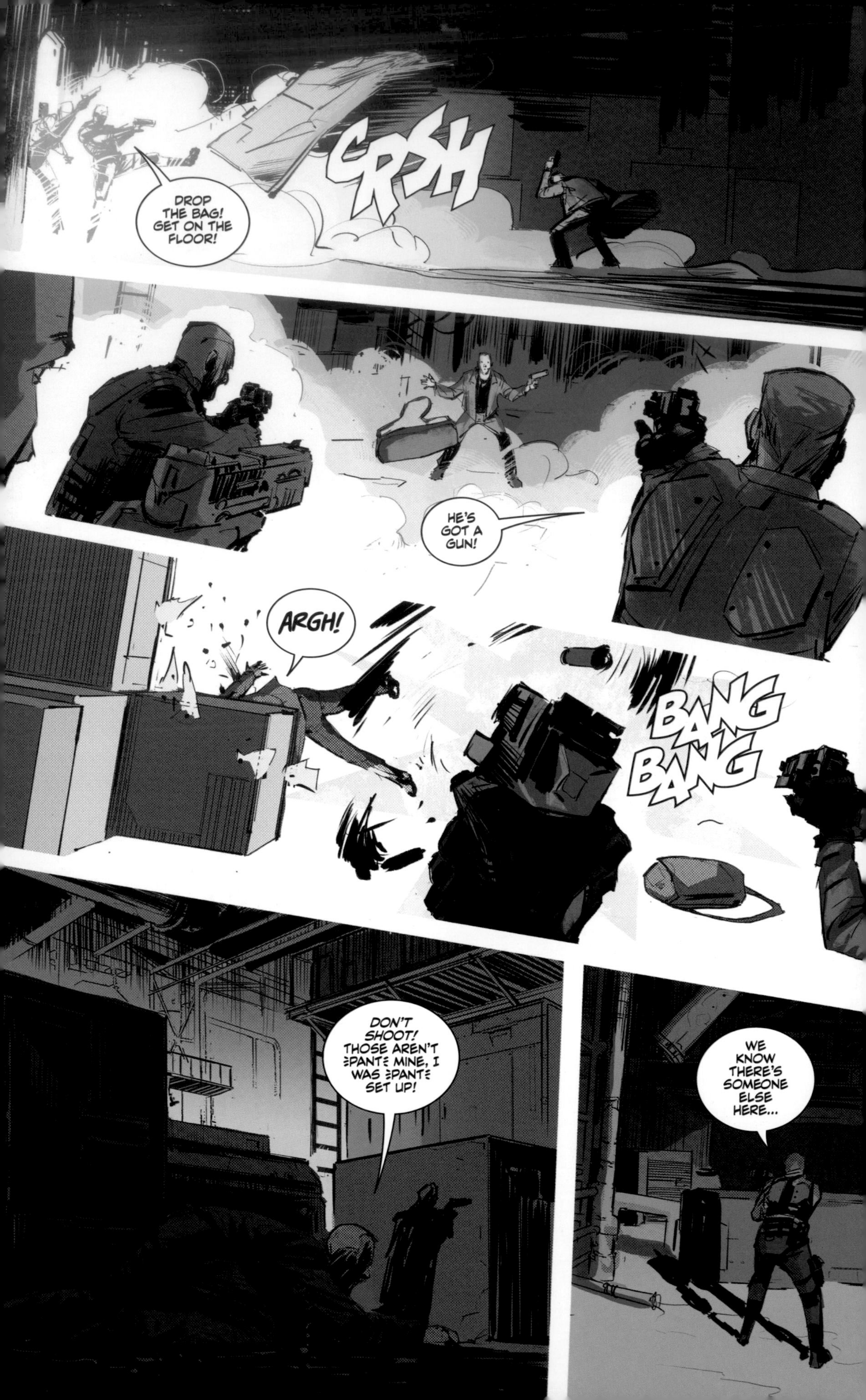
CRSH
DROP THE BAG! GET ON THE FLOOR!
HE'S GOT A GUN!
ARGH!
BANG BANG
DON'T SHOOT! THOSE AREN'T *PANT* MINE, I WAS *PANT* SET UP!
WE KNOW THERE'S SOMEONE ELSE HERE...

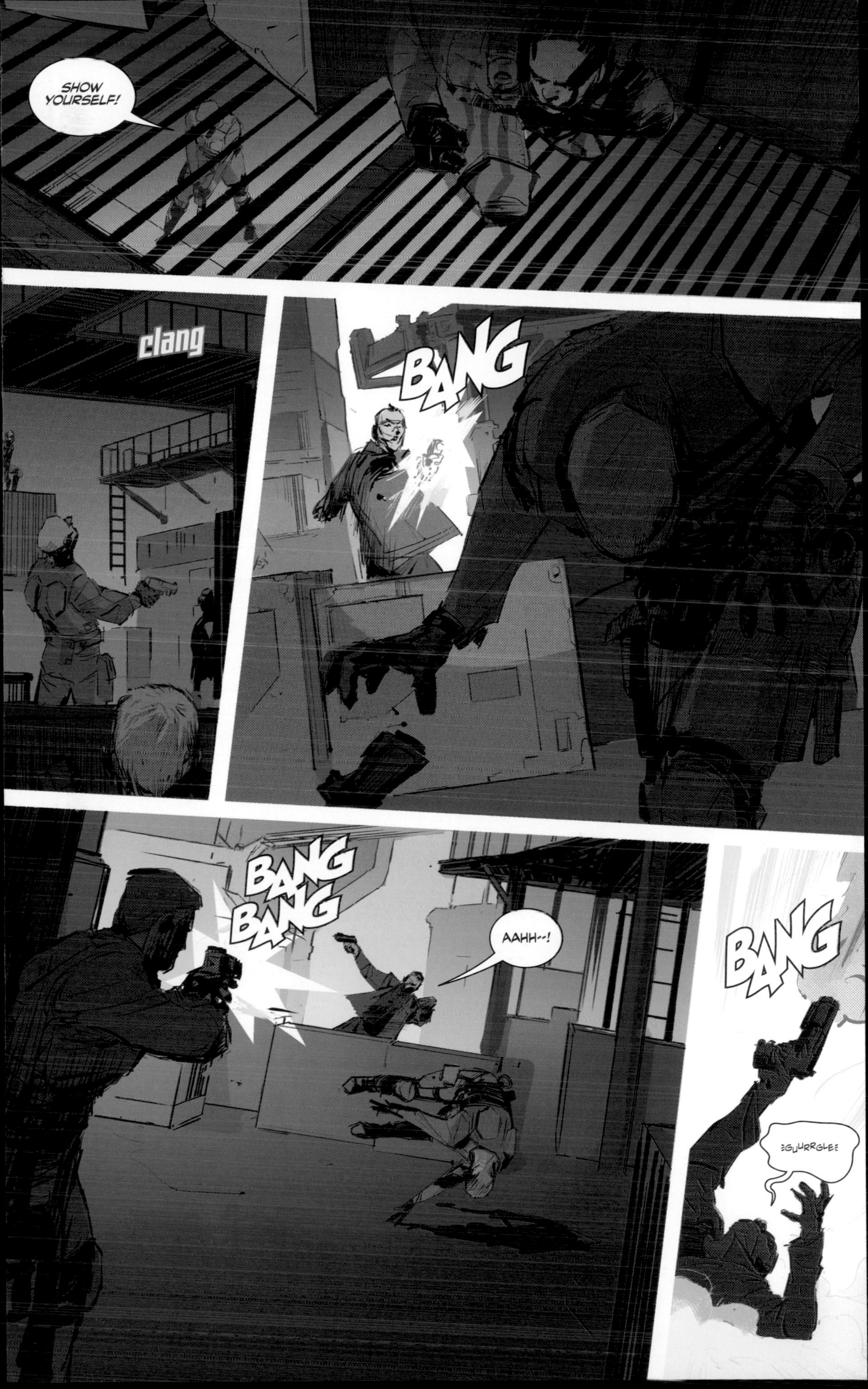
SHOW YOURSELF!
clang
BANG
BANG BANG
AAHH--!
BANG
GUURRGLE

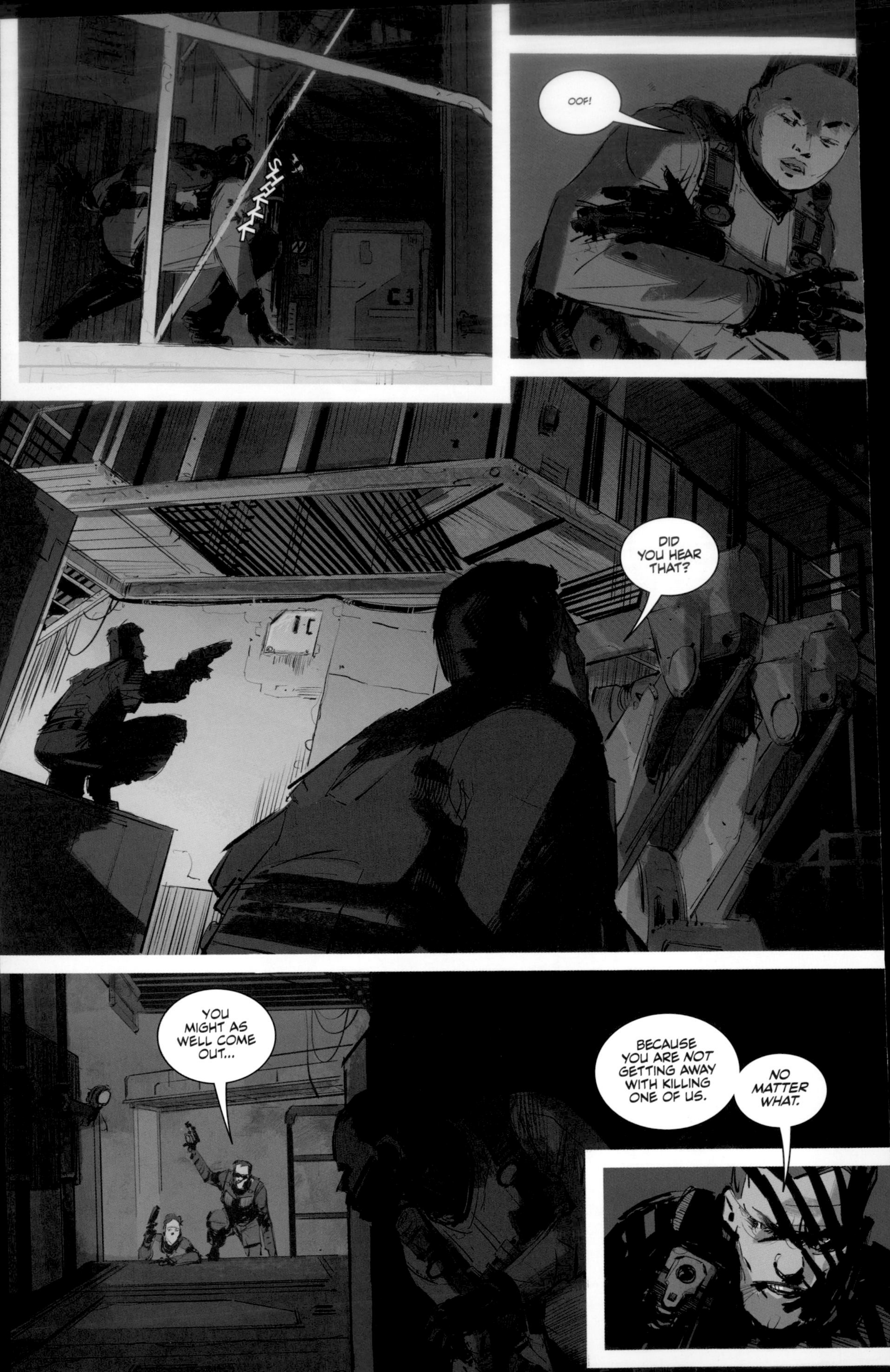
SHHKKK
OOF!
DID YOU HEAR THAT?
YOU MIGHT AS WELL COME OUT...
BECAUSE YOU ARE *NOT* GETTING AWAY WITH KILLING ONE OF US.
NO MATTER WHAT.

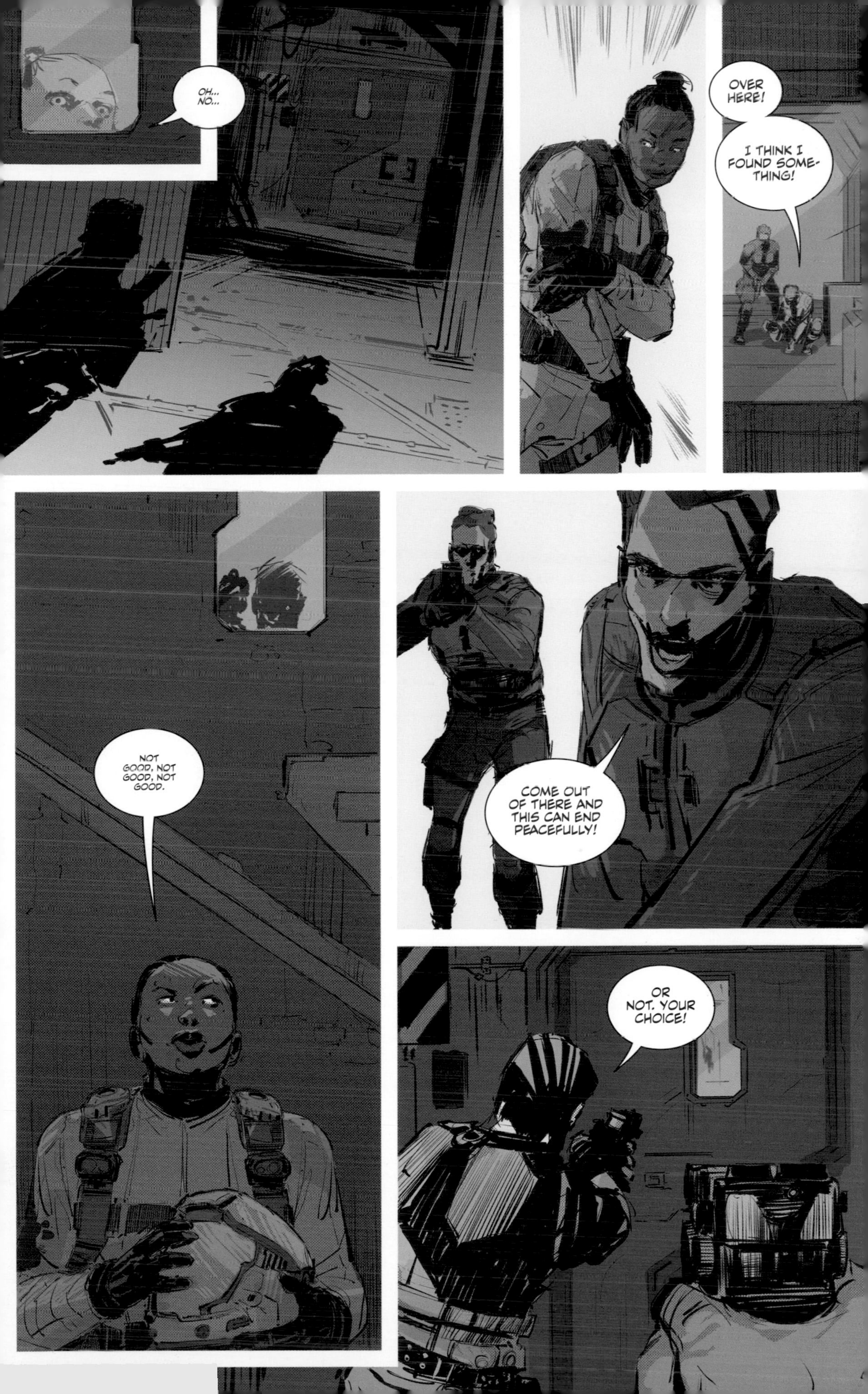
OH... NO...
OVER HERE!
I THINK I FOUND SOME-THING!
NOT GOOD, NOT GOOD, NOT GOOD.
COME OUT OF THERE AND THIS CAN END PEACEFULLY!
OR NOT. YOUR CHOICE!

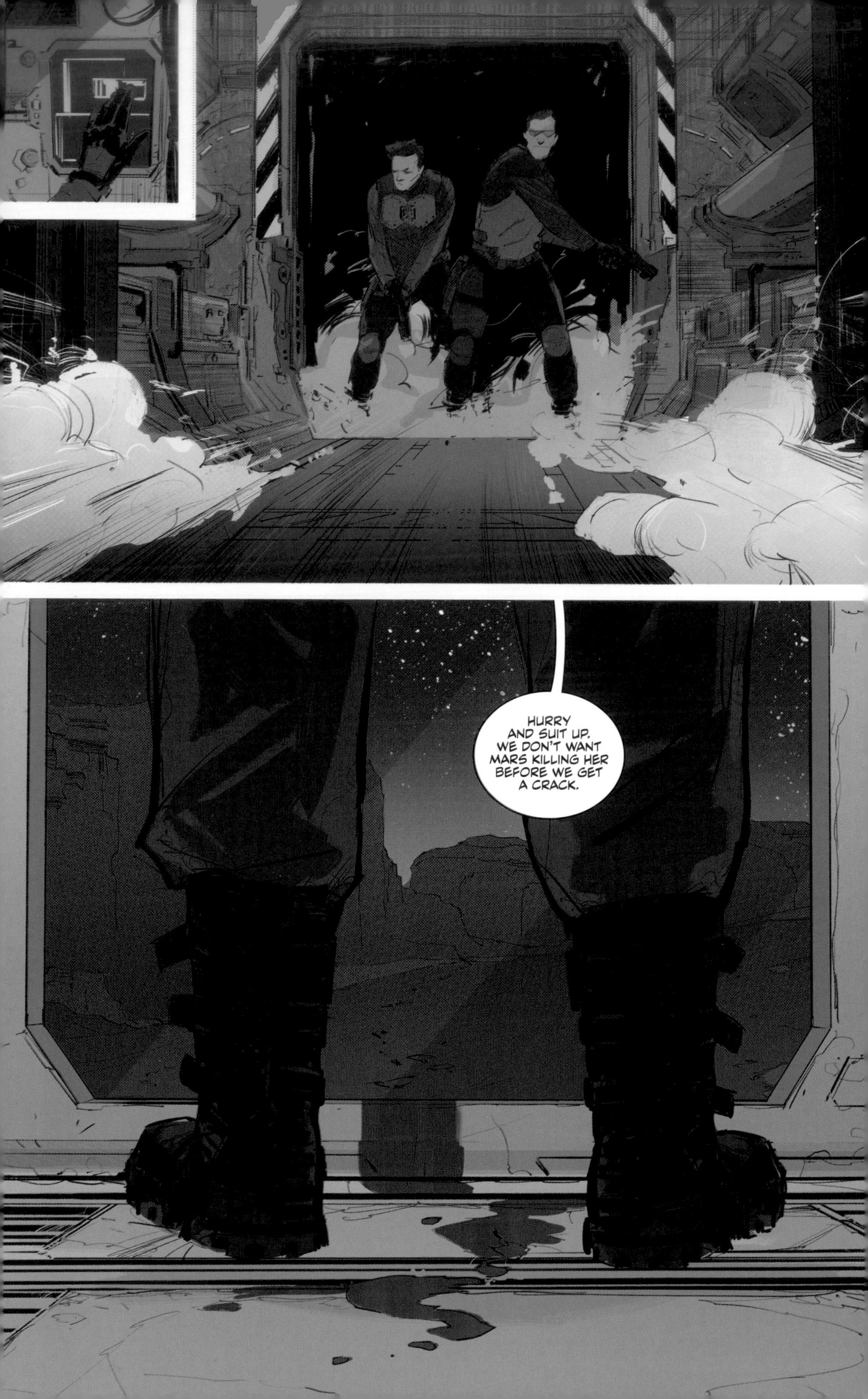
HURRY AND SUIT UP. WE DON'T WANT MARS KILLING HER BEFORE WE GET A CRACK.

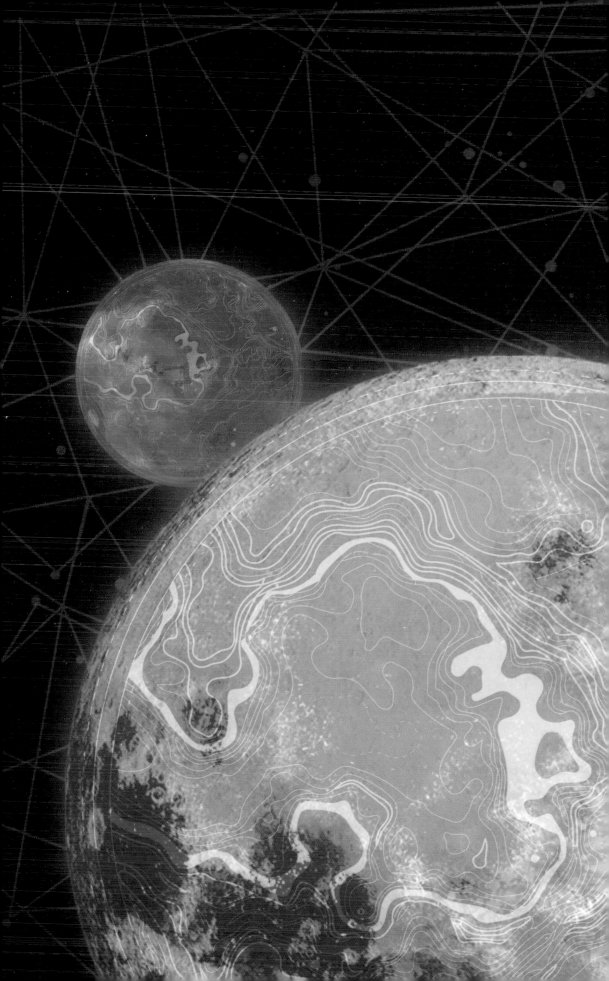

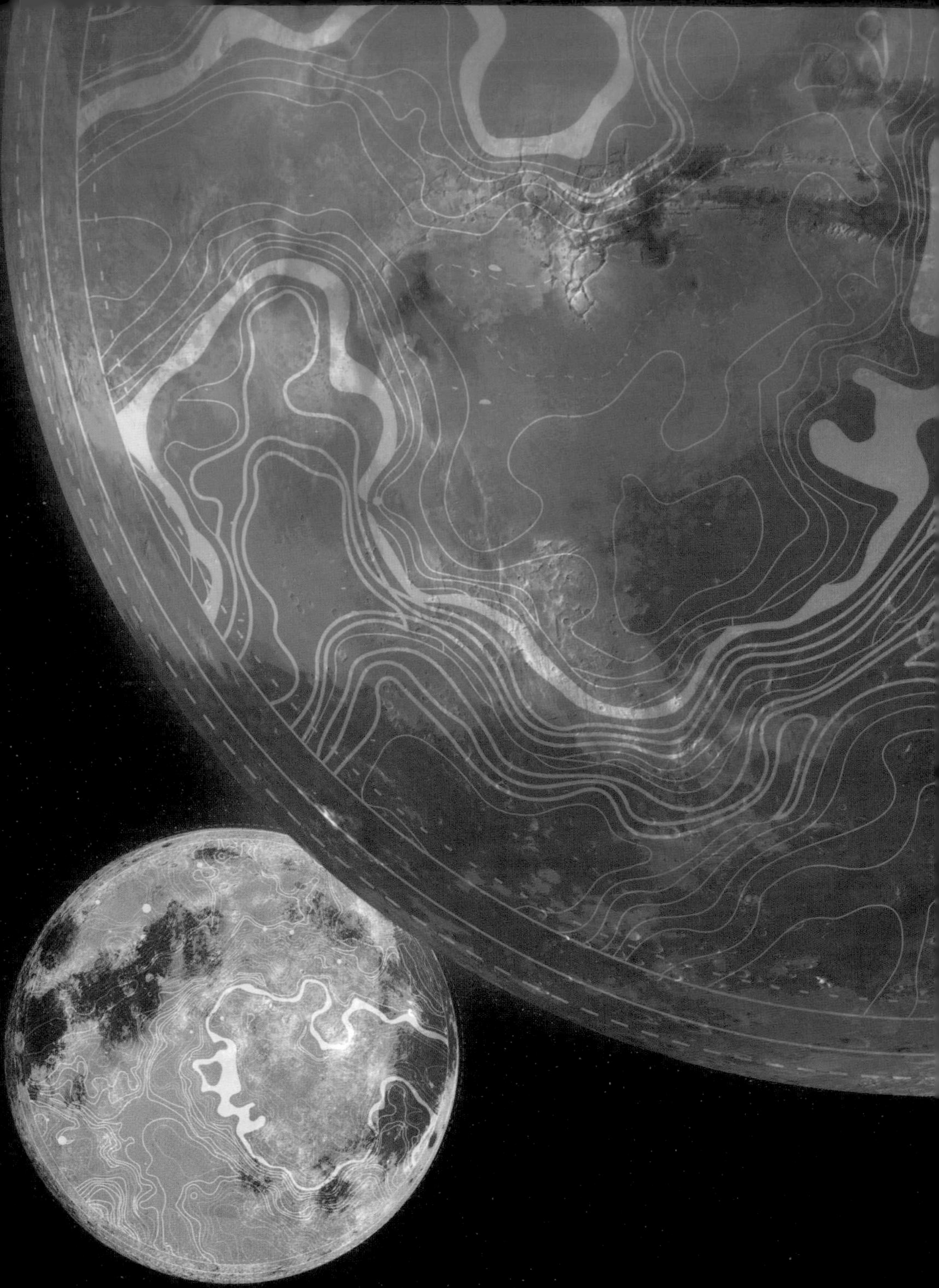

CHAPTER TWO

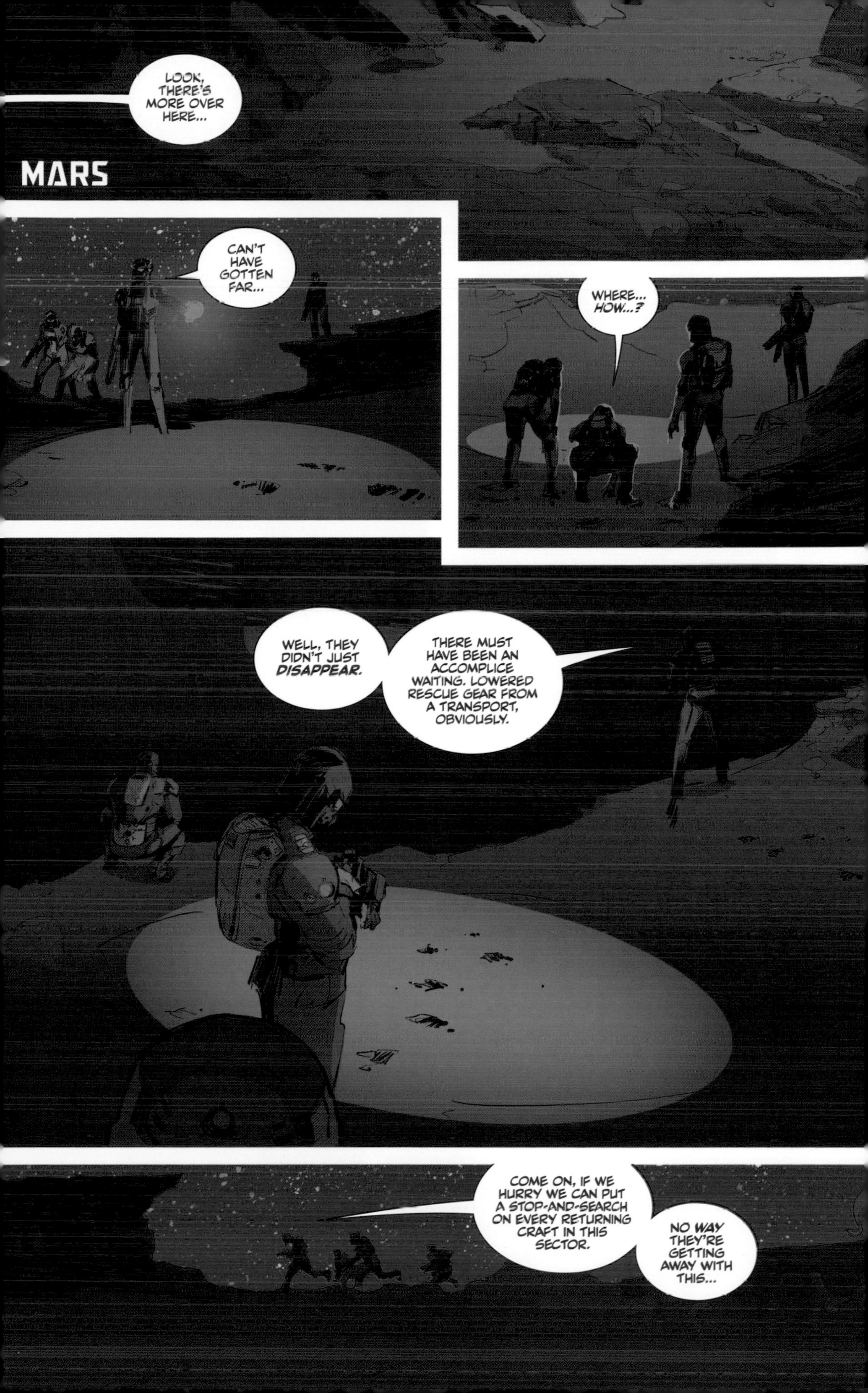
LOOK, THERE'S MORE OVER HERE...
MARS
CAN'T HAVE GOTTEN FAR...
WHERE... HOW...?
WELL, THEY DIDN'T JUST DISAPPEAR.
THERE MUST HAVE BEEN AN ACCOMPLICE WAITING. LOWERED RESCUE GEAR FROM A TRANSPORT, OBVIOUSLY.
COME ON, IF WE HURRY WE CAN PUT A STOP-AND-SEARCH ON EVERY RETURNING CRAFT IN THIS SECTOR.
NO WAY THEY'RE GETTING AWAY WITH THIS...

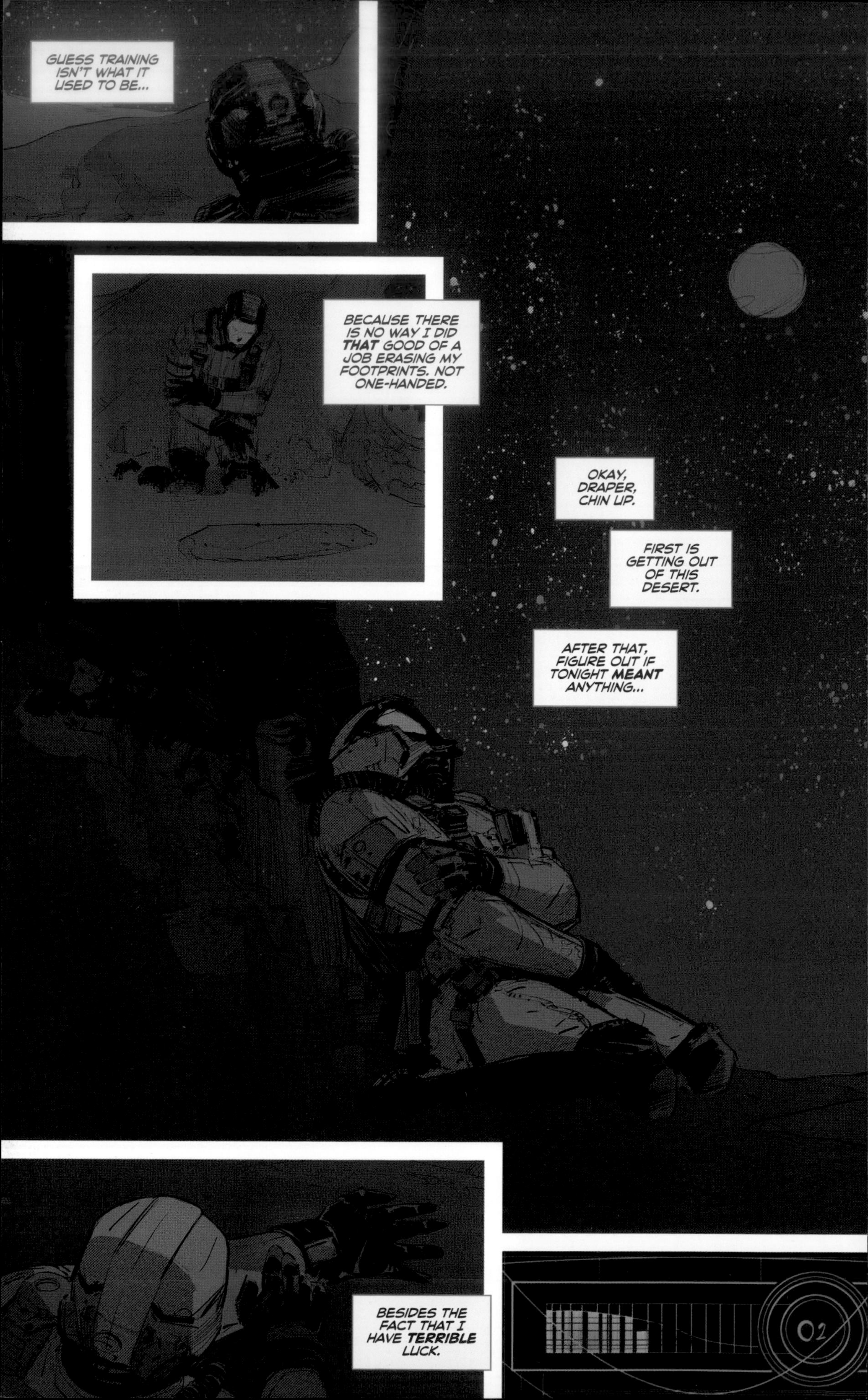
GUESS TRAINING ISN'T WHAT IT USED TO BE...
BECAUSE THERE IS NO WAY I DID **THAT** GOOD OF A JOB ERASING MY FOOTPRINTS. NOT ONE-HANDED.
OKAY, DRAPER, CHIN UP.
FIRST IS GETTING OUT OF THIS DESERT.
AFTER THAT, FIGURE OUT IF TONIGHT **MEANT** ANYTHING...
BESIDES THE FACT THAT I HAVE **TERRIBLE** LUCK.
O2

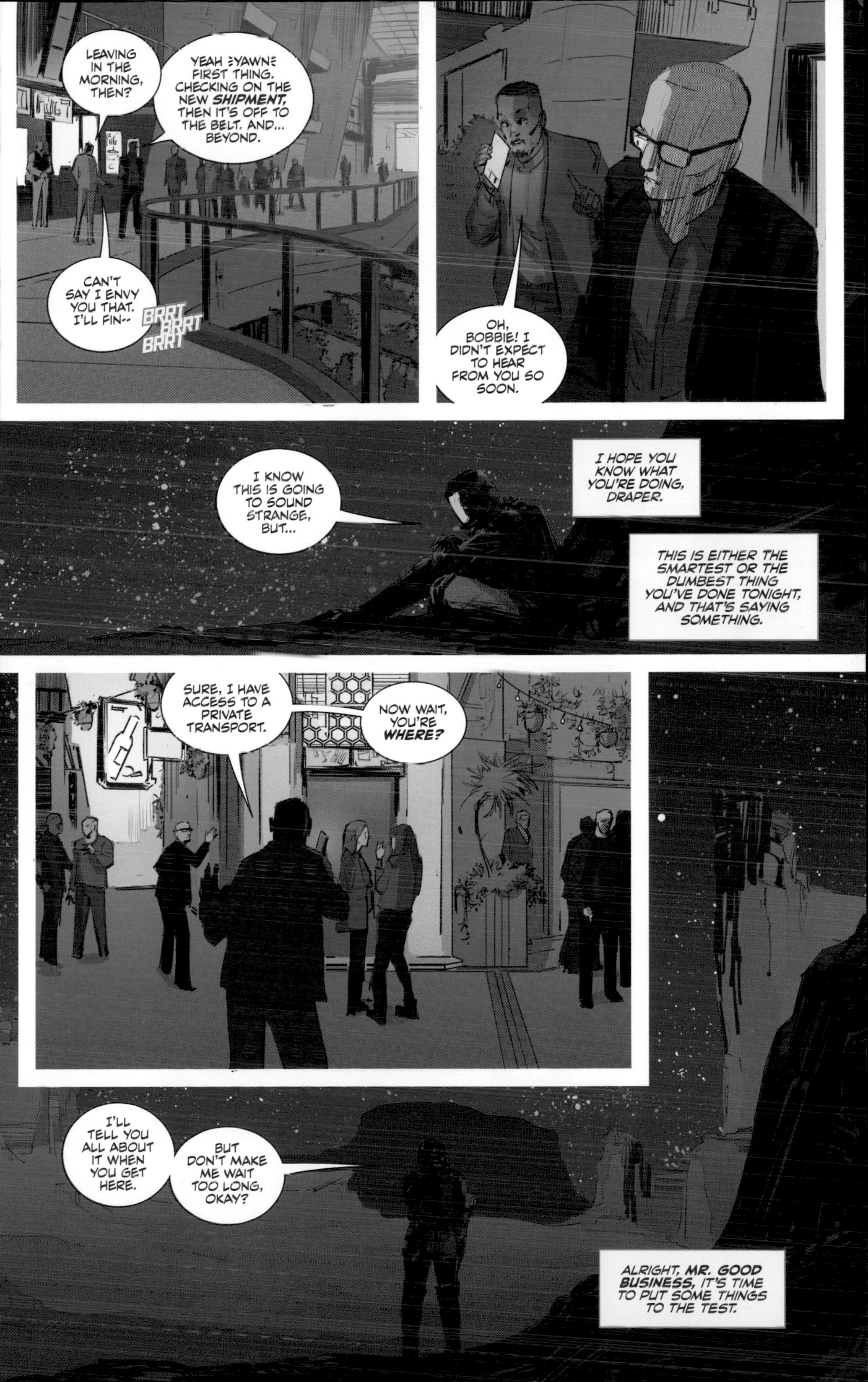
LEAVING IN THE MORNING, THEN?
YEAH =YAWN= FIRST THING. CHECKING ON THE NEW SHIPMENT, THEN IT'S OFF TO THE BELT. AND... BEYOND.
CAN'T SAY I ENVY YOU THAT. I'LL FIN--
BRRT BRRT BRRT
OH, BOBBIE! I DIDN'T EXPECT TO HEAR FROM YOU SO SOON.
I KNOW THIS IS GOING TO SOUND STRANGE, BUT...
I HOPE YOU KNOW WHAT YOU'RE DOING, DRAPER.
THIS IS EITHER THE SMARTEST OR THE DUMBEST THING YOU'VE DONE TONIGHT, AND THAT'S SAYING SOMETHING.
SURE, I HAVE ACCESS TO A PRIVATE TRANSPORT.
NOW WAIT, YOU'RE WHERE?
I'LL TELL YOU ALL ABOUT IT WHEN YOU GET HERE.
BUT DON'T MAKE ME WAIT TOO LONG, OKAY?
ALRIGHT, MR. GOOD BUSINESS, IT'S TIME TO PUT SOME THINGS TO THE TEST.

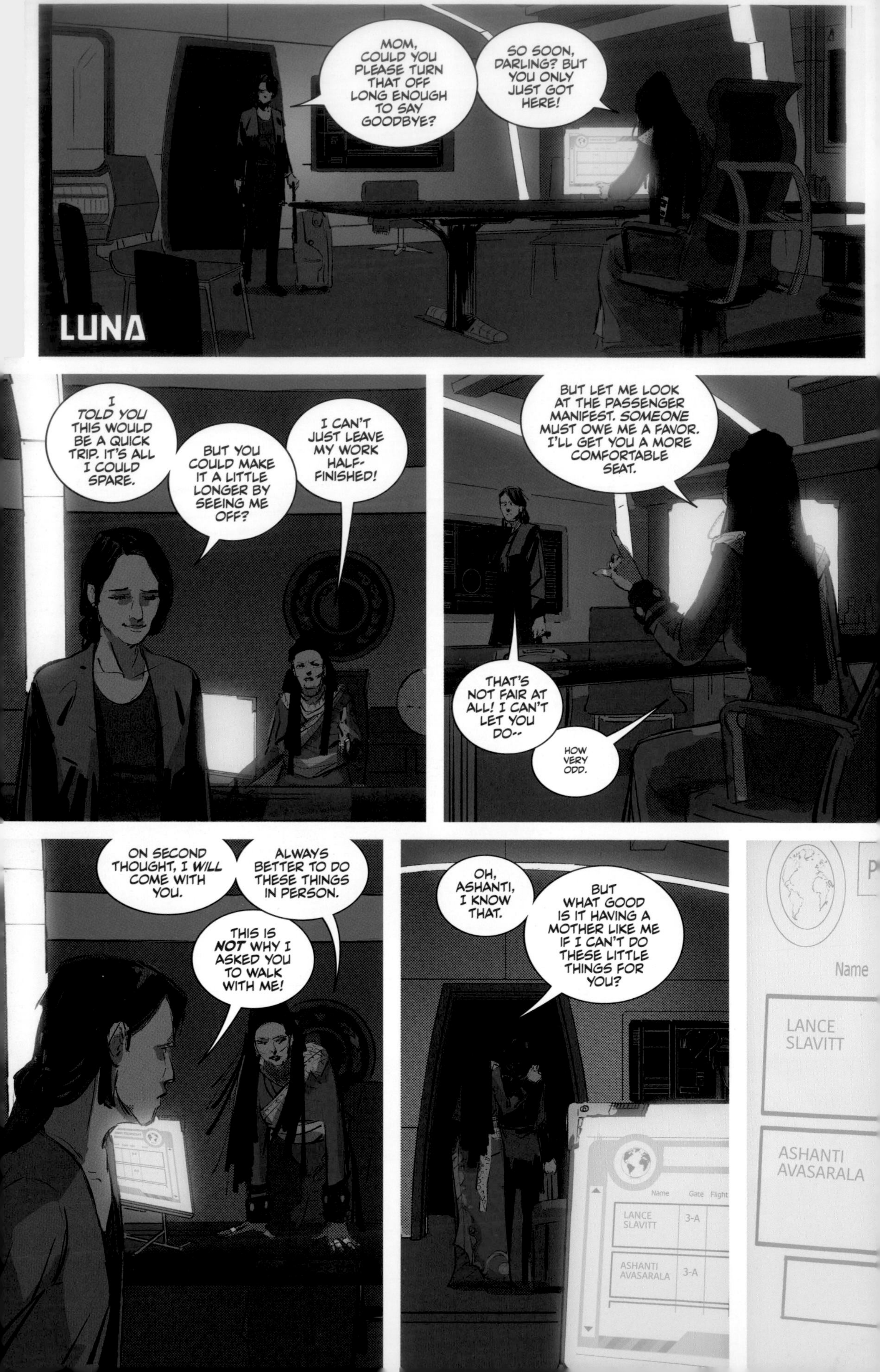
MOM, COULD YOU PLEASE TURN THAT OFF LONG ENOUGH TO SAY GOODBYE?
SO SOON, DARLING? BUT YOU ONLY JUST GOT HERE!
LUNA
I *TOLD YOU* THIS WOULD BE A QUICK TRIP. IT'S ALL I COULD SPARE.
BUT YOU COULD MAKE IT A LITTLE LONGER BY SEEING ME OFF?
I CAN'T JUST LEAVE MY WORK HALF-FINISHED!
BUT LET ME LOOK AT THE PASSENGER MANIFEST. *SOMEONE* MUST OWE ME A FAVOR. I'LL GET YOU A MORE COMFORTABLE SEAT.
THAT'S NOT FAIR AT ALL! I CAN'T LET YOU DO--
HOW VERY ODD.
ON SECOND THOUGHT, I *WILL* COME WITH YOU.
ALWAYS BETTER TO DO THESE THINGS IN PERSON.
THIS IS ***NOT*** WHY I ASKED YOU TO WALK WITH ME!
OH, ASHANTI, I KNOW THAT.
BUT WHAT GOOD IS IT HAVING A MOTHER LIKE ME IF I CAN'T DO THESE LITTLE THINGS FOR YOU?
Name
Gate
Flight
LANCE SLAVITT
3-A
ASHANTI AVASARALA
3-A
Name
LANCE SLAVITT
ASHANTI AVASARALA

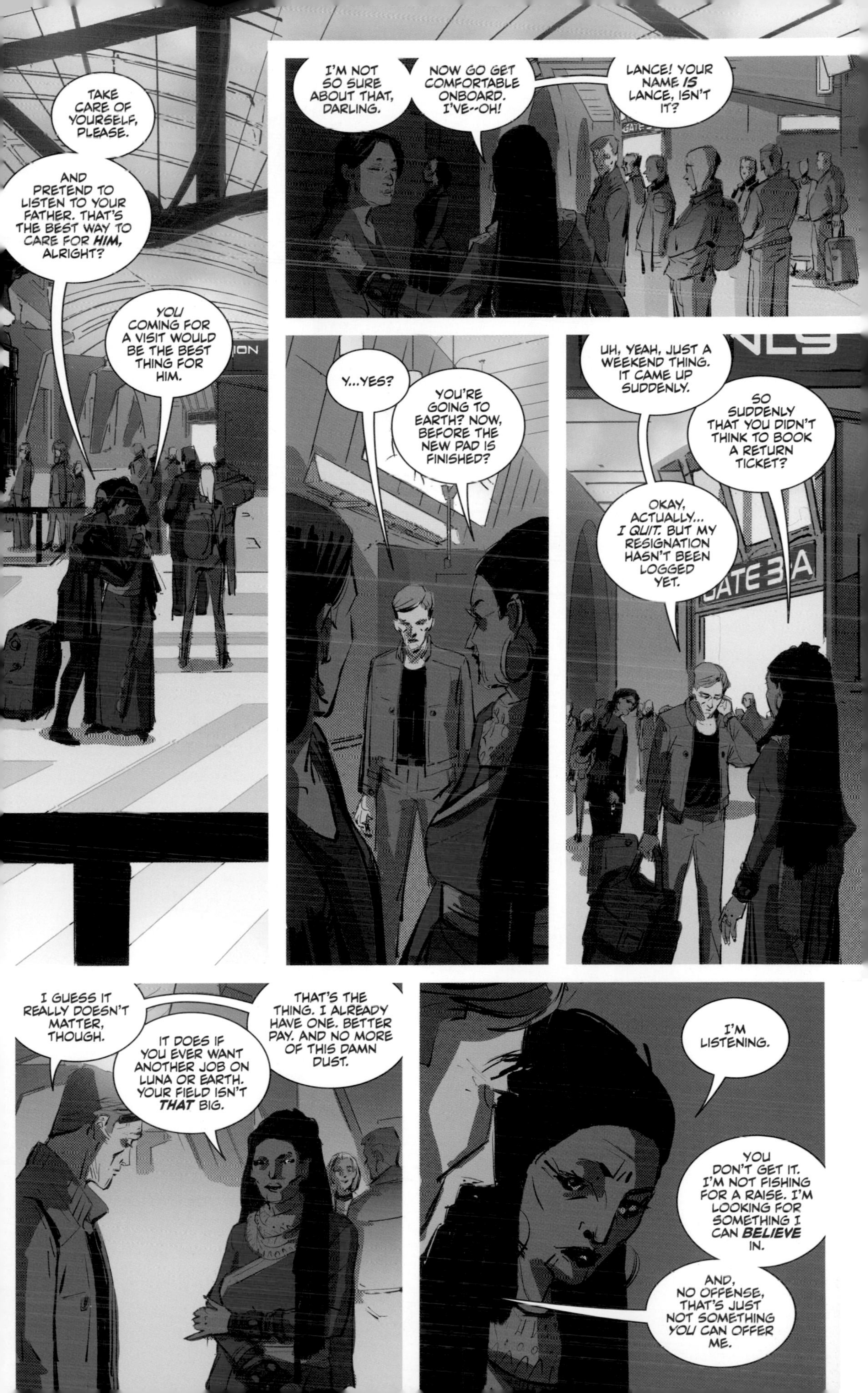
TAKE CARE OF YOURSELF, PLEASE.
AND PRETEND TO LISTEN TO YOUR FATHER. THAT'S THE BEST WAY TO CARE FOR *HIM*, ALRIGHT?
YOU COMING FOR A VISIT WOULD BE THE BEST THING FOR HIM.
I'M NOT SO SURE ABOUT THAT, DARLING.
NOW GO GET COMFORTABLE ONBOARD. I'VE--OH!
LANCE! YOUR NAME *IS* LANCE, ISN'T IT?
Y...YES?
YOU'RE GOING TO EARTH? NOW, BEFORE THE NEW PAD IS FINISHED?
UH, YEAH, JUST A WEEKEND THING. IT CAME UP SUDDENLY.
SO SUDDENLY THAT YOU DIDN'T THINK TO BOOK A RETURN TICKET?
OKAY, ACTUALLY... *I QUIT.* BUT MY RESIGNATION HASN'T BEEN LOGGED YET.
GATE 3-A
I GUESS IT REALLY DOESN'T MATTER, THOUGH.
IT DOES IF YOU EVER WANT ANOTHER JOB ON LUNA OR EARTH. YOUR FIELD ISN'T *THAT* BIG.
THAT'S THE THING. I ALREADY HAVE ONE. BETTER PAY. AND NO MORE OF THIS DAMN DUST.
I'M LISTENING.
YOU DON'T GET IT. I'M NOT FISHING FOR A RAISE. I'M LOOKING FOR SOMETHING I CAN *BELIEVE* IN.
AND, NO OFFENSE, THAT'S JUST NOT SOMETHING *YOU* CAN OFFER ME.

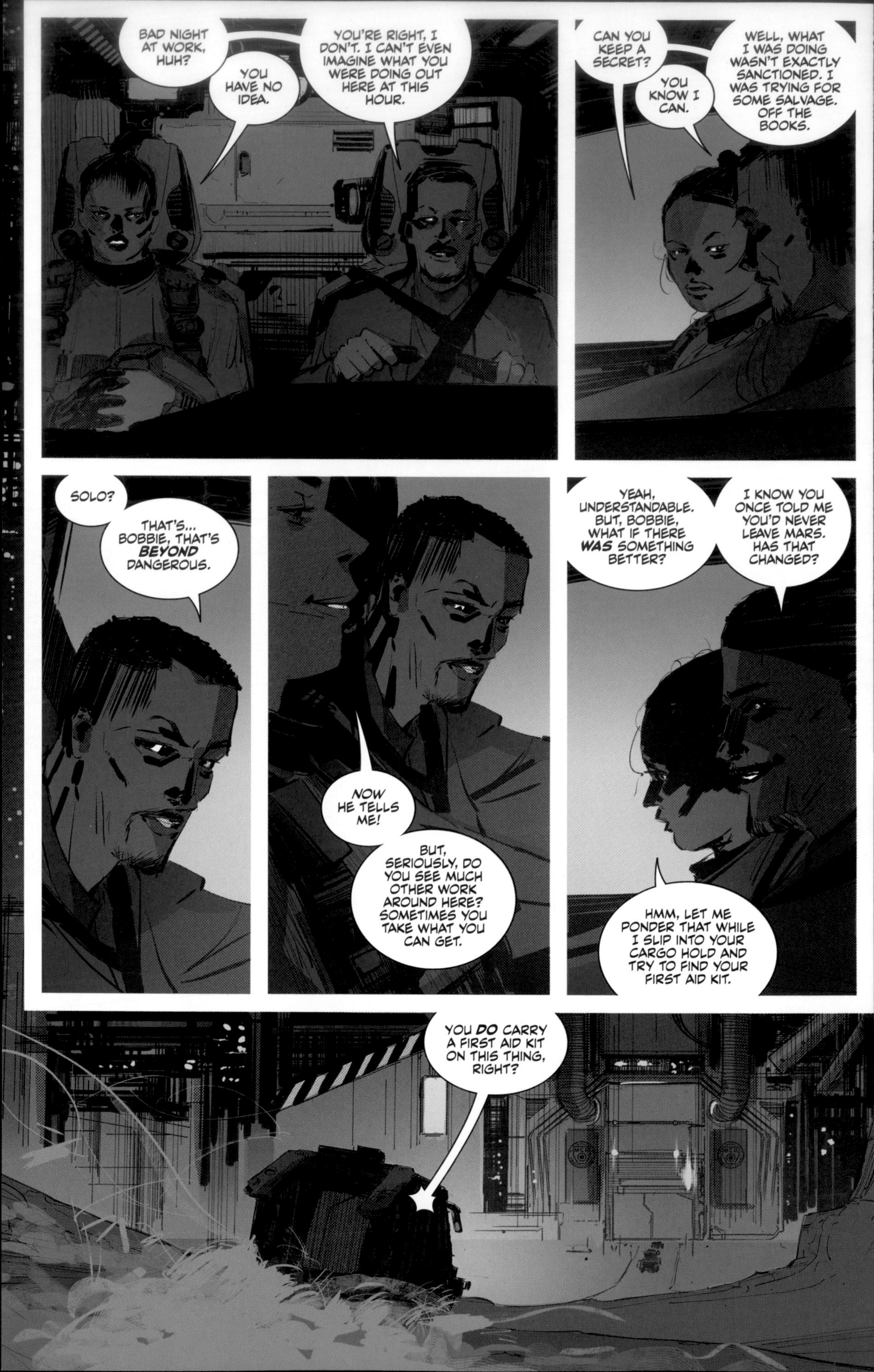
BAD NIGHT AT WORK, HUH?
YOU HAVE NO IDEA.
YOU'RE RIGHT, I DON'T. I CAN'T EVEN IMAGINE WHAT YOU WERE DOING OUT HERE AT THIS HOUR.
CAN YOU KEEP A SECRET?
YOU KNOW I CAN.
WELL, WHAT I WAS DOING WASN'T EXACTLY SANCTIONED. I WAS TRYING FOR SOME SALVAGE. OFF THE BOOKS.
SOLO?
THAT'S... BOBBIE, THAT'S *BEYOND* DANGEROUS.
NOW HE TELLS ME!
BUT, SERIOUSLY, DO YOU SEE MUCH OTHER WORK AROUND HERE? SOMETIMES YOU TAKE WHAT YOU CAN GET.
YEAH, UNDERSTANDABLE. BUT, BOBBIE, WHAT IF THERE *WAS* SOMETHING BETTER?
I KNOW YOU ONCE TOLD ME YOU'D NEVER LEAVE MARS. HAS THAT CHANGED?
HMM, LET ME PONDER THAT WHILE I SLIP INTO YOUR CARGO HOLD AND TRY TO FIND YOUR FIRST AID KIT.
YOU *DO* CARRY A FIRST AID KIT ON THIS THING, RIGHT?

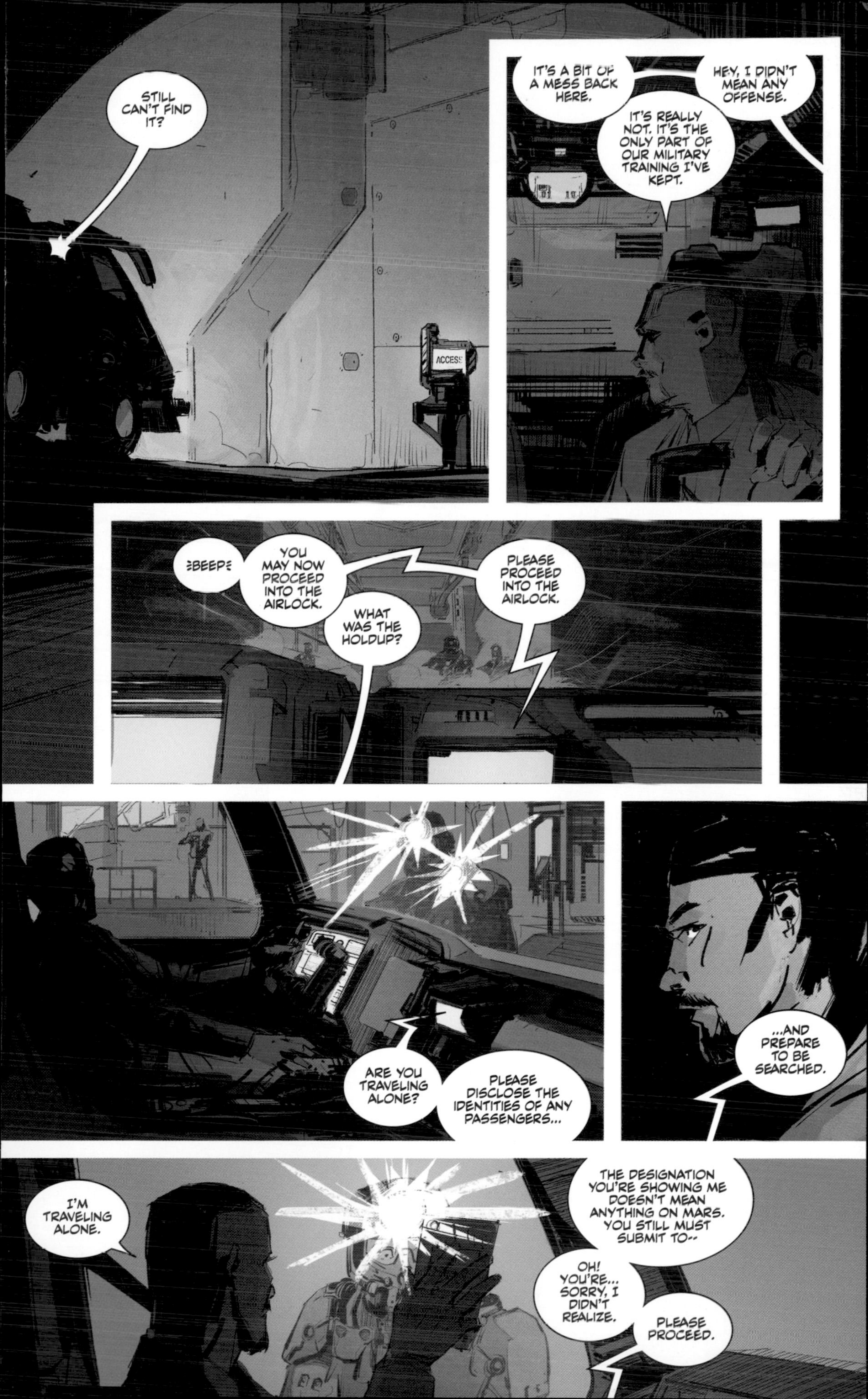
STILL CAN'T FIND IT?
IT'S A BIT OF A MESS BACK HERE.
HEY, I DIDN'T MEAN ANY OFFENSE.
IT'S REALLY NOT. IT'S THE ONLY PART OF OUR MILITARY TRAINING I'VE KEPT.
ACCESS
=BEEP=
YOU MAY NOW PROCEED INTO THE AIRLOCK.
PLEASE PROCEED INTO THE AIRLOCK.
WHAT WAS THE HOLDUP?
ARE YOU TRAVELING ALONE?
PLEASE DISCLOSE THE IDENTITIES OF ANY PASSENGERS...
...AND PREPARE TO BE SEARCHED.
I'M TRAVELING ALONE.
THE DESIGNATION YOU'RE SHOWING ME DOESN'T MEAN ANYTHING ON MARS. YOU STILL MUST SUBMIT TO--
OH! YOU'RE... SORRY, I DIDN'T REALIZE.
PLEASE PROCEED.

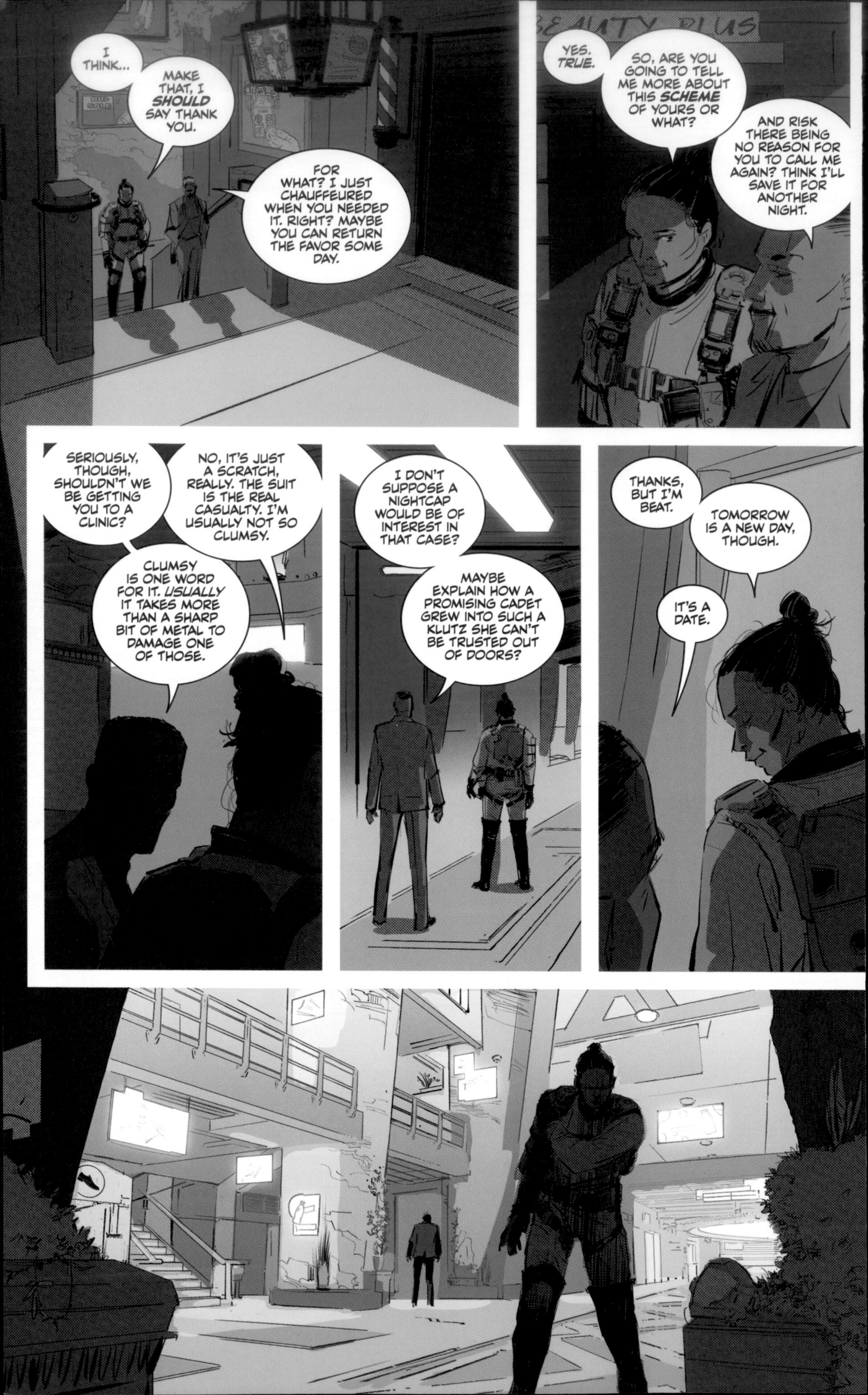

I THINK...
MAKE THAT, I SHOULD SAY THANK YOU.
FOR WHAT? I JUST CHAUFFEURED WHEN YOU NEEDED IT. RIGHT? MAYBE YOU CAN RETURN THE FAVOR SOME DAY.
BEAUTY PLUS
YES. TRUE.
SO, ARE YOU GOING TO TELL ME MORE ABOUT THIS SCHEME OF YOURS OR WHAT?
AND RISK THERE BEING NO REASON FOR YOU TO CALL ME AGAIN? THINK I'LL SAVE IT FOR ANOTHER NIGHT.
SERIOUSLY, THOUGH, SHOULDN'T WE BE GETTING YOU TO A CLINIC?
NO, IT'S JUST A SCRATCH, REALLY. THE SUIT IS THE REAL CASUALTY. I'M USUALLY NOT SO CLUMSY.
CLUMSY IS ONE WORD FOR IT. USUALLY IT TAKES MORE THAN A SHARP BIT OF METAL TO DAMAGE ONE OF THOSE.
I DON'T SUPPOSE A NIGHTCAP WOULD BE OF INTEREST IN THAT CASE?
MAYBE EXPLAIN HOW A PROMISING CADET GREW INTO SUCH A KLUTZ SHE CAN'T BE TRUSTED OUT OF DOORS?
THANKS, BUT I'M BEAT.
TOMORROW IS A NEW DAY, THOUGH.
IT'S A DATE.

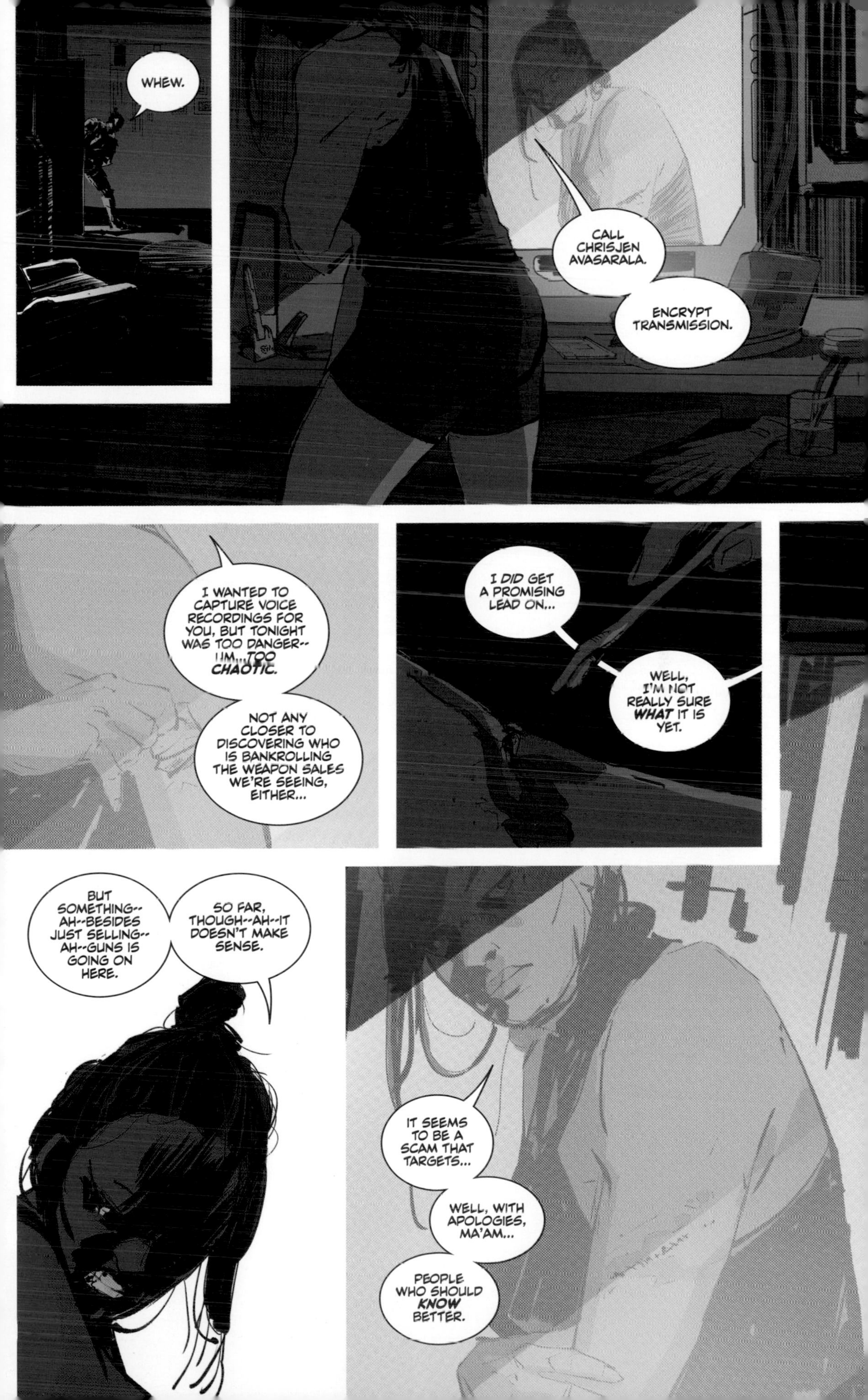
WHEW.
CALL CHRISJEN AVASARALA.
ENCRYPT TRANSMISSION.
I WANTED TO CAPTURE VOICE RECORDINGS FOR YOU, BUT TONIGHT WAS TOO DANGER-- UM...TOO CHAOTIC.
NOT ANY CLOSER TO DISCOVERING WHO IS BANKROLLING THE WEAPON SALES WE'RE SEEING, EITHER...
I DID GET A PROMISING LEAD ON...
WELL, I'M NOT REALLY SURE WHAT IT IS YET.
BUT SOMETHING-- AH--BESIDES JUST SELLING-- AH--GUNS IS GOING ON HERE.
SO FAR, THOUGH--AH--IT DOESN'T MAKE SENSE.
IT SEEMS TO BE A SCAM THAT TARGETS...
WELL, WITH APOLOGIES, MA'AM...
PEOPLE WHO SHOULD KNOW BETTER.

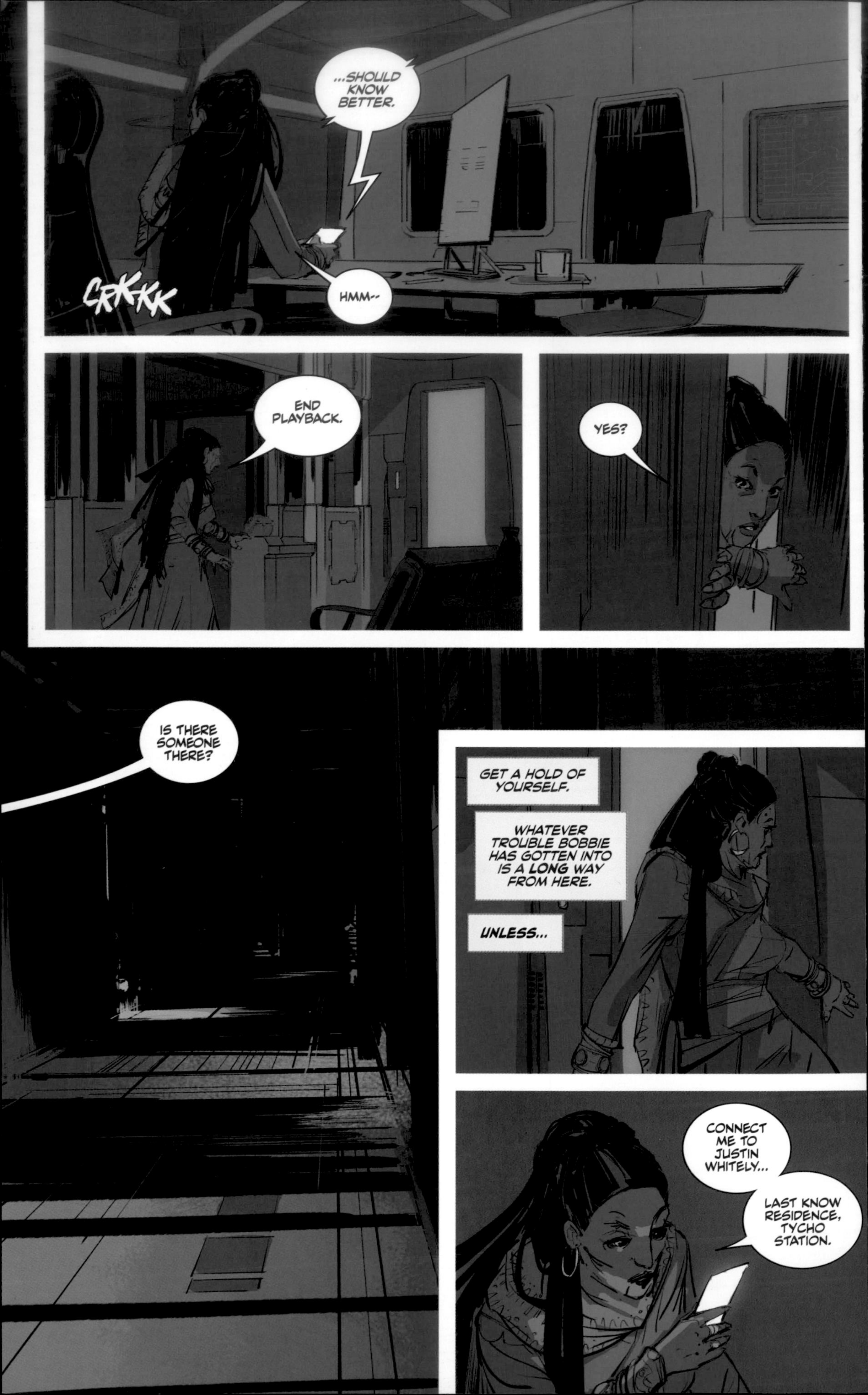
...SHOULD KNOW BETTER.
HMM--
CRKKK
END PLAYBACK.
YES?
IS THERE SOMEONE THERE?
GET A HOLD OF YOURSELF.
WHATEVER TROUBLE BOBBIE HAS GOTTEN INTO IS A LONG WAY FROM HERE.
UNLESS...
CONNECT ME TO JUSTIN WHITELY...
LAST KNOW RESIDENCE, TYCHO STATION.

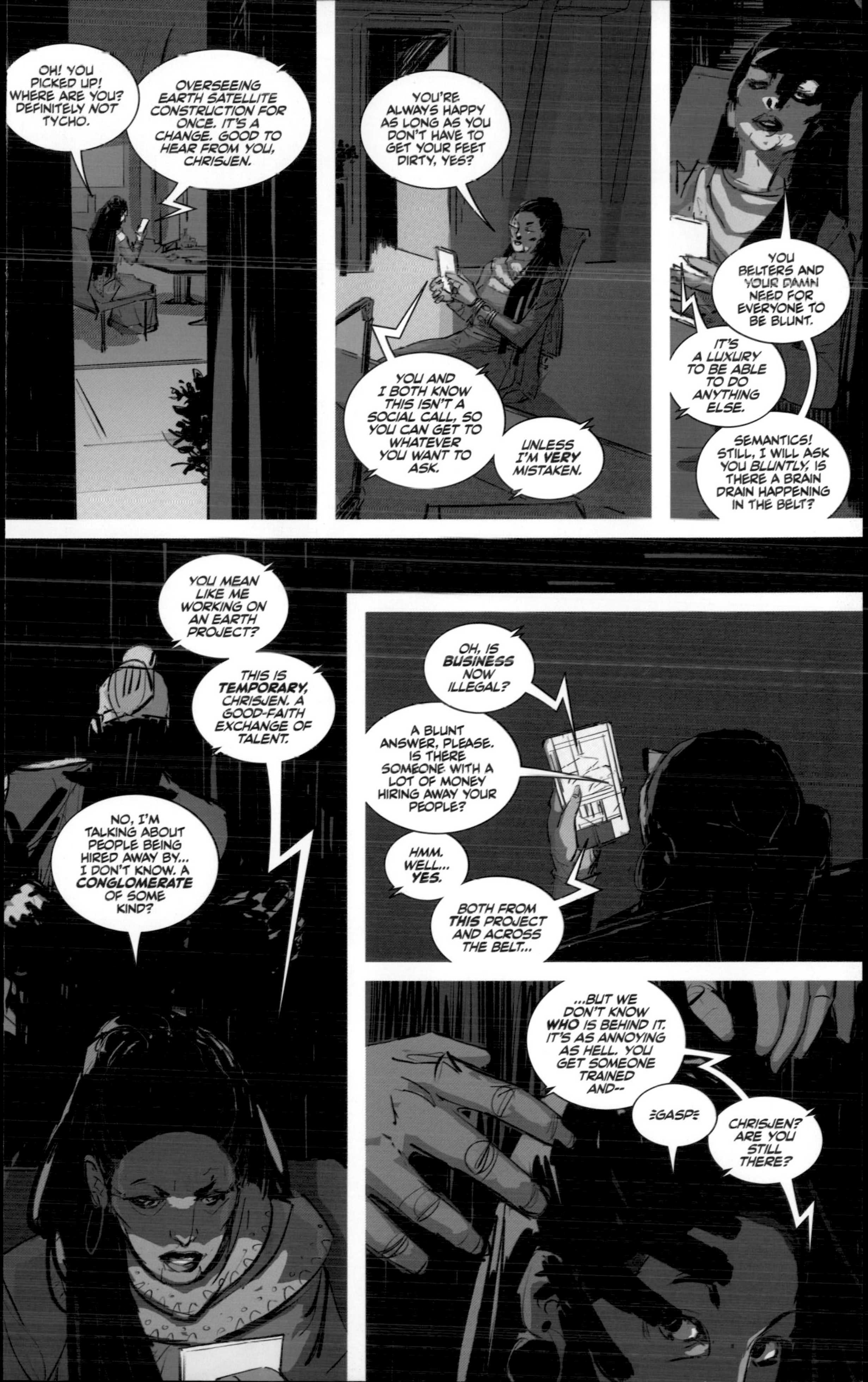

OH! YOU PICKED UP! WHERE ARE YOU? DEFINITELY NOT TYCHO.
OVERSEEING EARTH SATELLITE CONSTRUCTION FOR ONCE. IT'S A CHANGE. GOOD TO HEAR FROM YOU, CHRISJEN.
YOU'RE ALWAYS HAPPY AS LONG AS YOU DON'T HAVE TO GET YOUR FEET DIRTY, YES?
YOU AND I BOTH KNOW THIS ISN'T A SOCIAL CALL, SO YOU CAN GET TO WHATEVER YOU WANT TO ASK.
UNLESS I'M VERY MISTAKEN.
YOU BELTERS AND YOUR DAMN NEED FOR EVERYONE TO BE BLUNT.
IT'S A LUXURY TO BE ABLE TO DO ANYTHING ELSE.
SEMANTICS! STILL, I WILL ASK YOU BLUNTLY, IS THERE A BRAIN DRAIN HAPPENING IN THE BELT?
YOU MEAN LIKE ME WORKING ON AN EARTH PROJECT?
THIS IS TEMPORARY, CHRISJEN. A GOOD-FAITH EXCHANGE OF TALENT.
NO, I'M TALKING ABOUT PEOPLE BEING HIRED AWAY BY... I DON'T KNOW. A CONGLOMERATE OF SOME KIND?
OH, IS BUSINESS NOW ILLEGAL?
A BLUNT ANSWER, PLEASE. IS THERE SOMEONE WITH A LOT OF MONEY HIRING AWAY YOUR PEOPLE?
HMM. WELL... YES.
BOTH FROM THIS PROJECT AND ACROSS THE BELT...
...BUT WE DON'T KNOW WHO IS BEHIND IT. IT'S AS ANNOYING AS HELL. YOU GET SOMEONE TRAINED AND--
=GASP=
CHRISJEN? ARE YOU STILL THERE?

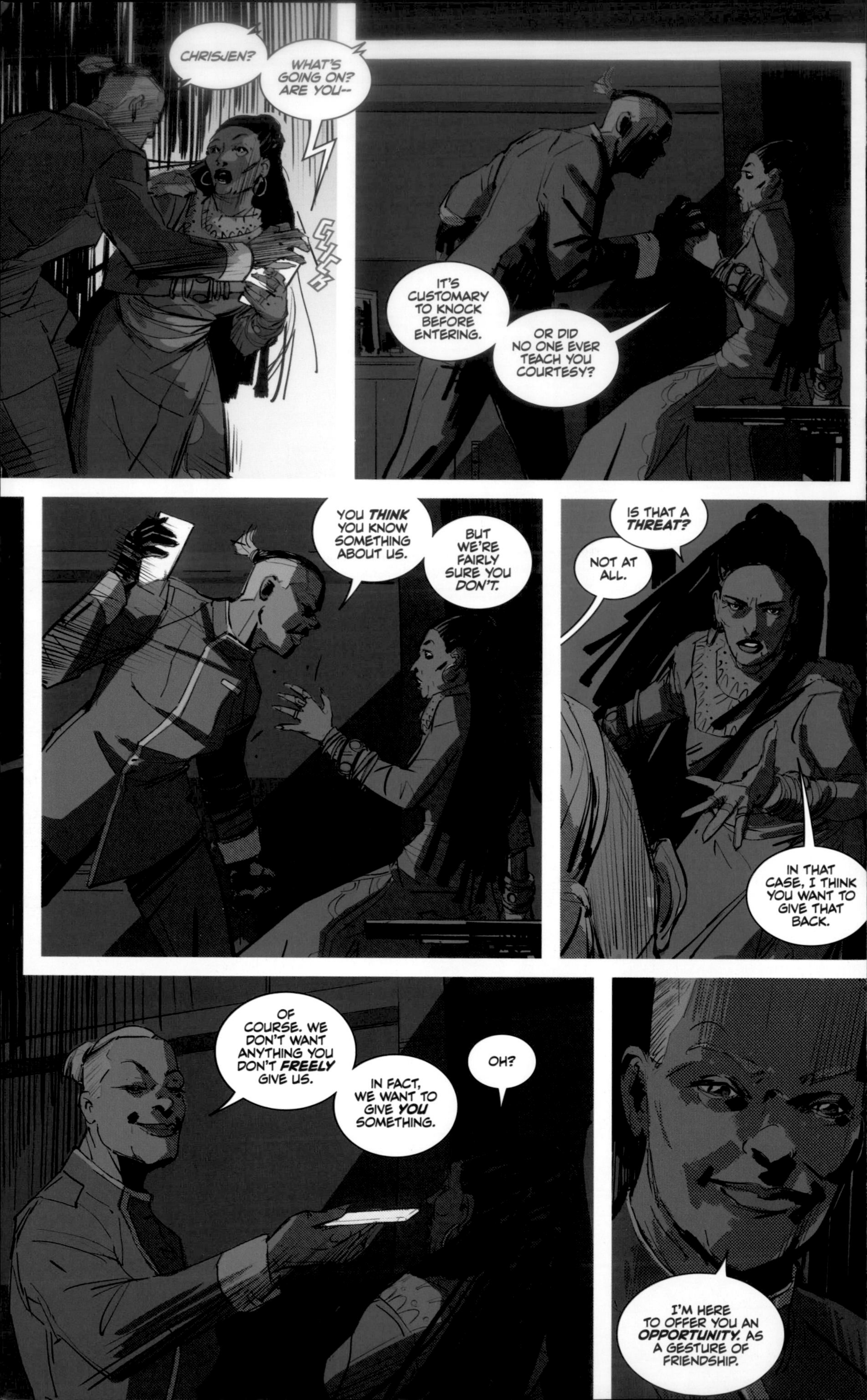
CHRISJEN?
WHAT'S GOING ON? ARE YOU--
IT'S CUSTOMARY TO KNOCK BEFORE ENTERING.
OR DID NO ONE EVER TEACH YOU COURTESY?
YOU *THINK* YOU KNOW SOMETHING ABOUT US.
BUT WE'RE FAIRLY SURE YOU *DON'T.*
IS THAT A *THREAT?*
NOT AT ALL.
IN THAT CASE, I THINK YOU WANT TO GIVE THAT BACK.
OF COURSE. WE DON'T WANT ANYTHING YOU DON'T *FREELY* GIVE US.
IN FACT, WE WANT TO GIVE *YOU* SOMETHING.
OH?
I'M HERE TO OFFER YOU AN *OPPORTUNITY.* AS A GESTURE OF FRIENDSHIP.

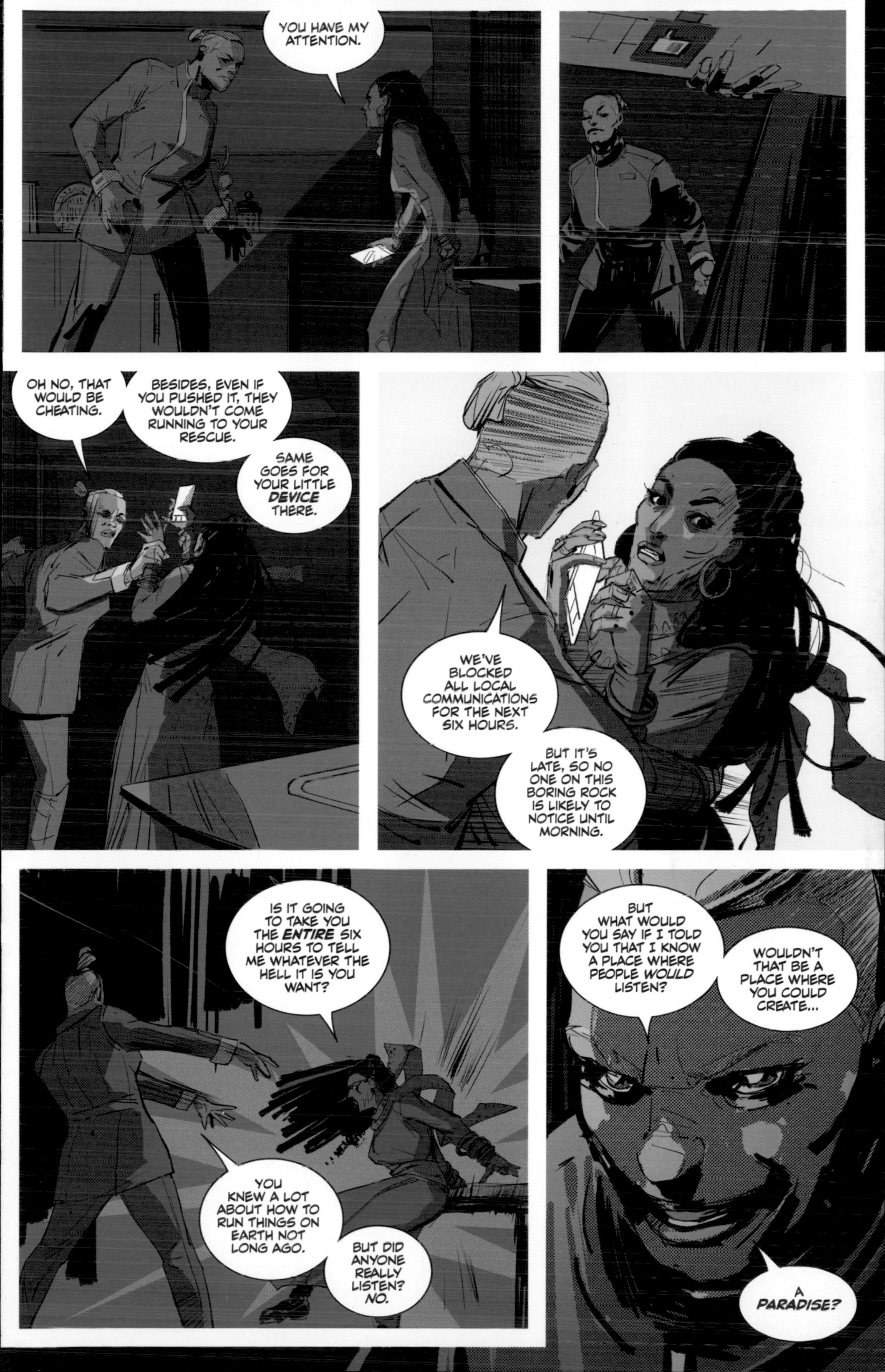
YOU HAVE MY ATTENTION.
OH NO, THAT WOULD BE CHEATING.
BESIDES, EVEN IF YOU PUSHED IT, THEY WOULDN'T COME RUNNING TO YOUR RESCUE.
SAME GOES FOR YOUR LITTLE DEVICE THERE.
WE'VE BLOCKED ALL LOCAL COMMUNICATIONS FOR THE NEXT SIX HOURS.
BUT IT'S LATE, SO NO ONE ON THIS BORING ROCK IS LIKELY TO NOTICE UNTIL MORNING.
IS IT GOING TO TAKE YOU THE ENTIRE SIX HOURS TO TELL ME WHATEVER THE HELL IT IS YOU WANT?
YOU KNEW A LOT ABOUT HOW TO RUN THINGS ON EARTH NOT LONG AGO.
BUT DID ANYONE REALLY LISTEN? NO.
BUT WHAT WOULD YOU SAY IF I TOLD YOU THAT I KNOW A PLACE WHERE PEOPLE WOULD LISTEN?
WOULDN'T THAT BE A PLACE WHERE YOU COULD CREATE...
A PARADISE?

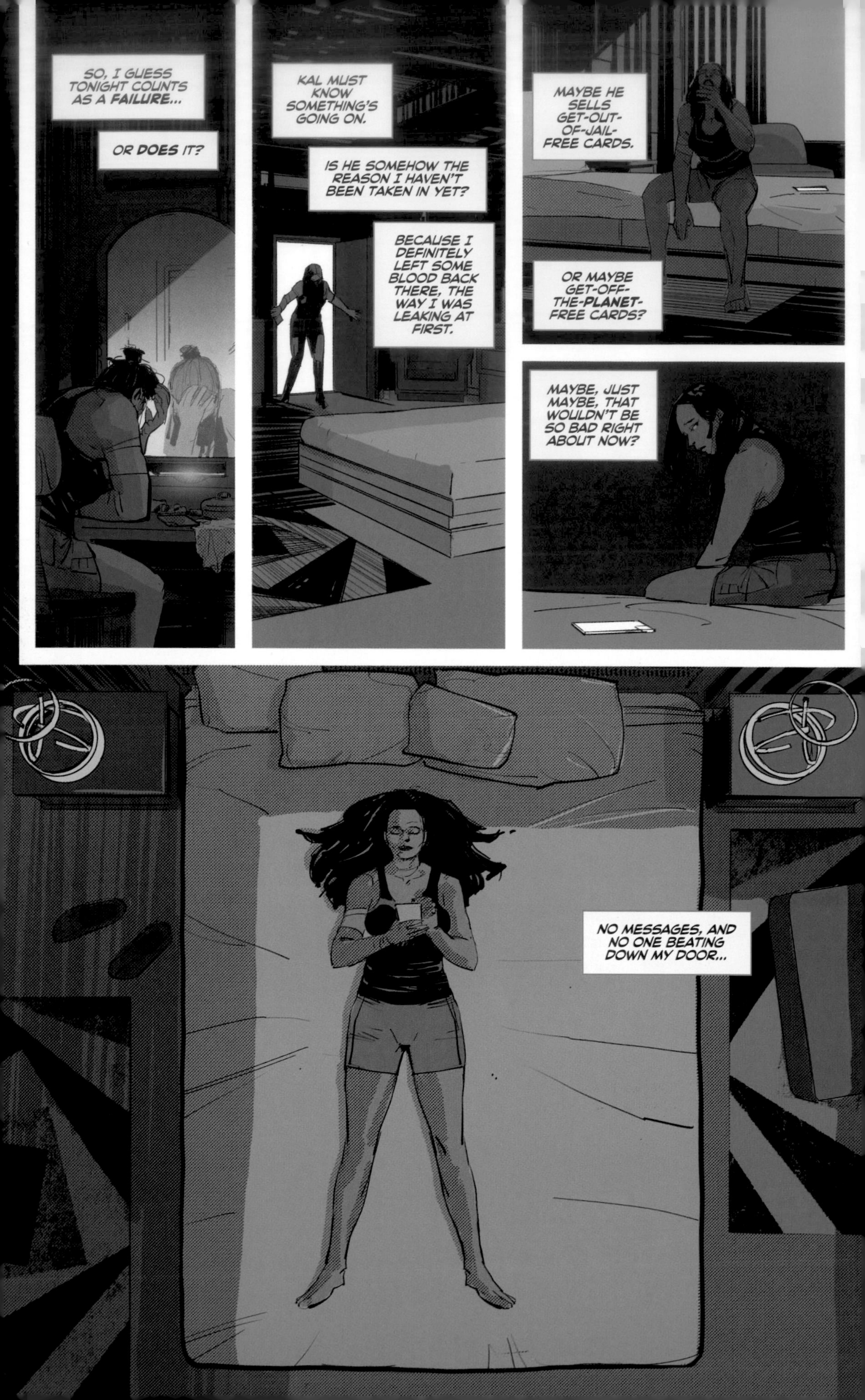
SO, I GUESS TONIGHT COUNTS AS A **FAILURE**...
OR **DOES** IT?
KAL MUST KNOW SOMETHING'S GOING ON.
IS HE SOMEHOW THE REASON I HAVEN'T BEEN TAKEN IN YET?
BECAUSE I DEFINITELY LEFT SOME BLOOD BACK THERE, THE WAY I WAS LEAKING AT FIRST.
MAYBE HE SELLS GET-OUT-OF-JAIL-FREE CARDS.
OR MAYBE GET-OFF-THE-**PLANET**-FREE CARDS?
MAYBE, JUST MAYBE, THAT WOULDN'T BE SO BAD RIGHT ABOUT NOW?
NO MESSAGES, AND NO ONE BEATING DOWN MY DOOR...

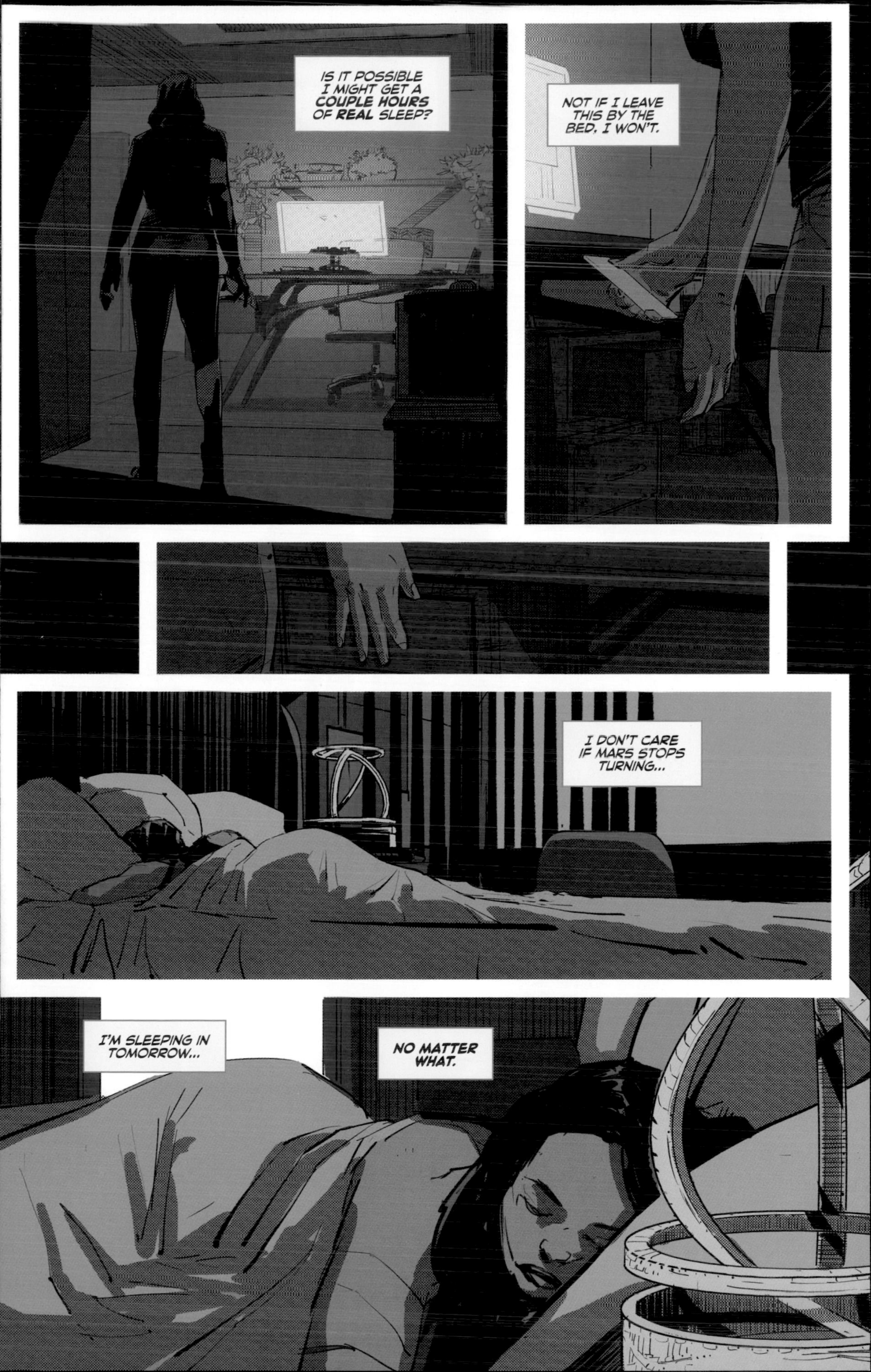
IS IT POSSIBLE I MIGHT GET A COUPLE HOURS OF REAL SLEEP?
NOT IF I LEAVE THIS BY THE BED, I WON'T.
I DON'T CARE IF MARS STOPS TURNING...
I'M SLEEPING IN TOMORROW...
NO MATTER WHAT.

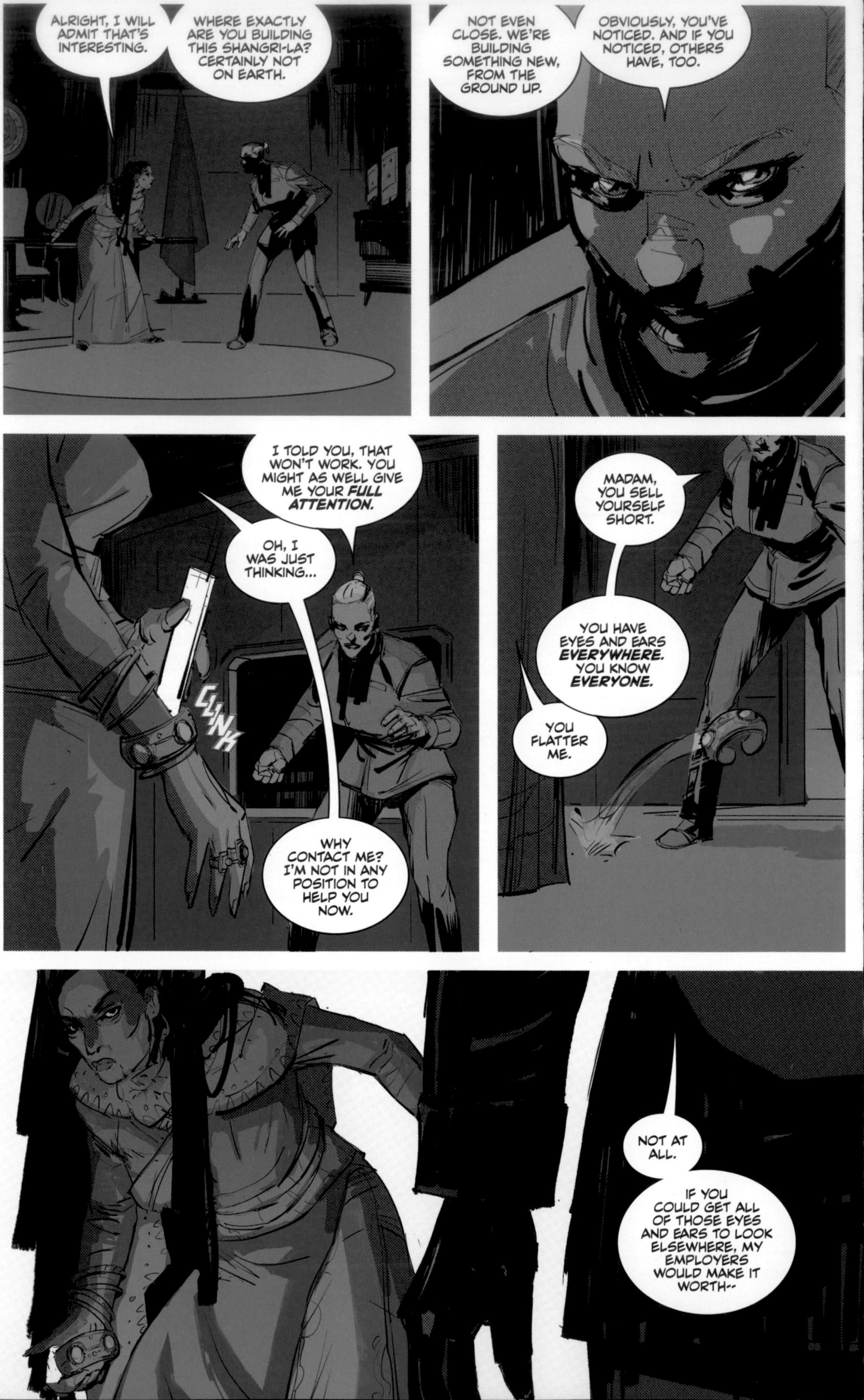
ALRIGHT, I WILL ADMIT THAT'S INTERESTING.
WHERE EXACTLY ARE YOU BUILDING THIS SHANGRI-LA? CERTAINLY NOT ON EARTH.
NOT EVEN CLOSE. WE'RE BUILDING SOMETHING NEW, FROM THE GROUND UP.
OBVIOUSLY, YOU'VE NOTICED. AND IF YOU NOTICED, OTHERS HAVE, TOO.
I TOLD YOU, THAT WON'T WORK. YOU MIGHT AS WELL GIVE ME YOUR FULL ATTENTION.
OH, I WAS JUST THINKING...
CLINK
WHY CONTACT ME? I'M NOT IN ANY POSITION TO HELP YOU NOW.
MADAM, YOU SELL YOURSELF SHORT.
YOU HAVE EYES AND EARS EVERYWHERE. YOU KNOW EVERYONE.
YOU FLATTER ME.
NOT AT ALL.
IF YOU COULD GET ALL OF THOSE EYES AND EARS TO LOOK ELSEWHERE, MY EMPLOYERS WOULD MAKE IT WORTH--

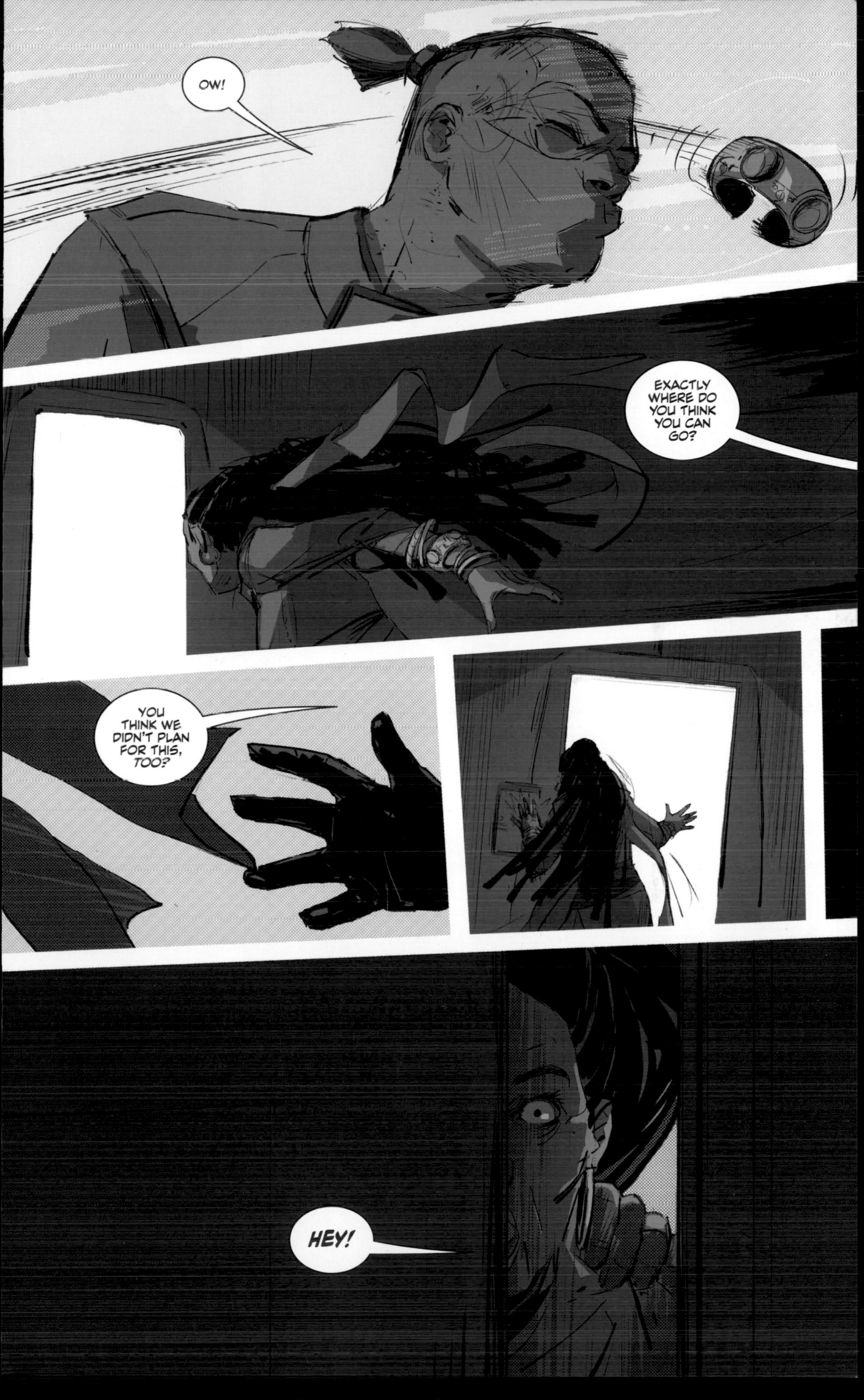
OW!
EXACTLY WHERE DO YOU THINK YOU CAN GO?
YOU THINK WE DIDN'T PLAN FOR THIS, TOO?
HEY!

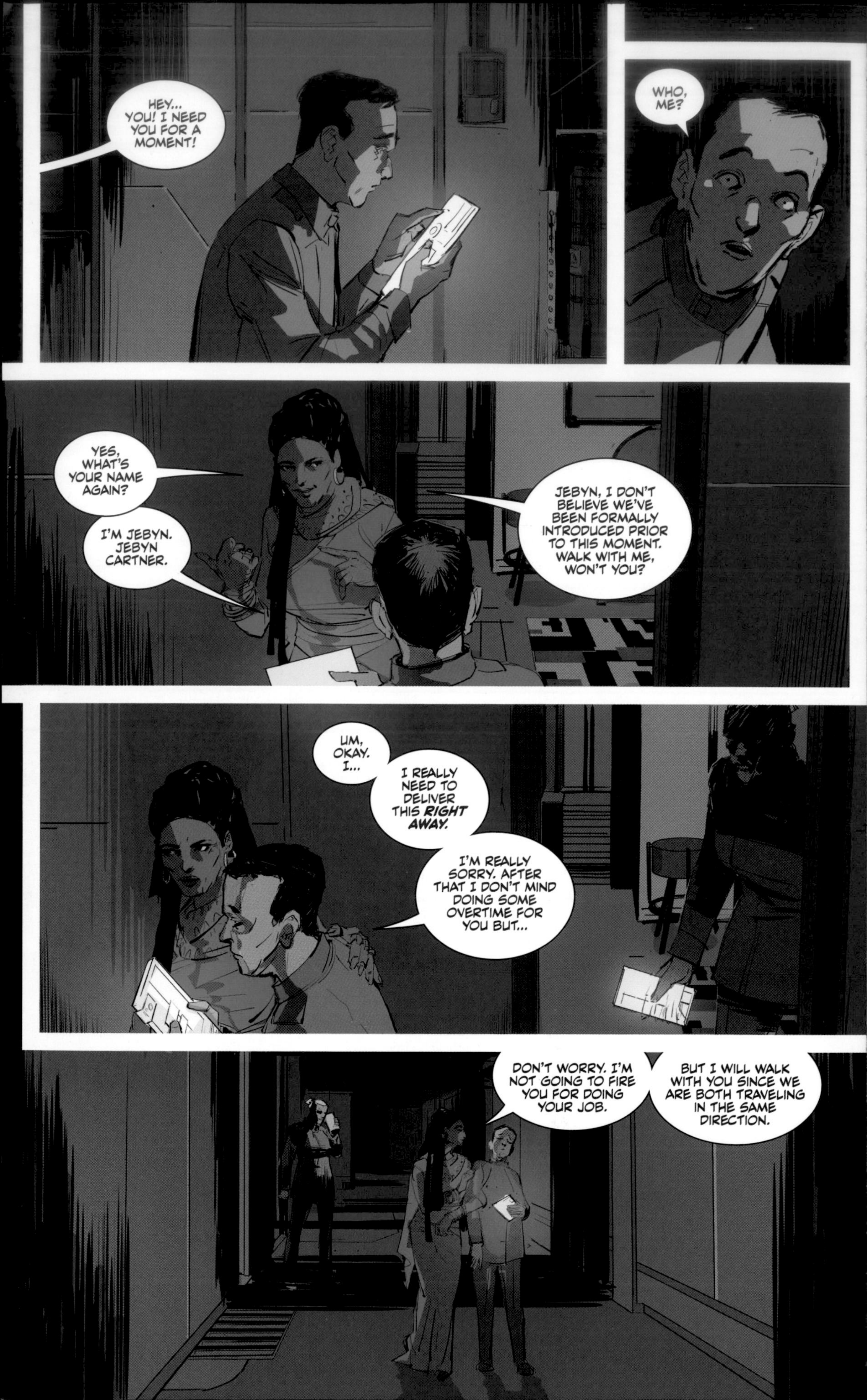
HEY... YOU! I NEED YOU FOR A MOMENT!
WHO, ME?
YES, WHAT'S YOUR NAME AGAIN?
I'M JEBYN. JEBYN CARTNER.
JEBYN, I DON'T BELIEVE WE'VE BEEN FORMALLY INTRODUCED PRIOR TO THIS MOMENT. WALK WITH ME, WON'T YOU?
UM, OKAY. I...
I REALLY NEED TO DELIVER THIS *RIGHT AWAY.*
I'M REALLY SORRY. AFTER THAT I DON'T MIND DOING SOME OVERTIME FOR YOU BUT...
DON'T WORRY. I'M NOT GOING TO FIRE YOU FOR DOING YOUR JOB.
BUT I WILL WALK WITH YOU SINCE WE ARE BOTH TRAVELING IN THE SAME DIRECTION.

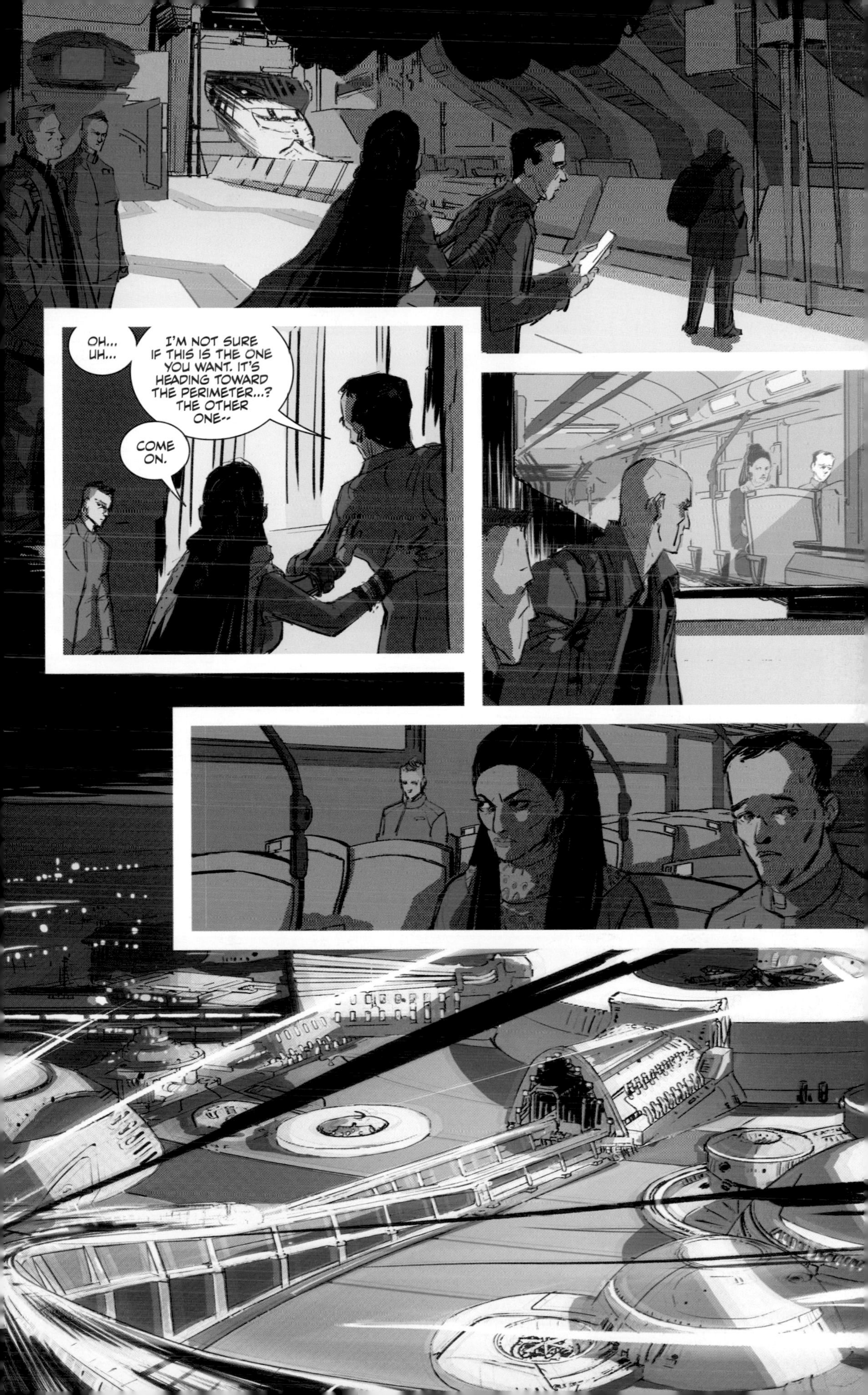
OH... UH...
I'M NOT SURE IF THIS IS THE ONE YOU WANT. IT'S HEADING TOWARD THE PERIMETER...? THE OTHER ONE--
COME ON.

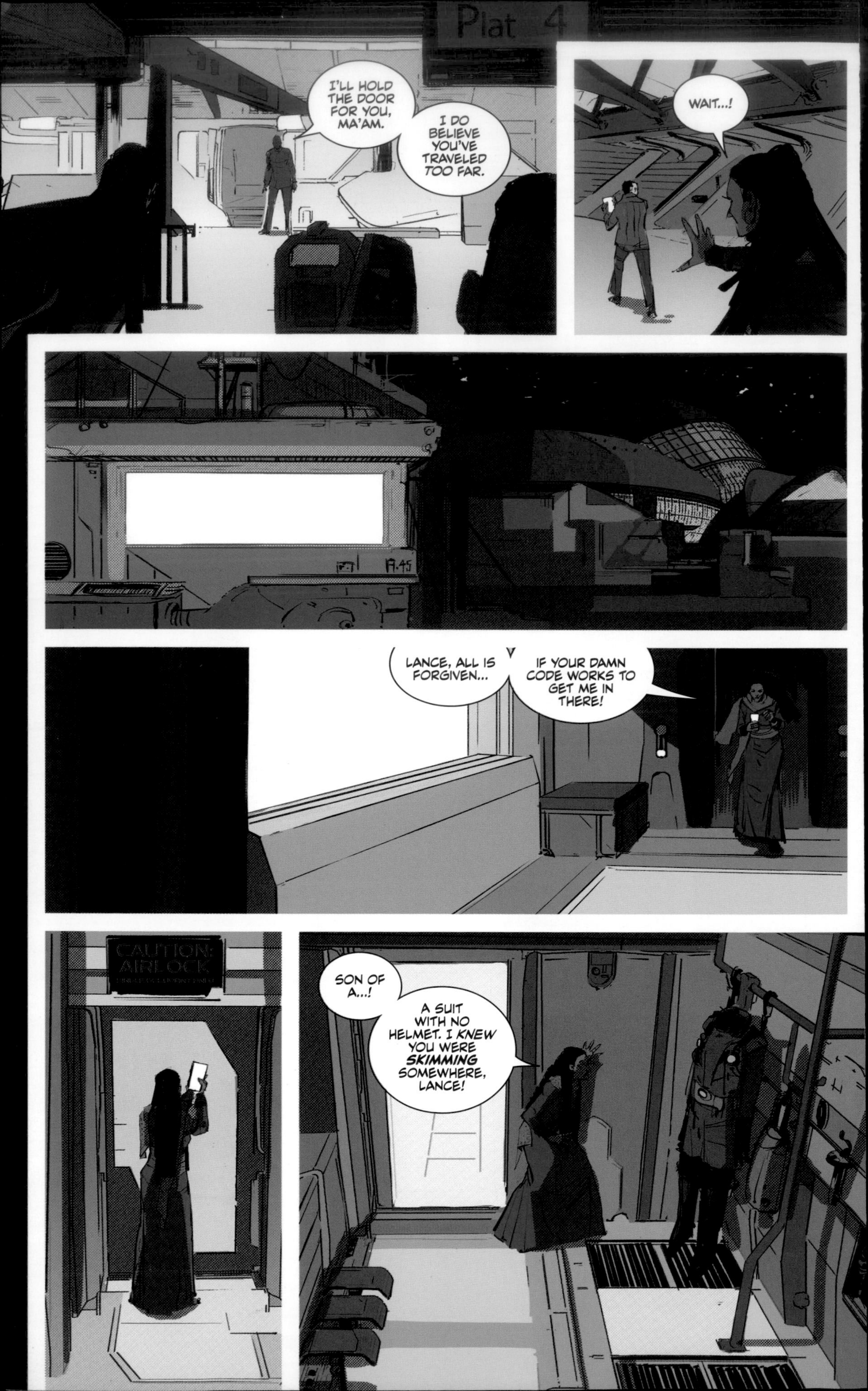
Plat 4
I'LL HOLD THE DOOR FOR YOU, MA'AM.
I DO BELIEVE YOU'VE TRAVELED *TOO FAR.*
WAIT...!
LANCE, ALL IS FORGIVEN...
IF YOUR DAMN CODE WORKS TO GET ME IN THERE!
CAUTION: AIRLOCK
SON OF A...!
A SUIT WITH NO HELMET. I *KNEW* YOU WERE ***SKIMMING*** SOMEWHERE, LANCE!

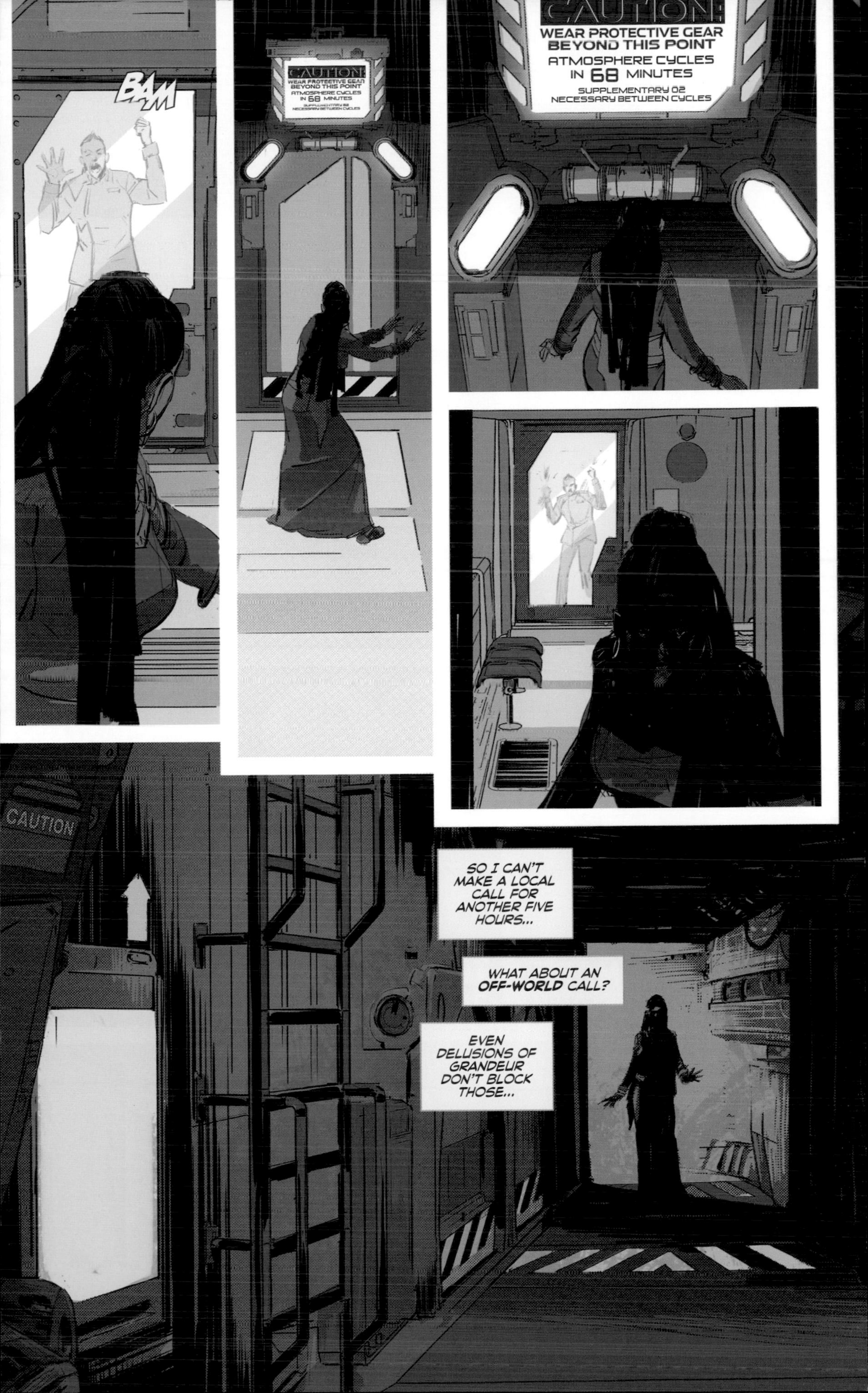
BAM
CAUTION!
WEAR PROTECTIVE GEAR
BEYOND THIS POINT
ATMOSPHERE CYCLES
IN 68 MINUTES
CAUTION!
WEAR PROTECTIVE GEAR
BEYOND THIS POINT
ATMOSPHERE CYCLES
IN 68 MINUTES
SUPPLEMENTARY O2
NECESSARY BETWEEN CYCLES
CAUTION
SO I CAN'T MAKE A LOCAL CALL FOR ANOTHER FIVE HOURS...
WHAT ABOUT AN ***OFF-WORLD*** CALL?
EVEN DELUSIONS OF GRANDEUR DON'T BLOCK THOSE...

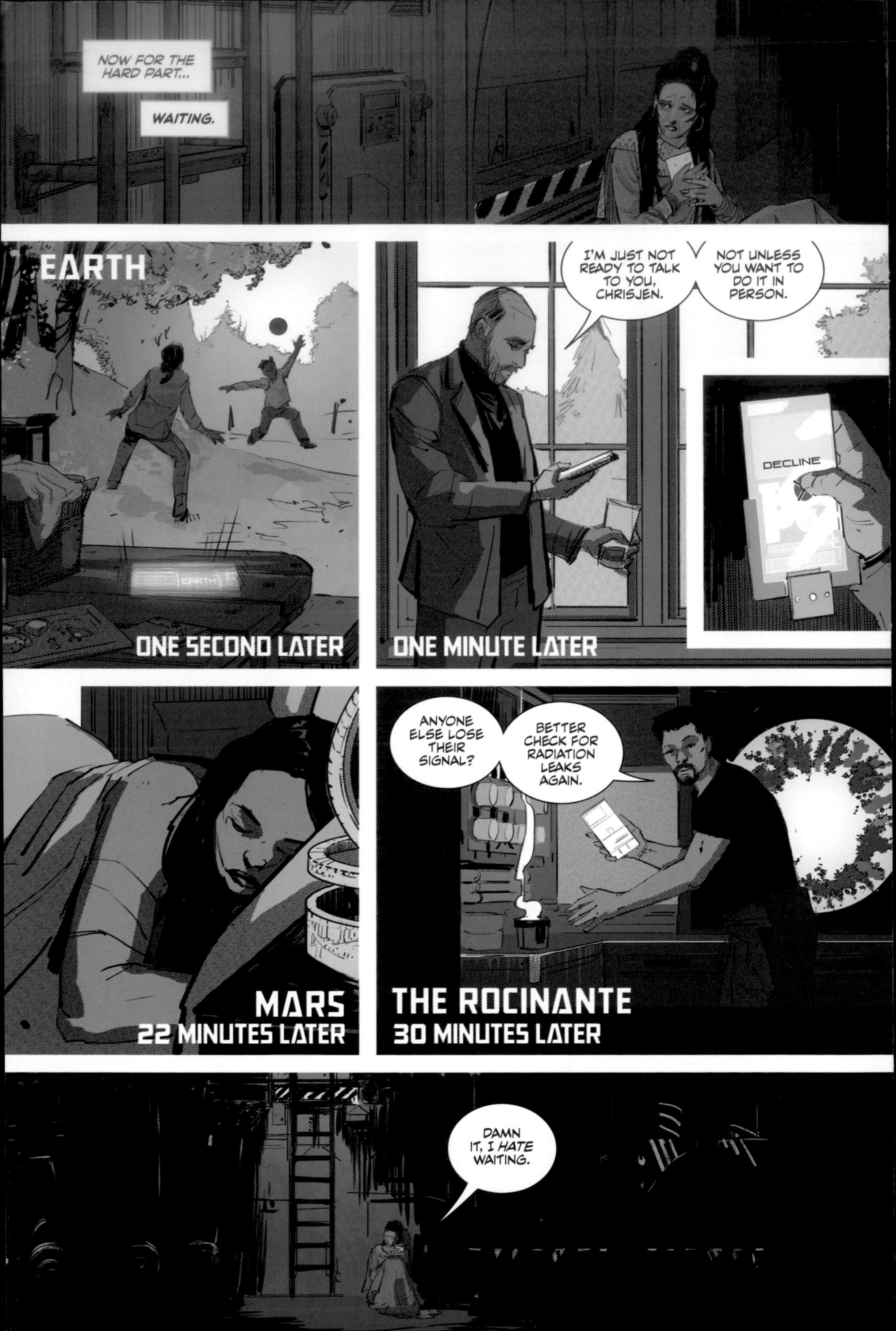

NOW FOR THE HARD PART...
WAITING.
EARTH
EARTH
ONE SECOND LATER
I'M JUST NOT READY TO TALK TO YOU, CHRISJEN.
NOT UNLESS YOU WANT TO DO IT IN PERSON.
DECLINE
ONE MINUTE LATER
MARS
22 MINUTES LATER
ANYONE ELSE LOSE THEIR SIGNAL?
BETTER CHECK FOR RADIATION LEAKS AGAIN.
THE ROCINANTE
30 MINUTES LATER
DAMN IT, I *HATE* WAITING.

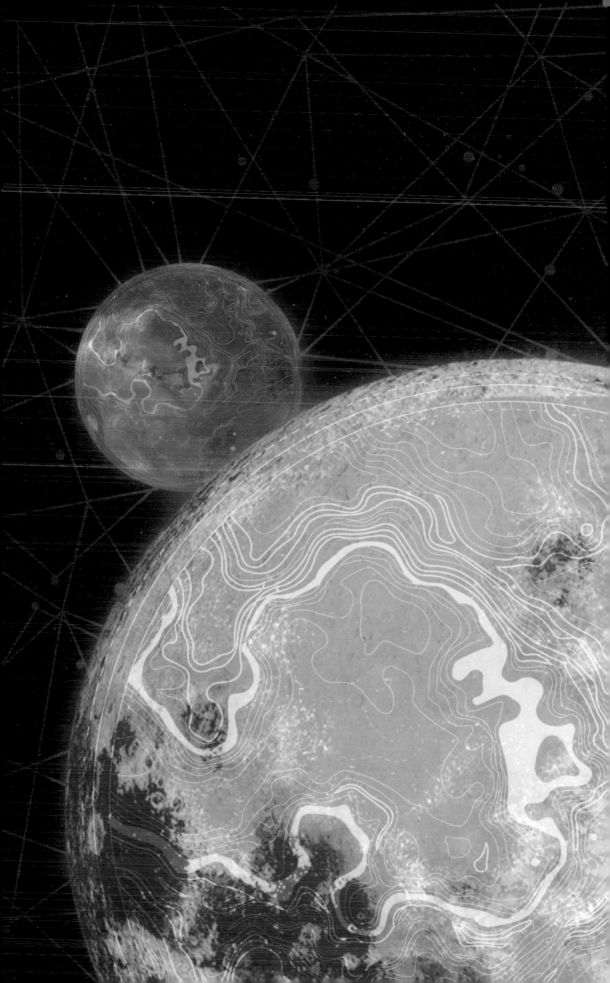

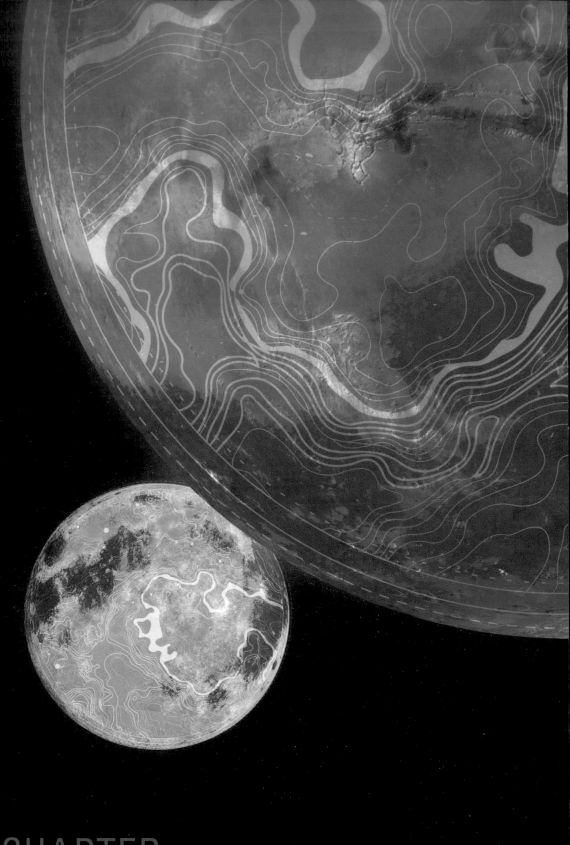

CHAPTER
THREE

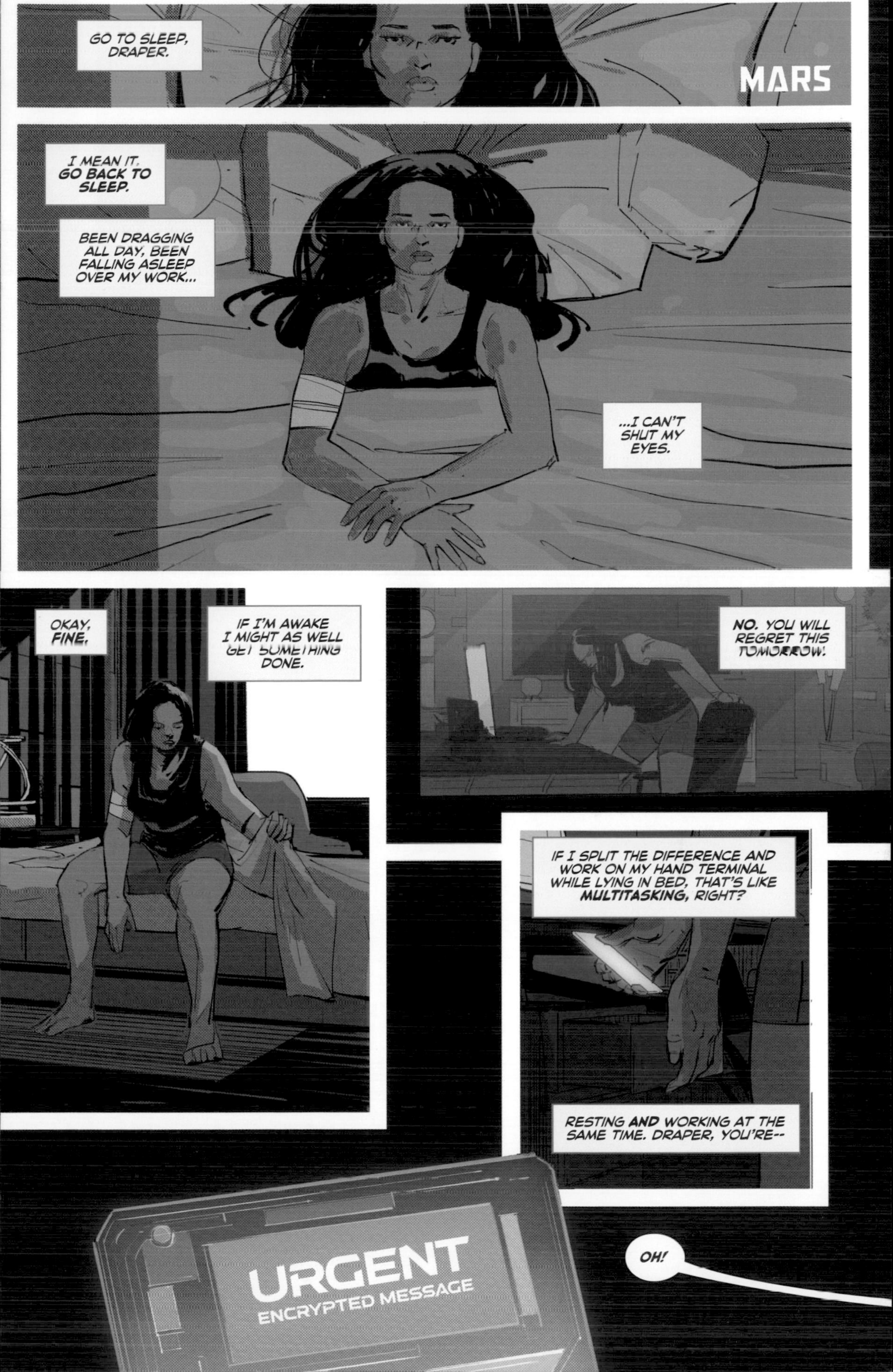

GO TO SLEEP, DRAPER.
MARS
I MEAN IT. GO BACK TO SLEEP.
BEEN DRAGGING ALL DAY, BEEN FALLING ASLEEP OVER MY WORK...
...I CAN'T SHUT MY EYES.
OKAY, FINE.
IF I'M AWAKE I MIGHT AS WELL GET SOMETHING DONE.
NO. YOU WILL REGRET THIS TOMORROW.
IF I SPLIT THE DIFFERENCE AND WORK ON MY HAND TERMINAL WHILE LYING IN BED, THAT'S LIKE MULTITASKING, RIGHT?
RESTING AND WORKING AT THE SAME TIME. DRAPER, YOU'RE--
URGENT
ENCRYPTED MESSAGE
OH!

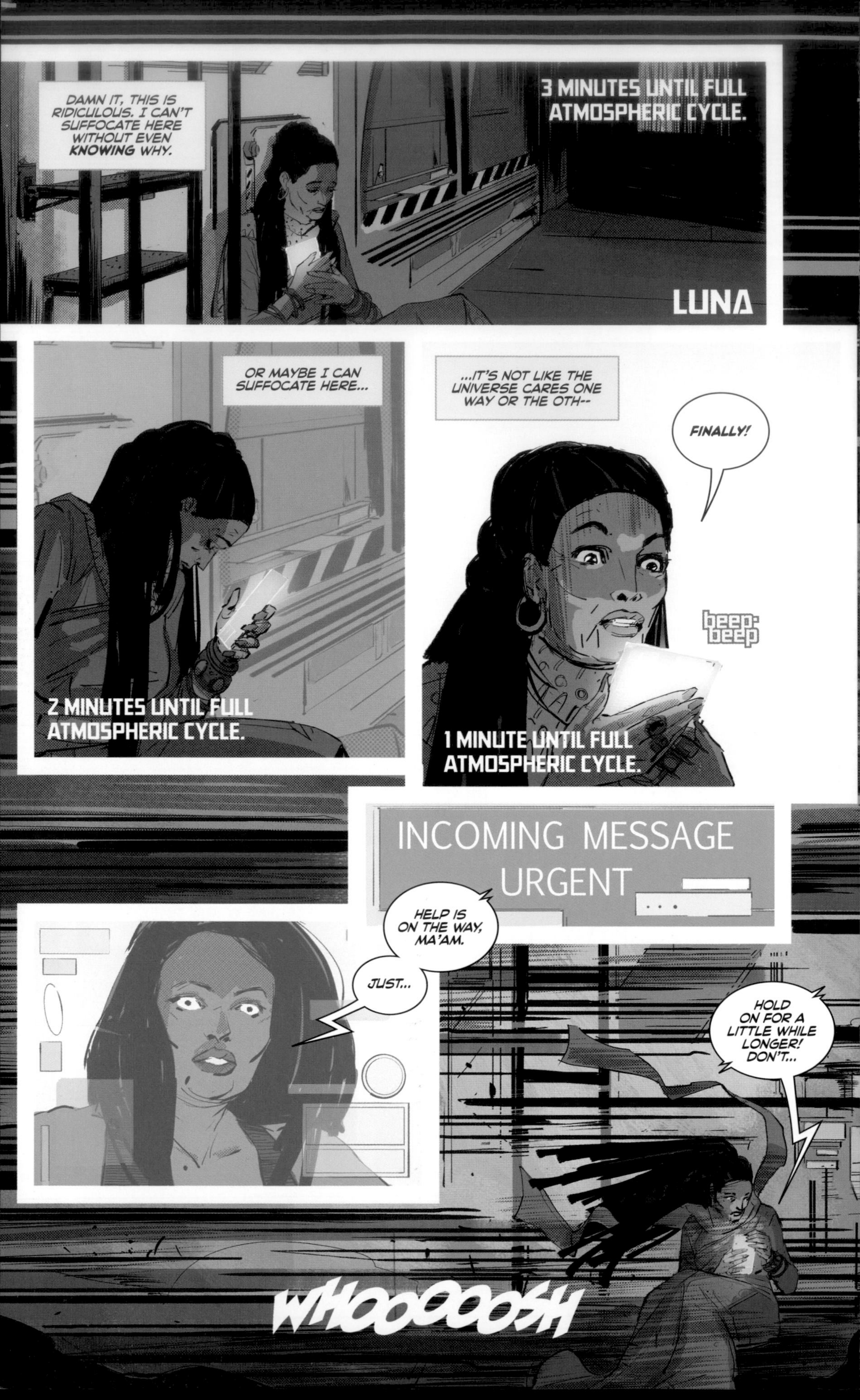
DAMN IT, THIS IS RIDICULOUS. I CAN'T SUFFOCATE HERE WITHOUT EVEN KNOWING WHY.
3 MINUTES UNTIL FULL ATMOSPHERIC CYCLE.
LUNA
OR MAYBE I CAN SUFFOCATE HERE...
2 MINUTES UNTIL FULL ATMOSPHERIC CYCLE.
...IT'S NOT LIKE THE UNIVERSE CARES ONE WAY OR THE OTH--
FINALLY!
beep-beep
1 MINUTE UNTIL FULL ATMOSPHERIC CYCLE.
INCOMING MESSAGE
URGENT
HELP IS ON THE WAY, MA'AM.
JUST...
HOLD ON FOR A LITTLE WHILE LONGER! DON'T...
WHOOOOOSH

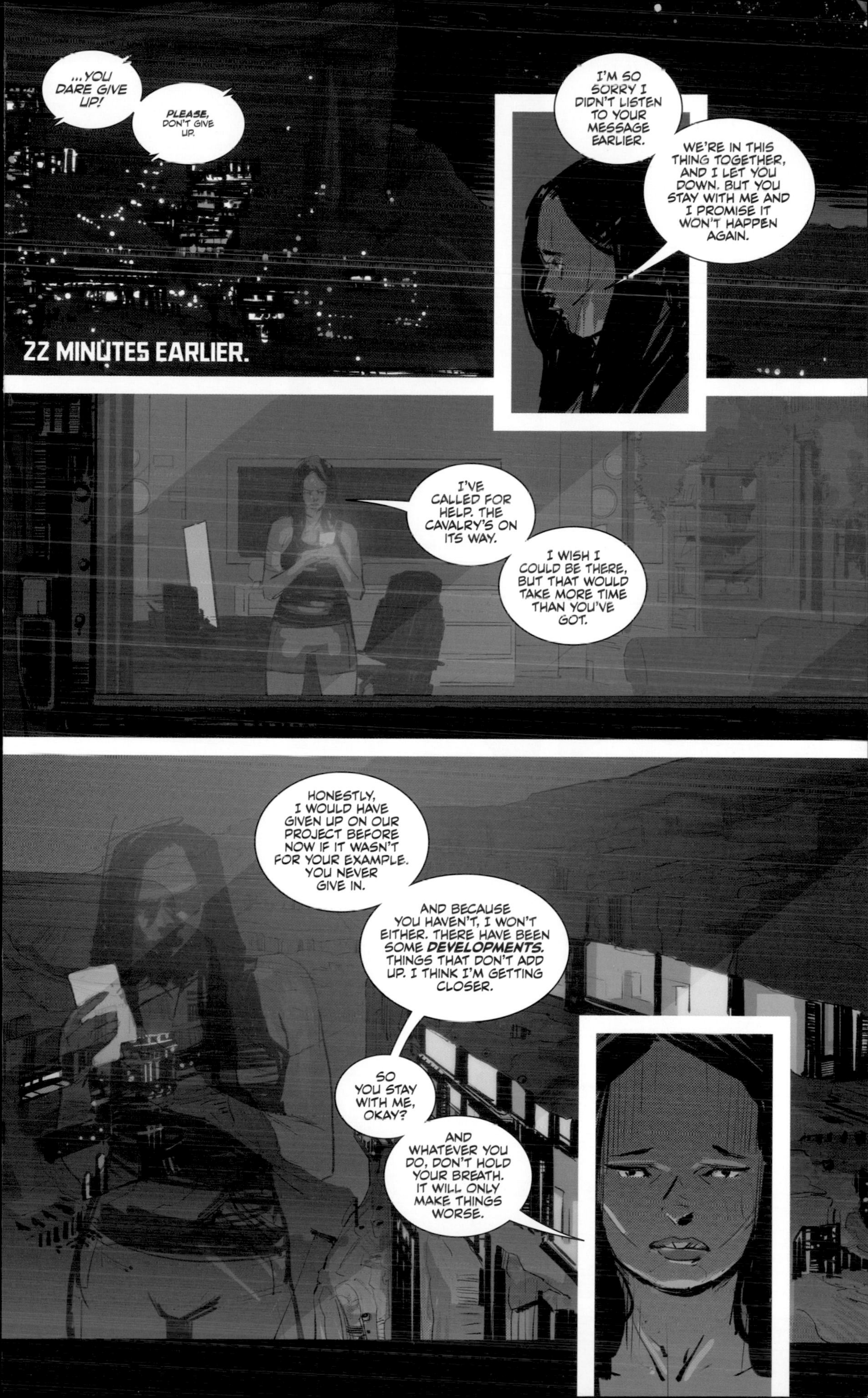
...YOU DARE GIVE UP!
PLEASE, DON'T GIVE UP.
22 MINUTES EARLIER.
I'M SO SORRY I DIDN'T LISTEN TO YOUR MESSAGE EARLIER.
WE'RE IN THIS THING TOGETHER, AND I LET YOU DOWN. BUT YOU STAY WITH ME AND I PROMISE IT WON'T HAPPEN AGAIN.
I'VE CALLED FOR HELP. THE CAVALRY'S ON ITS WAY.
I WISH I COULD BE THERE, BUT THAT WOULD TAKE MORE TIME THAN YOU'VE GOT.
HONESTLY, I WOULD HAVE GIVEN UP ON OUR PROJECT BEFORE NOW IF IT WASN'T FOR YOUR EXAMPLE. YOU NEVER GIVE IN.
AND BECAUSE YOU HAVEN'T, I WON'T EITHER. THERE HAVE BEEN SOME DEVELOPMENTS. THINGS THAT DON'T ADD UP. I THINK I'M GETTING CLOSER.
SO YOU STAY WITH ME, OKAY?
AND WHATEVER YOU DO, DON'T HOLD YOUR BREATH. IT WILL ONLY MAKE THINGS WORSE.

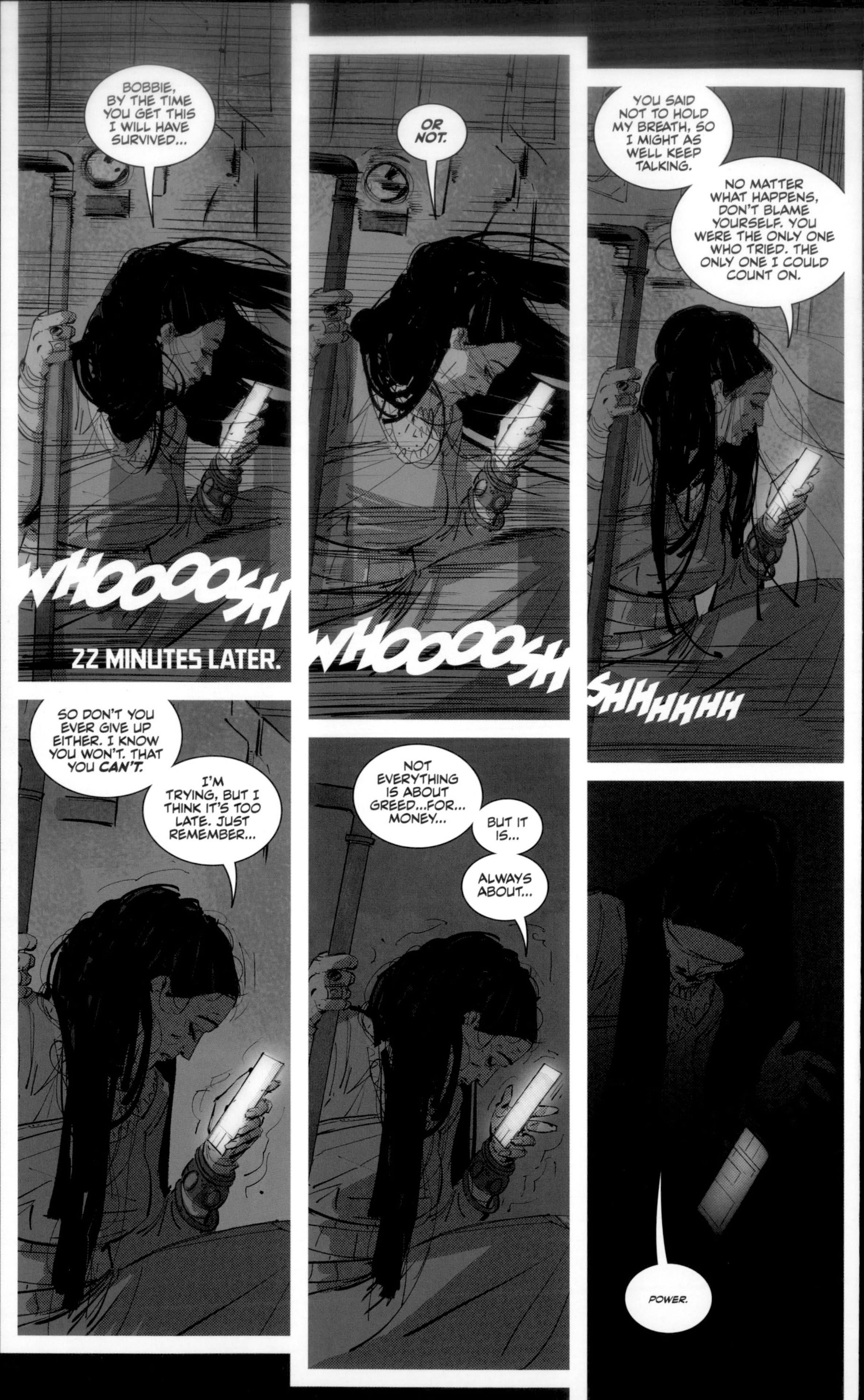
BOBBIE, BY THE TIME YOU GET THIS I WILL HAVE SURVIVED...
WHOOOOSH
22 MINUTES LATER.
OR NOT.
WHOOOOSH
YOU SAID NOT TO HOLD MY BREATH, SO I MIGHT AS WELL KEEP TALKING.
NO MATTER WHAT HAPPENS, DON'T BLAME YOURSELF. YOU WERE THE ONLY ONE WHO TRIED. THE ONLY ONE I COULD COUNT ON.
SHHHHHH
SO DON'T YOU EVER GIVE UP EITHER. I KNOW YOU WON'T. THAT YOU CAN'T.
I'M TRYING, BUT I THINK IT'S TOO LATE. JUST REMEMBER...
NOT EVERYTHING IS ABOUT GREED...FOR... MONEY...
BUT IT IS...
ALWAYS ABOUT...
POWER.

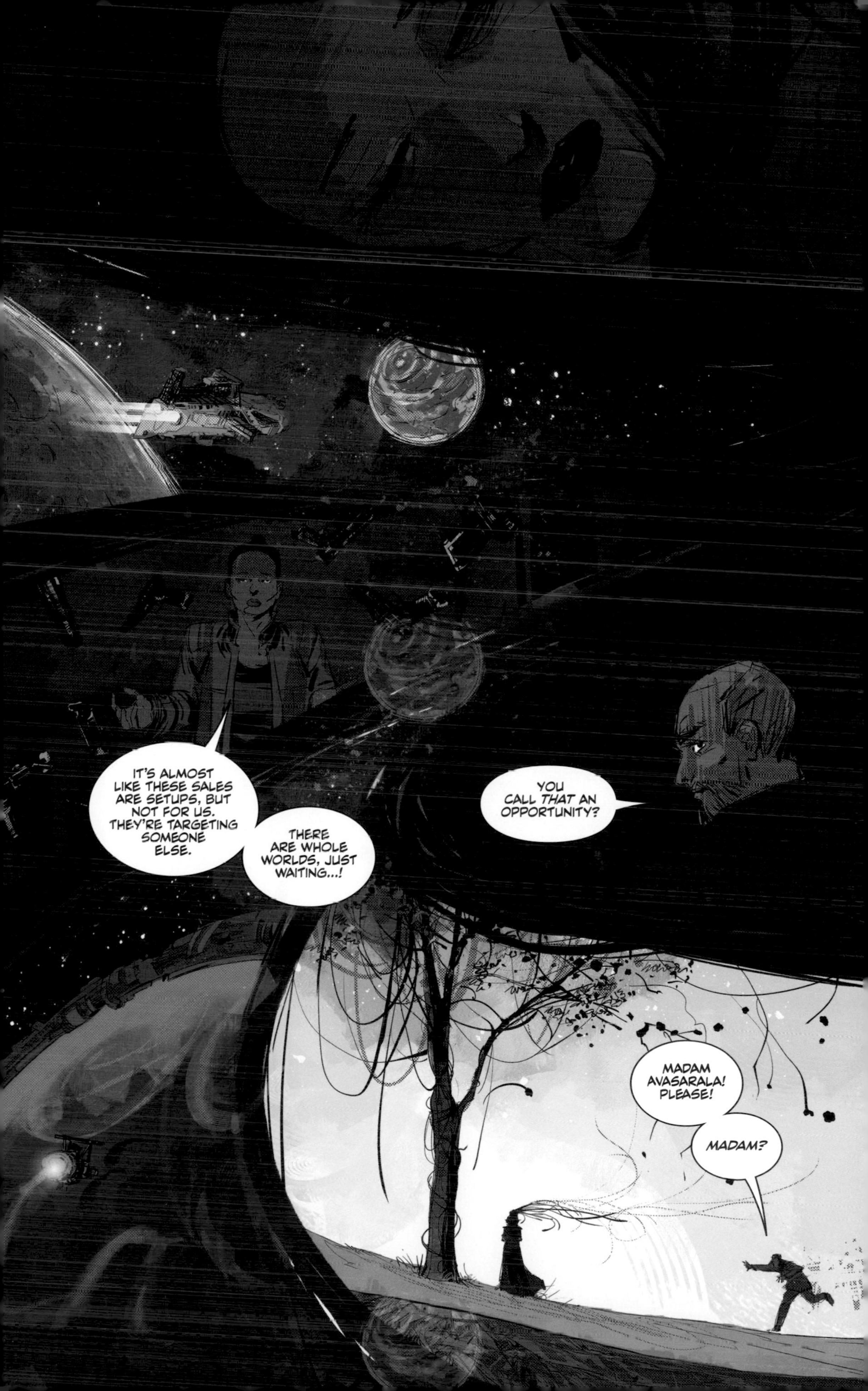
IT'S ALMOST LIKE THESE SALES ARE SETUPS, BUT NOT FOR US. THEY'RE TARGETING SOMEONE ELSE.
THERE ARE WHOLE WORLDS, JUST WAITING...!
YOU CALL *THAT* AN OPPORTUNITY?
MADAM AVASARALA! PLEASE!
MADAM?

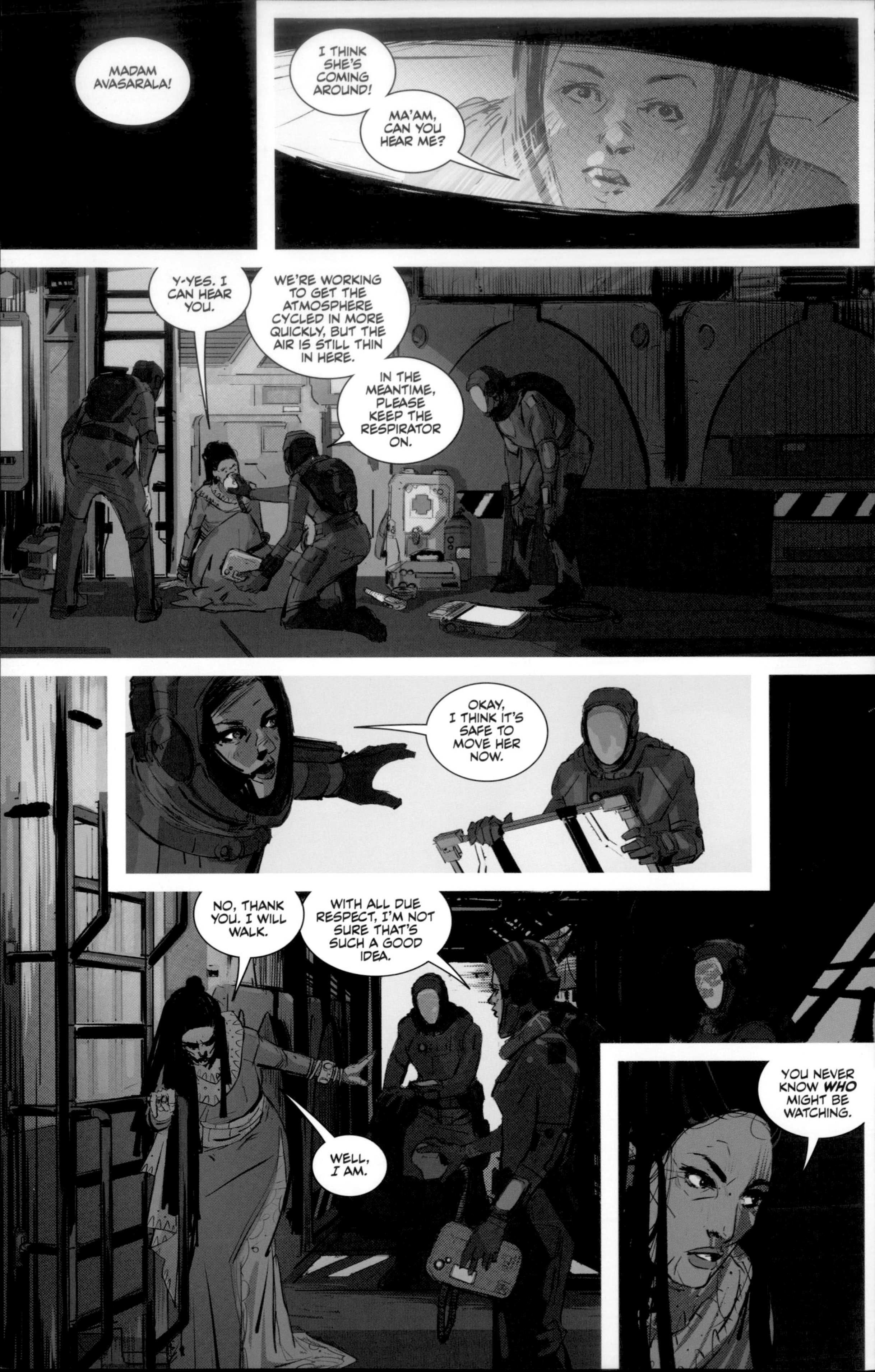
MADAM AVASARALA!
I THINK SHE'S COMING AROUND!
MA'AM, CAN YOU HEAR ME?
Y-YES. I CAN HEAR YOU.
WE'RE WORKING TO GET THE ATMOSPHERE CYCLED IN MORE QUICKLY, BUT THE AIR IS STILL THIN IN HERE.
IN THE MEANTIME, PLEASE KEEP THE RESPIRATOR ON.
OKAY, I THINK IT'S SAFE TO MOVE HER NOW.
NO, THANK YOU. I WILL WALK.
WITH ALL DUE RESPECT, I'M NOT SURE THAT'S SUCH A GOOD IDEA.
WELL, *I* AM.
YOU NEVER KNOW ***WHO*** MIGHT BE WATCHING.

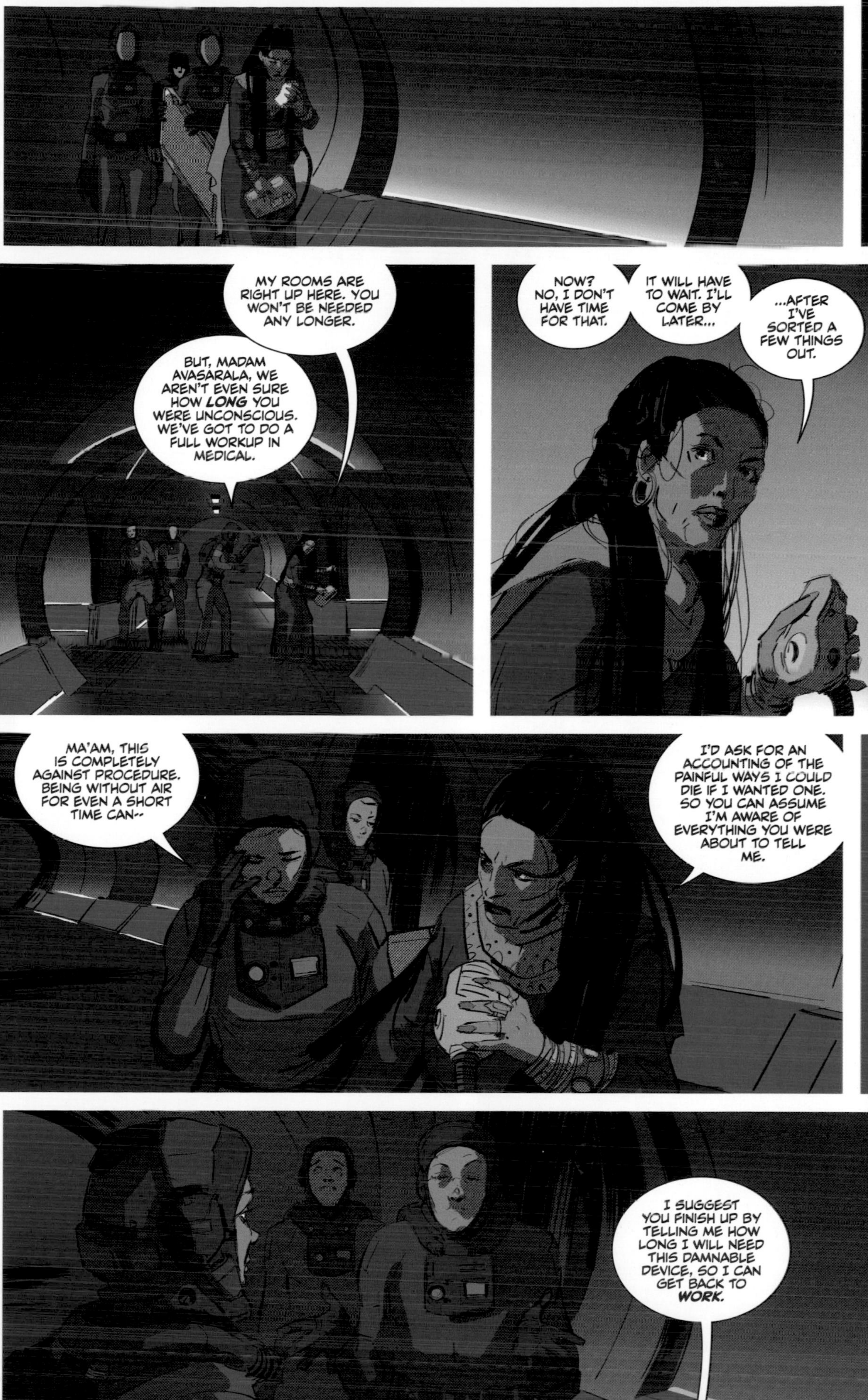
MY ROOMS ARE RIGHT UP HERE. YOU WON'T BE NEEDED ANY LONGER.
BUT, MADAM AVASARALA, WE AREN'T EVEN SURE HOW LONG YOU WERE UNCONSCIOUS. WE'VE GOT TO DO A FULL WORKUP IN MEDICAL.
NOW? NO, I DON'T HAVE TIME FOR THAT.
IT WILL HAVE TO WAIT. I'LL COME BY LATER...
...AFTER I'VE SORTED A FEW THINGS OUT.
MA'AM, THIS IS COMPLETELY AGAINST PROCEDURE. BEING WITHOUT AIR FOR EVEN A SHORT TIME CAN--
I'D ASK FOR AN ACCOUNTING OF THE PAINFUL WAYS I COULD DIE IF I WANTED ONE. SO YOU CAN ASSUME I'M AWARE OF EVERYTHING YOU WERE ABOUT TO TELL ME.
I SUGGEST YOU FINISH UP BY TELLING ME HOW LONG I WILL NEED THIS DAMNABLE DEVICE, SO I CAN GET BACK TO WORK.

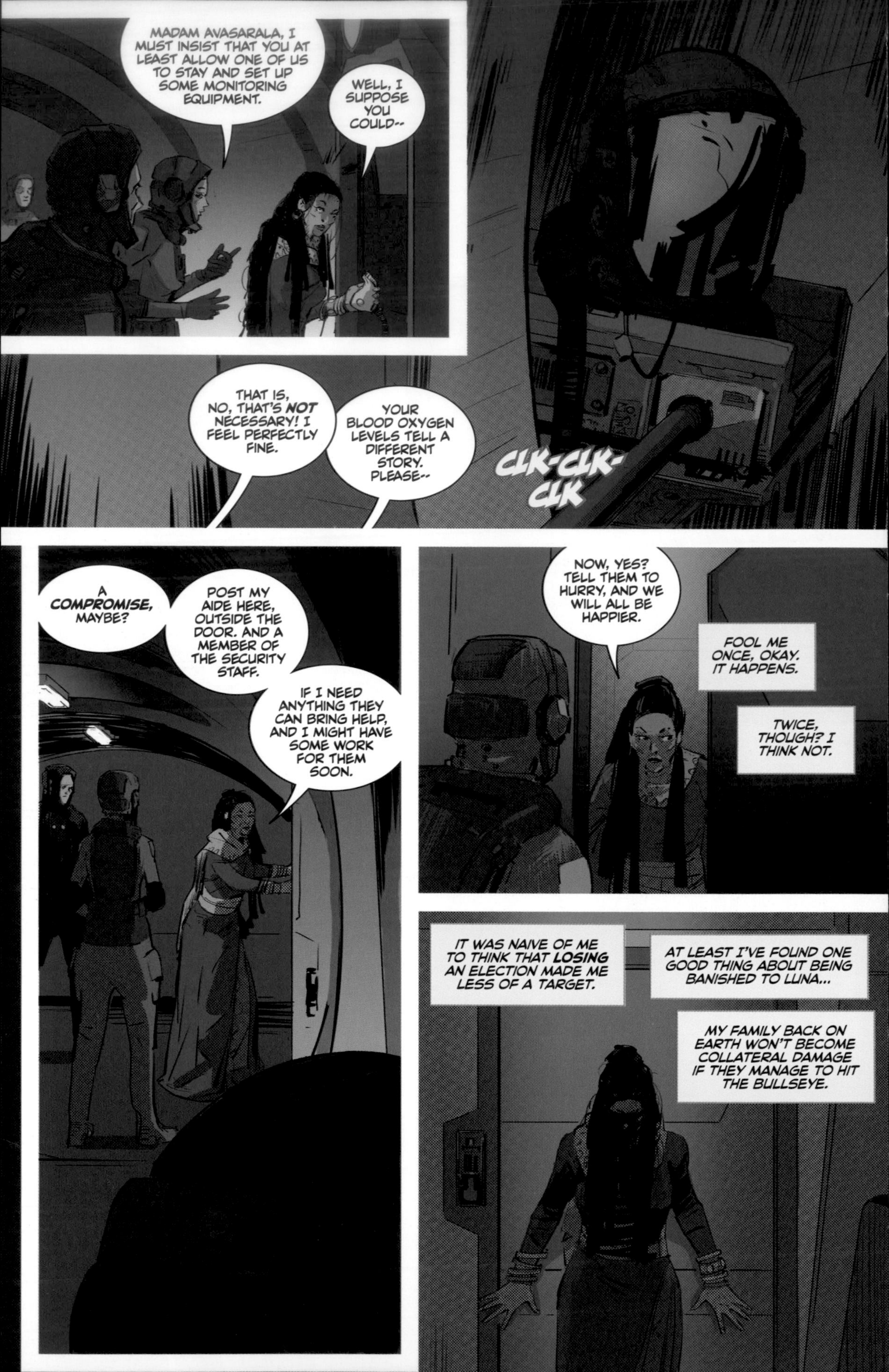
MADAM AVASARALA, I MUST INSIST THAT YOU AT LEAST ALLOW ONE OF US TO STAY AND SET UP SOME MONITORING EQUIPMENT.
WELL, I SUPPOSE YOU COULD--
THAT IS, NO, THAT'S **NOT** NECESSARY! I FEEL PERFECTLY FINE.
YOUR BLOOD OXYGEN LEVELS TELL A DIFFERENT STORY. PLEASE--
CLK-CLK-CLK
A **COMPROMISE,** MAYBE?
POST MY AIDE HERE, OUTSIDE THE DOOR. AND A MEMBER OF THE SECURITY STAFF.
IF I NEED ANYTHING THEY CAN BRING HELP, AND I MIGHT HAVE SOME WORK FOR THEM SOON.
NOW, YES? TELL THEM TO HURRY, AND WE WILL ALL BE HAPPIER.
FOOL ME ONCE, OKAY. IT HAPPENS.
TWICE, THOUGH? I THINK NOT.
IT WAS NAIVE OF ME TO THINK THAT ***LOSING*** *AN ELECTION MADE ME LESS OF A TARGET.*
AT LEAST I'VE FOUND ONE GOOD THING ABOUT BEING BANISHED TO LUNA...
MY FAMILY BACK ON EARTH WON'T BECOME COLLATERAL DAMAGE IF THEY MANAGE TO HIT THE BULLSEYE.

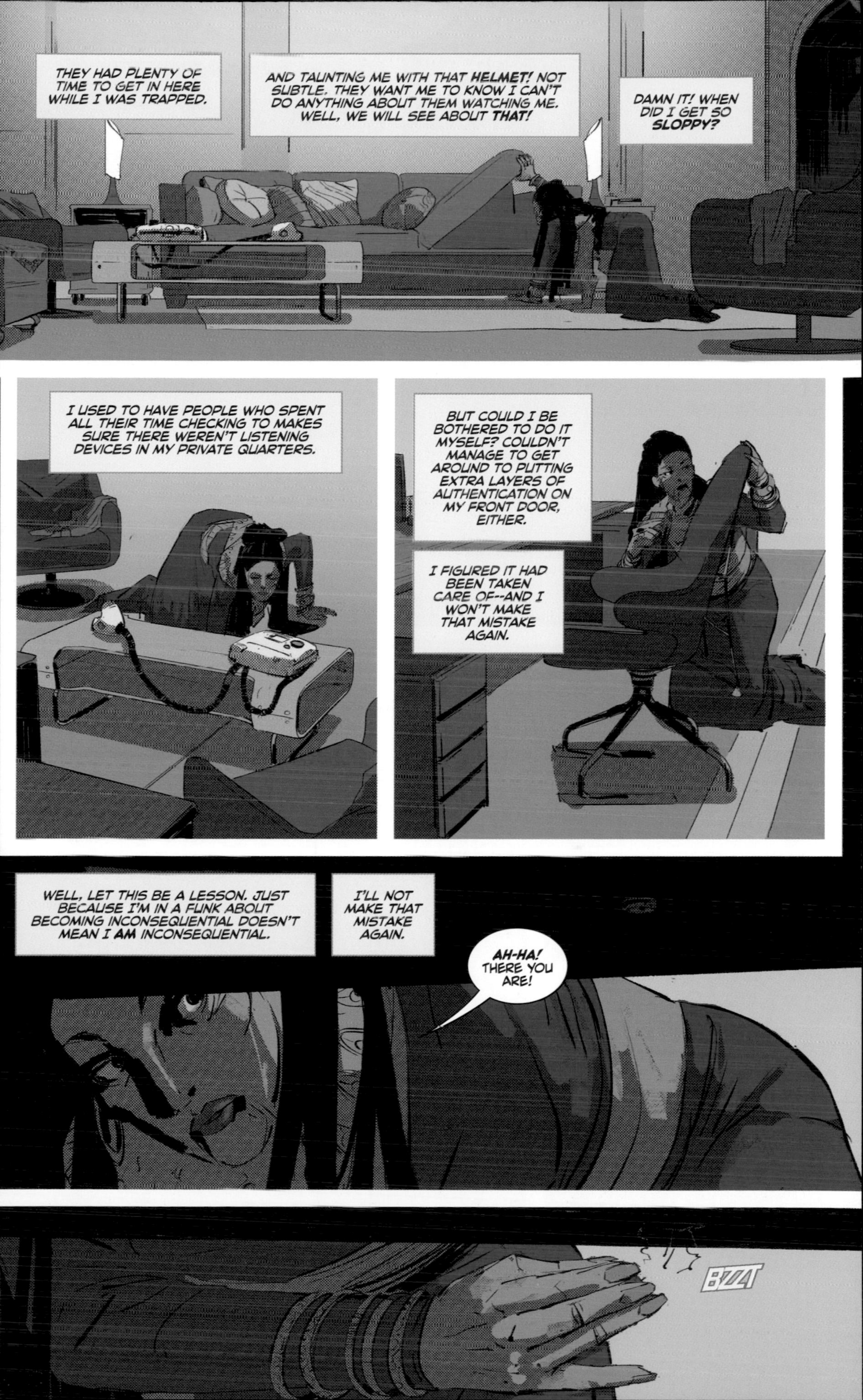
THEY HAD PLENTY OF TIME TO GET IN HERE WHILE I WAS TRAPPED.
AND TAUNTING ME WITH THAT **HELMET!** NOT SUBTLE. THEY WANT ME TO KNOW I CAN'T DO ANYTHING ABOUT THEM WATCHING ME. WELL, WE WILL SEE ABOUT **THAT!**
DAMN IT! WHEN DID I GET SO **SLOPPY?**
I USED TO HAVE PEOPLE WHO SPENT ALL THEIR TIME CHECKING TO MAKES SURE THERE WEREN'T LISTENING DEVICES IN MY PRIVATE QUARTERS.
BUT COULD I BE BOTHERED TO DO IT MYSELF? COULDN'T MANAGE TO GET AROUND TO PUTTING EXTRA LAYERS OF AUTHENTICATION ON MY FRONT DOOR, EITHER.
I FIGURED IT HAD BEEN TAKEN CARE OF--AND I WON'T MAKE THAT MISTAKE AGAIN.
WELL, LET THIS BE A LESSON. JUST BECAUSE I'M IN A FUNK ABOUT BECOMING INCONSEQUENTIAL DOESN'T MEAN I **AM** INCONSEQUENTIAL.
I'LL NOT MAKE THAT MISTAKE AGAIN.
AH-HA! THERE YOU ARE!
BZZT

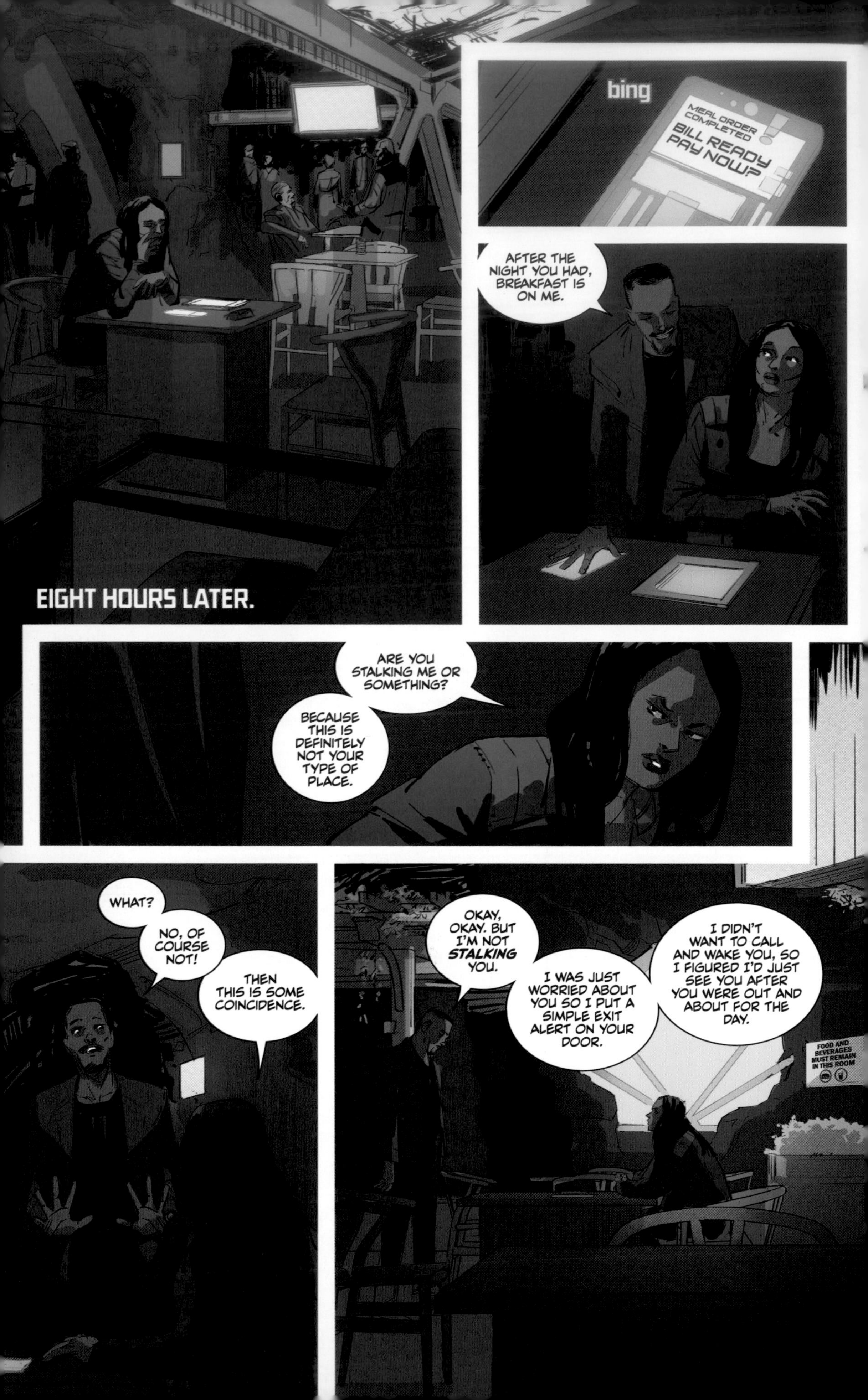
EIGHT HOURS LATER.
bing
MEAL ORDER COMPLETED
BILL READY
PAY NOW?
AFTER THE NIGHT YOU HAD, BREAKFAST IS ON ME.
ARE YOU STALKING ME OR SOMETHING?
BECAUSE THIS IS DEFINITELY NOT YOUR TYPE OF PLACE.
WHAT?
NO, OF COURSE NOT!
THEN THIS IS SOME COINCIDENCE.
OKAY, OKAY. BUT I'M NOT *STALKING* YOU.
I WAS JUST WORRIED ABOUT YOU SO I PUT A SIMPLE EXIT ALERT ON YOUR DOOR.
I DIDN'T WANT TO CALL AND WAKE YOU, SO I FIGURED I'D JUST SEE YOU AFTER YOU WERE OUT AND ABOUT FOR THE DAY.
FOOD AND BEVERAGES MUST REMAIN IN THIS ROOM

YOU DID? YOU NEED ACCESS TO THE MAIN POWER GRID IN THIS SECTION FOR THAT. LOW LEVEL ACCESS, BUT--

HEY, I SAID I HAD A LOT OF *FRIENDS.* BUT IF I WAS BEING NEFARIOUS, WOULD I HAVE TOLD YOU ABOUT IT?

I *KNOW* YOU CAN TAKE CARE OF YOURSELF.

YOU ALWAYS HAVE. I ACTUALLY FEEL SORRY FOR ANYONE WHO THINKS OTHERWISE.

BUT THERE ARE SOME THINGS THAT YOU NEED A FRIEND FOR. LIKE THIS.

LIKE WHAT?

LIKE TO SURPRISE YOU WITH A GIFT!

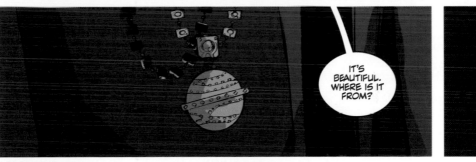

IT'S BEAUTIFUL. WHERE IS IT FROM?

I KEEP TELLING YOU, MY WORK RESULTS IN ALL SORTS OF LITTLE PERKS.

I WASN'T GOING TO WEAR THIS MYSELF, SO I THOUGHT I'D PASS IT ON.

IT'S NO BIG DEAL, REALLY. JUST THOUGHT YOU MIGHT LIKE IT.

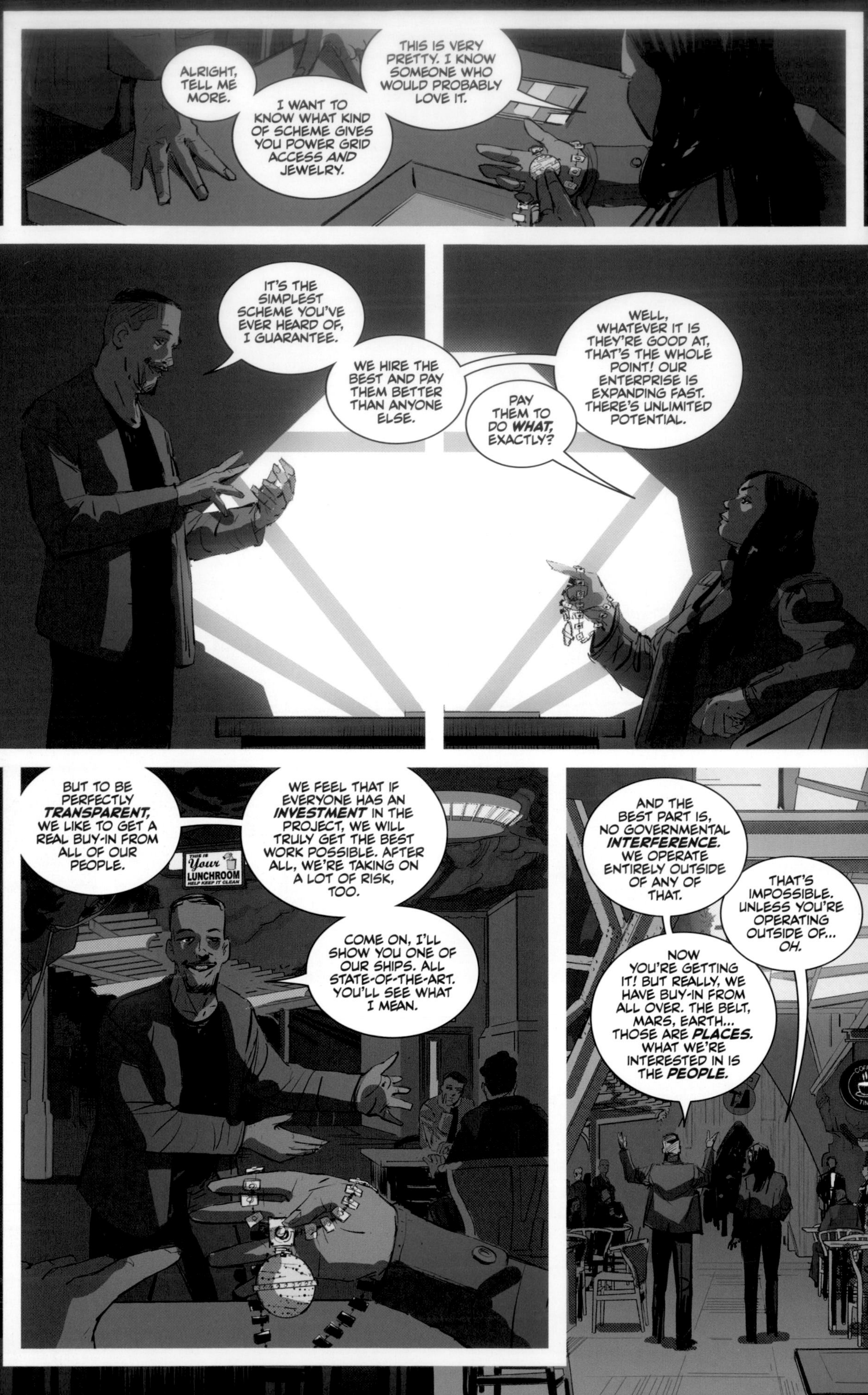
ALRIGHT, TELL ME MORE.
I WANT TO KNOW WHAT KIND OF SCHEME GIVES YOU POWER GRID ACCESS *AND* JEWELRY.
THIS IS VERY PRETTY. I KNOW SOMEONE WHO WOULD PROBABLY LOVE IT.
IT'S THE SIMPLEST SCHEME YOU'VE EVER HEARD OF, I GUARANTEE.
WE HIRE THE BEST AND PAY THEM BETTER THAN ANYONE ELSE.
PAY THEM TO DO ***WHAT,*** EXACTLY?
WELL, WHATEVER IT IS THEY'RE GOOD AT, THAT'S THE WHOLE POINT! OUR ENTERPRISE IS EXPANDING FAST. THERE'S UNLIMITED POTENTIAL.
BUT TO BE PERFECTLY ***TRANSPARENT,*** WE LIKE TO GET A REAL BUY-IN FROM ALL OF OUR PEOPLE.
THIS IS Your LUNCHROOM
WE FEEL THAT IF EVERYONE HAS AN ***INVESTMENT*** IN THE PROJECT, WE WILL TRULY GET THE BEST WORK POSSIBLE. AFTER ALL, WE'RE TAKING ON A LOT OF RISK, TOO.
COME ON, I'LL SHOW YOU ONE OF OUR SHIPS. ALL STATE-OF-THE-ART. YOU'LL SEE WHAT I MEAN.
AND THE BEST PART IS, NO GOVERNMENTAL ***INTERFERENCE.*** WE OPERATE ENTIRELY OUTSIDE OF ANY OF THAT.
THAT'S IMPOSSIBLE. UNLESS YOU'RE OPERATING OUTSIDE OF... *OH.*
NOW YOU'RE GETTING IT! BUT REALLY, WE HAVE BUY-IN FROM ALL OVER. THE BELT, MARS, EARTH... THOSE ARE ***PLACES.*** WHAT WE'RE INTERESTED IN IS THE ***PEOPLE.***

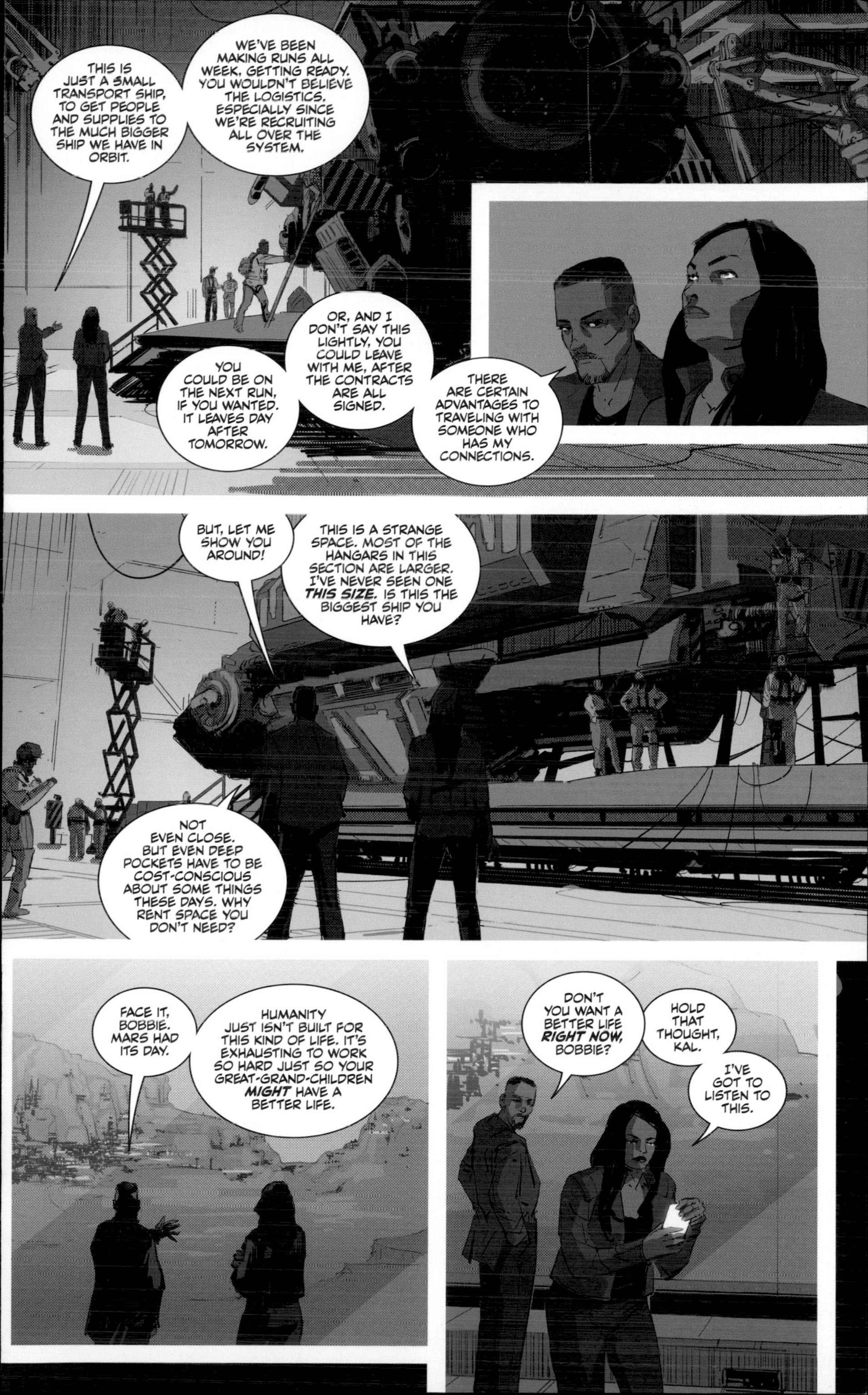
THIS IS JUST A SMALL TRANSPORT SHIP, TO GET PEOPLE AND SUPPLIES TO THE MUCH BIGGER SHIP WE HAVE IN ORBIT.
WE'VE BEEN MAKING RUNS ALL WEEK, GETTING READY. YOU WOULDN'T BELIEVE THE LOGISTICS. ESPECIALLY SINCE WE'RE RECRUITING ALL OVER THE SYSTEM.
YOU COULD BE ON THE NEXT RUN, IF YOU WANTED. IT LEAVES DAY AFTER TOMORROW.
OR, AND I DON'T SAY THIS LIGHTLY, YOU COULD LEAVE WITH ME, AFTER THE CONTRACTS ARE ALL SIGNED.
THERE ARE CERTAIN ADVANTAGES TO TRAVELING WITH SOMEONE WHO HAS MY CONNECTIONS.
BUT, LET ME SHOW YOU AROUND!
THIS IS A STRANGE SPACE. MOST OF THE HANGARS IN THIS SECTION ARE LARGER. I'VE NEVER SEEN ONE ***THIS SIZE.*** IS THIS THE BIGGEST SHIP YOU HAVE?
NOT EVEN CLOSE. BUT EVEN DEEP POCKETS HAVE TO BE COST-CONSCIOUS ABOUT SOME THINGS THESE DAYS. WHY RENT SPACE YOU DON'T NEED?
FACE IT, BOBBIE. MARS HAD ITS DAY.
HUMANITY JUST ISN'T BUILT FOR THIS KIND OF LIFE. IT'S EXHAUSTING TO WORK SO HARD JUST SO YOUR GREAT-GRAND-CHILDREN ***MIGHT*** HAVE A BETTER LIFE.
DON'T YOU WANT A BETTER LIFE ***RIGHT NOW,*** BOBBIE?
HOLD THAT THOUGHT, KAL.
I'VE GOT TO LISTEN TO THIS.

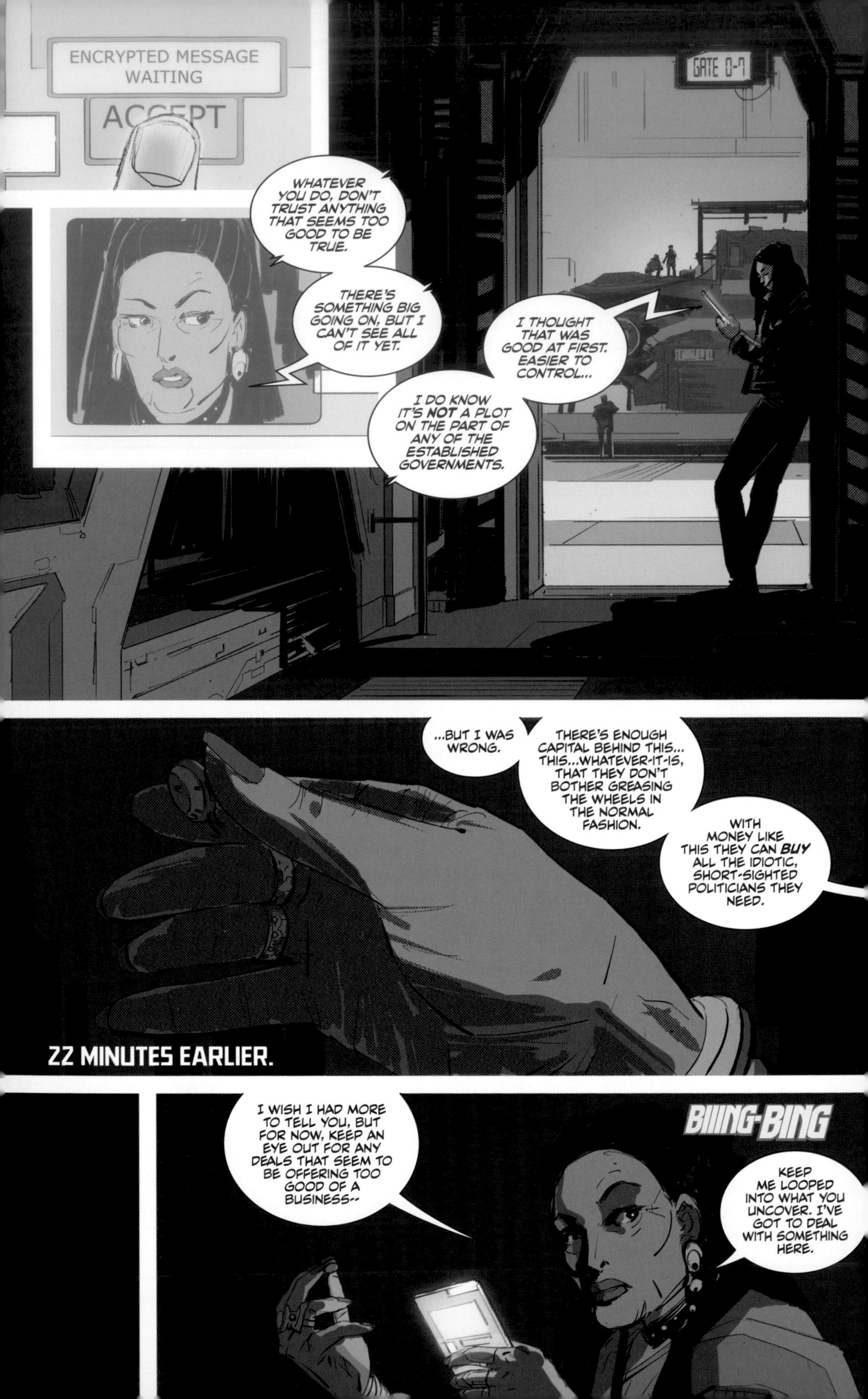
ENCRYPTED MESSAGE WAITING
ACCEPT
WHATEVER YOU DO, DON'T TRUST ANYTHING THAT SEEMS TOO GOOD TO BE TRUE.
THERE'S SOMETHING BIG GOING ON, BUT I CAN'T SEE ALL OF IT YET.
I THOUGHT THAT WAS GOOD AT FIRST. EASIER TO CONTROL...
I DO KNOW IT'S NOT A PLOT ON THE PART OF ANY OF THE ESTABLISHED GOVERNMENTS.
GATE D-7
...BUT I WAS WRONG.
THERE'S ENOUGH CAPITAL BEHIND THIS... THIS...WHATEVER-IT-IS, THAT THEY DON'T BOTHER GREASING THE WHEELS IN THE NORMAL FASHION.
WITH MONEY LIKE THIS THEY CAN BUY ALL THE IDIOTIC, SHORT-SIGHTED POLITICIANS THEY NEED.
22 MINUTES EARLIER.
I WISH I HAD MORE TO TELL YOU, BUT FOR NOW, KEEP AN EYE OUT FOR ANY DEALS THAT SEEM TO BE OFFERING TOO GOOD OF A BUSINESS--
BIIING-BING
KEEP ME LOOPED INTO WHAT YOU UNCOVER. I'VE GOT TO DEAL WITH SOMETHING HERE.

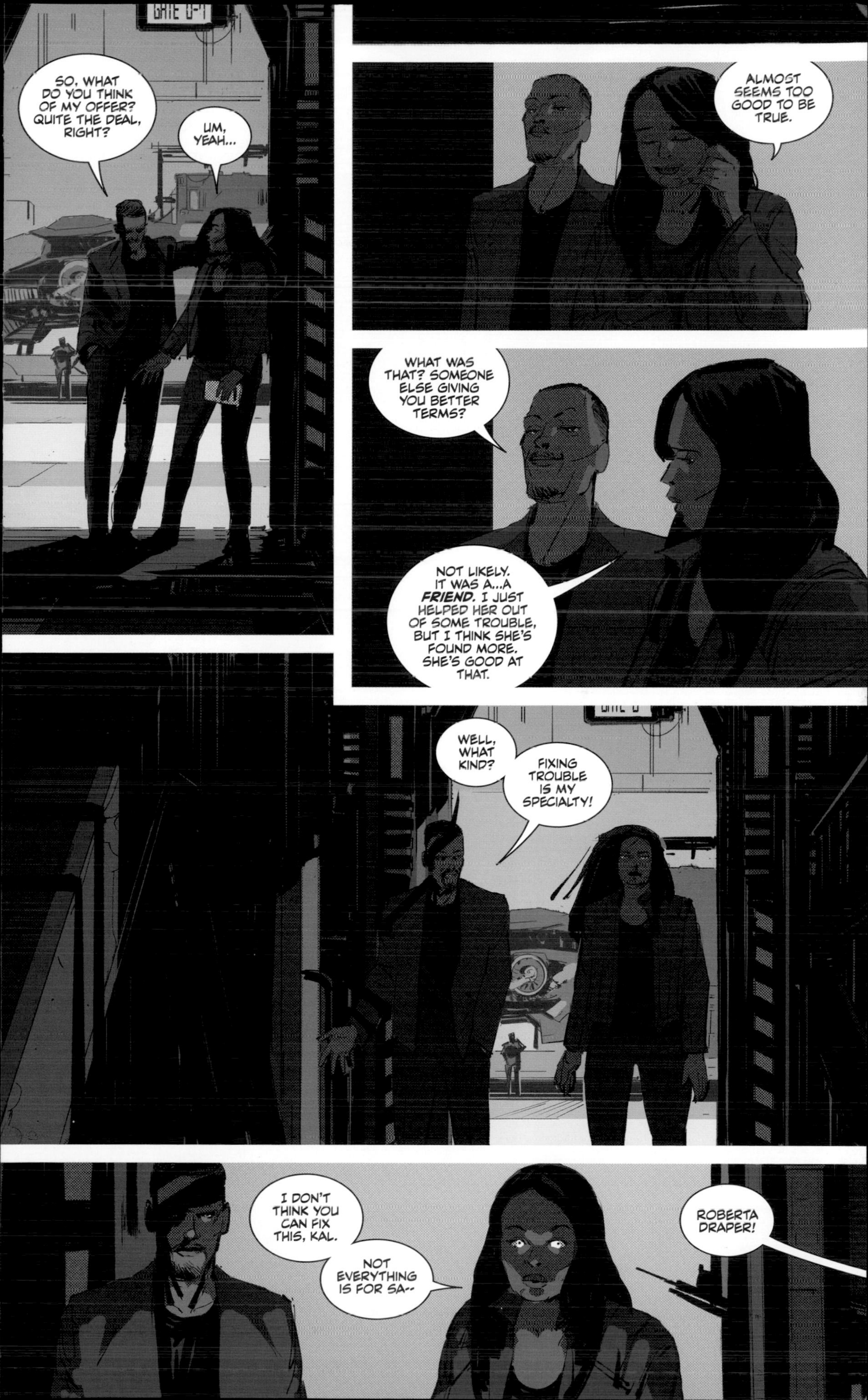
GATE D-1
SO, WHAT DO YOU THINK OF MY OFFER? QUITE THE DEAL, RIGHT?
UM, YEAH...
ALMOST SEEMS TOO GOOD TO BE TRUE.
WHAT WAS THAT? SOMEONE ELSE GIVING YOU BETTER TERMS?
NOT LIKELY. IT WAS A...A FRIEND. I JUST HELPED HER OUT OF SOME TROUBLE, BUT I THINK SHE'S FOUND MORE. SHE'S GOOD AT THAT.
WELL, WHAT KIND?
FIXING TROUBLE IS MY SPECIALTY!
I DON'T THINK YOU CAN FIX THIS, KAL.
NOT EVERYTHING IS FOR SA--
ROBERTA DRAPER!

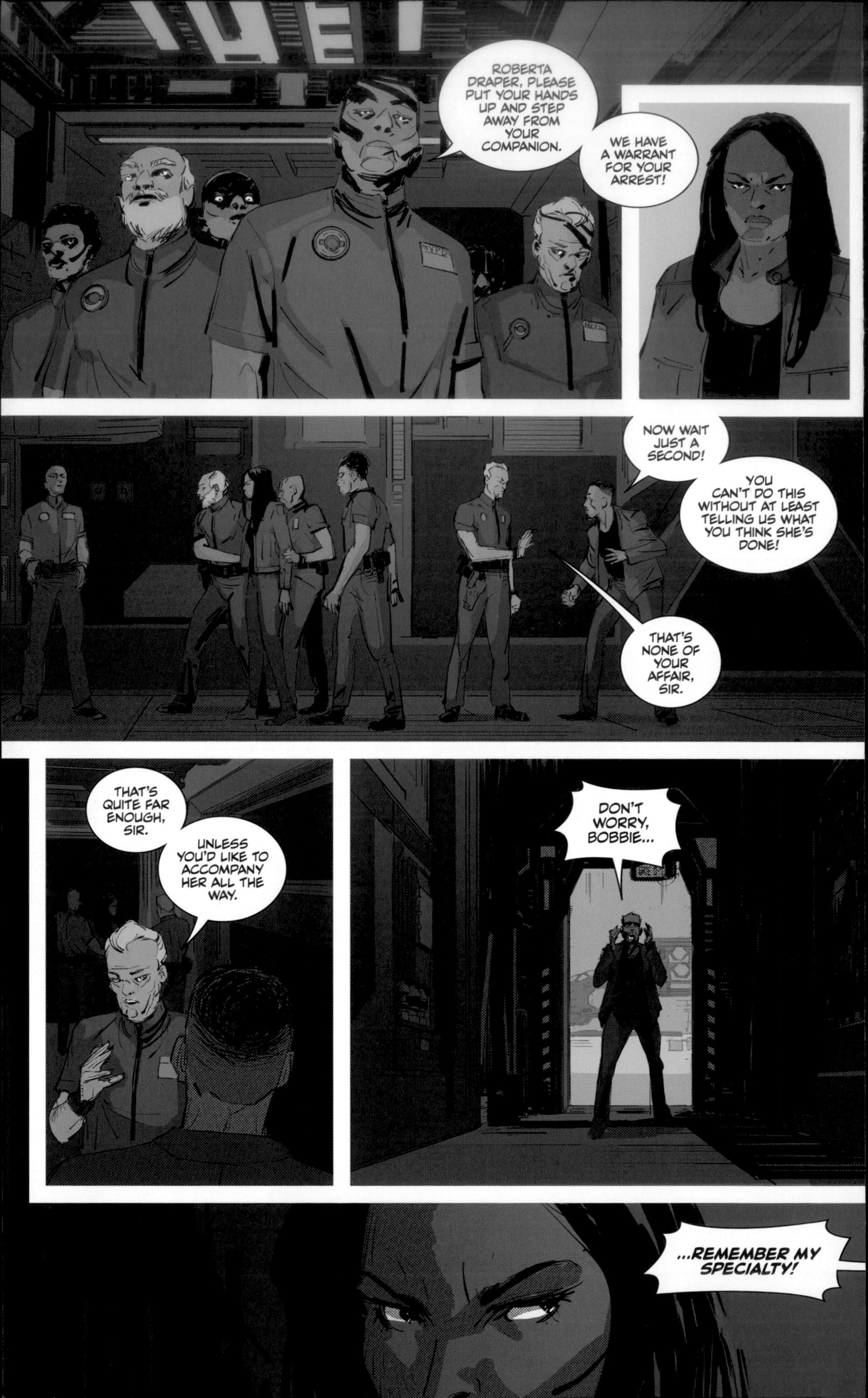
ROBERTA DRAPER, PLEASE PUT YOUR HANDS UP AND STEP AWAY FROM YOUR COMPANION.
WE HAVE A WARRANT FOR YOUR ARREST!
NOW WAIT JUST A SECOND!
YOU CAN'T DO THIS WITHOUT AT LEAST TELLING US WHAT YOU THINK SHE'S DONE!
THAT'S NONE OF YOUR AFFAIR, SIR.
THAT'S QUITE FAR ENOUGH, SIR.
UNLESS YOU'D LIKE TO ACCOMPANY HER ALL THE WAY.
DON'T WORRY, BOBBIE...
...REMEMBER MY SPECIALTY!

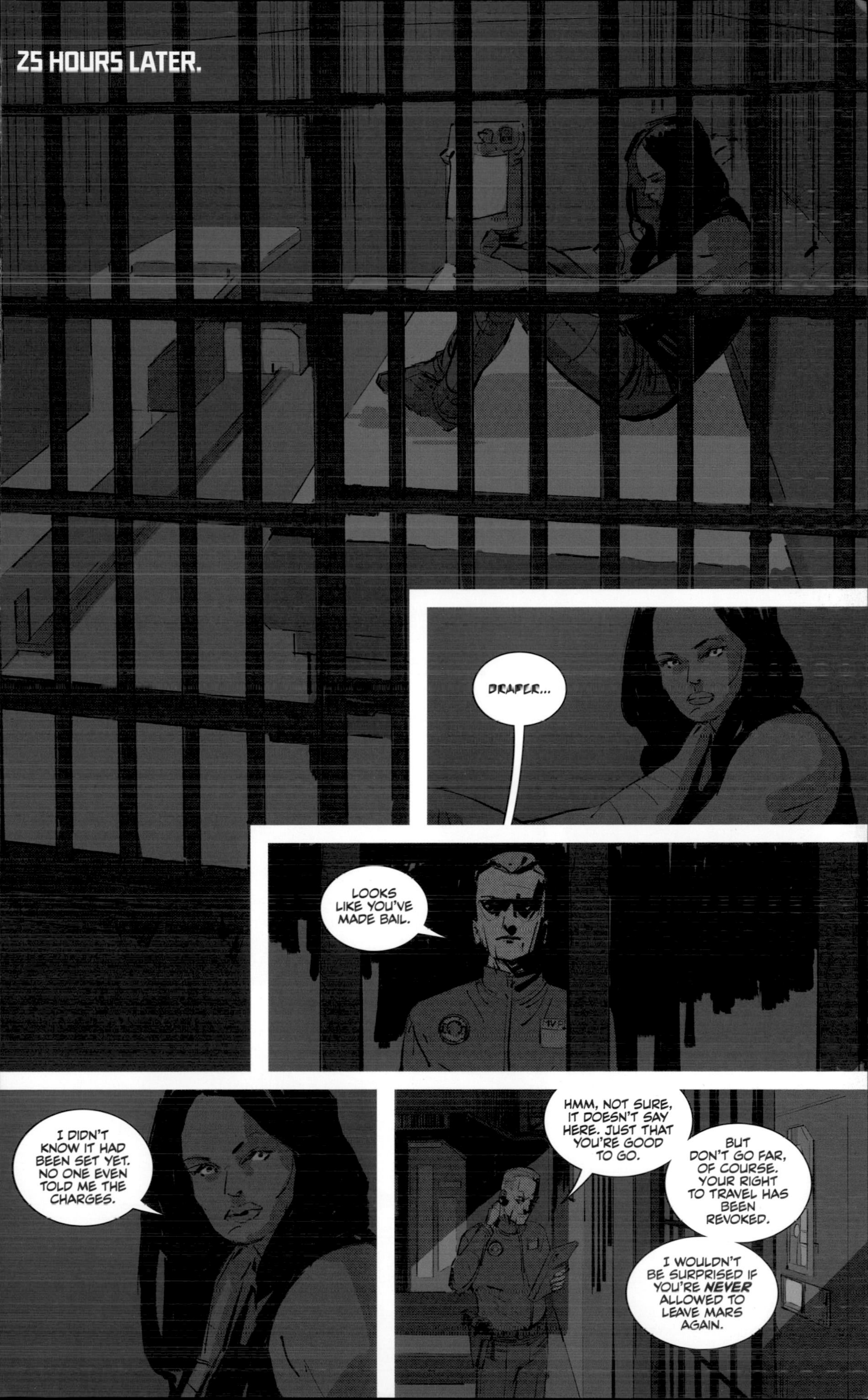
25 HOURS LATER.
DRAPER...
LOOKS LIKE YOU'VE MADE BAIL.
I DIDN'T KNOW IT HAD BEEN SET YET. NO ONE EVEN TOLD ME THE CHARGES.
HMM, NOT SURE, IT DOESN'T SAY HERE. JUST THAT YOU'RE GOOD TO GO.
BUT DON'T GO FAR, OF COURSE. YOUR RIGHT TO TRAVEL HAS BEEN REVOKED.
I WOULDN'T BE SURPRISED IF YOU'RE *NEVER* ALLOWED TO LEAVE MARS AGAIN.

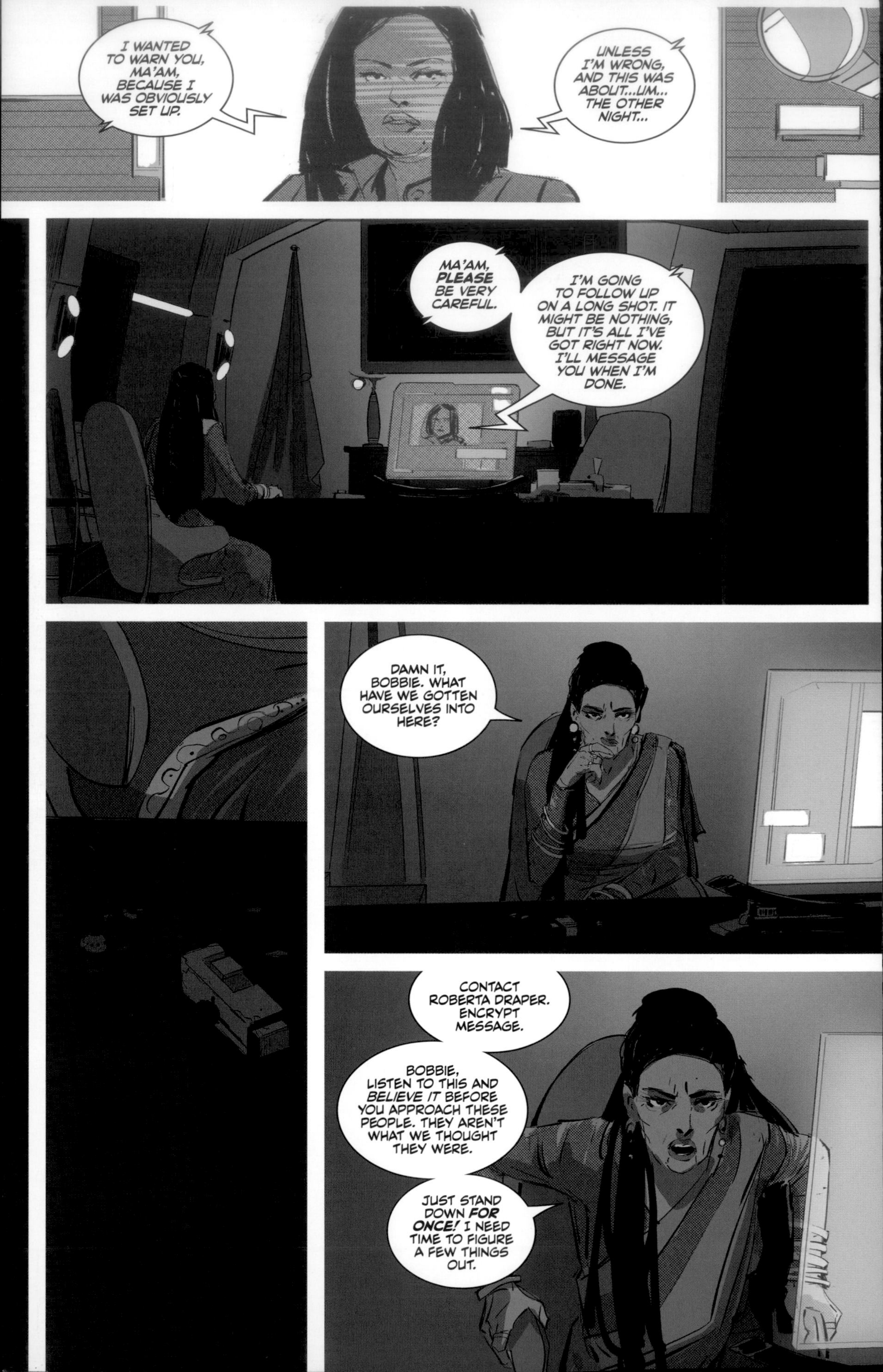
I WANTED TO WARN YOU, MA'AM, BECAUSE I WAS OBVIOUSLY SET UP.
UNLESS I'M WRONG, AND THIS WAS ABOUT...UM... THE OTHER NIGHT...
MA'AM, PLEASE BE VERY CAREFUL.
I'M GOING TO FOLLOW UP ON A LONG SHOT. IT MIGHT BE NOTHING, BUT IT'S ALL I'VE GOT RIGHT NOW. I'LL MESSAGE YOU WHEN I'M DONE.
DAMN IT, BOBBIE. WHAT HAVE WE GOTTEN OURSELVES INTO HERE?
CONTACT ROBERTA DRAPER. ENCRYPT MESSAGE.
BOBBIE, LISTEN TO THIS AND BELIEVE IT BEFORE YOU APPROACH THESE PEOPLE. THEY AREN'T WHAT WE THOUGHT THEY WERE.
JUST STAND DOWN FOR ONCE! I NEED TIME TO FIGURE A FEW THINGS OUT.

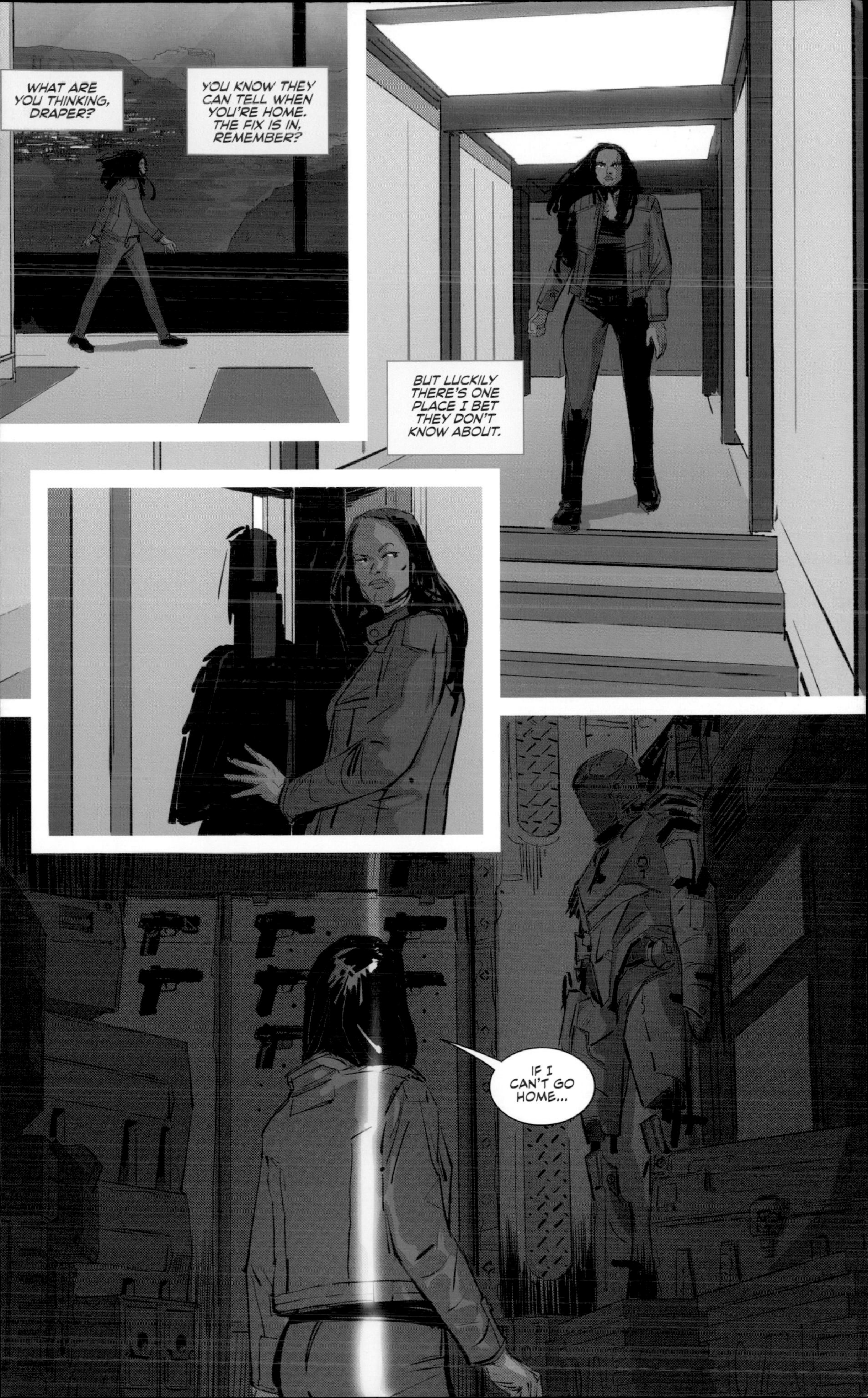
WHAT ARE YOU THINKING, DRAPER?
YOU KNOW THEY CAN TELL WHEN YOU'RE HOME. THE FIX IS IN, REMEMBER?
BUT LUCKILY THERE'S ONE PLACE I BET THEY DON'T KNOW ABOUT.
IF I CAN'T GO HOME...

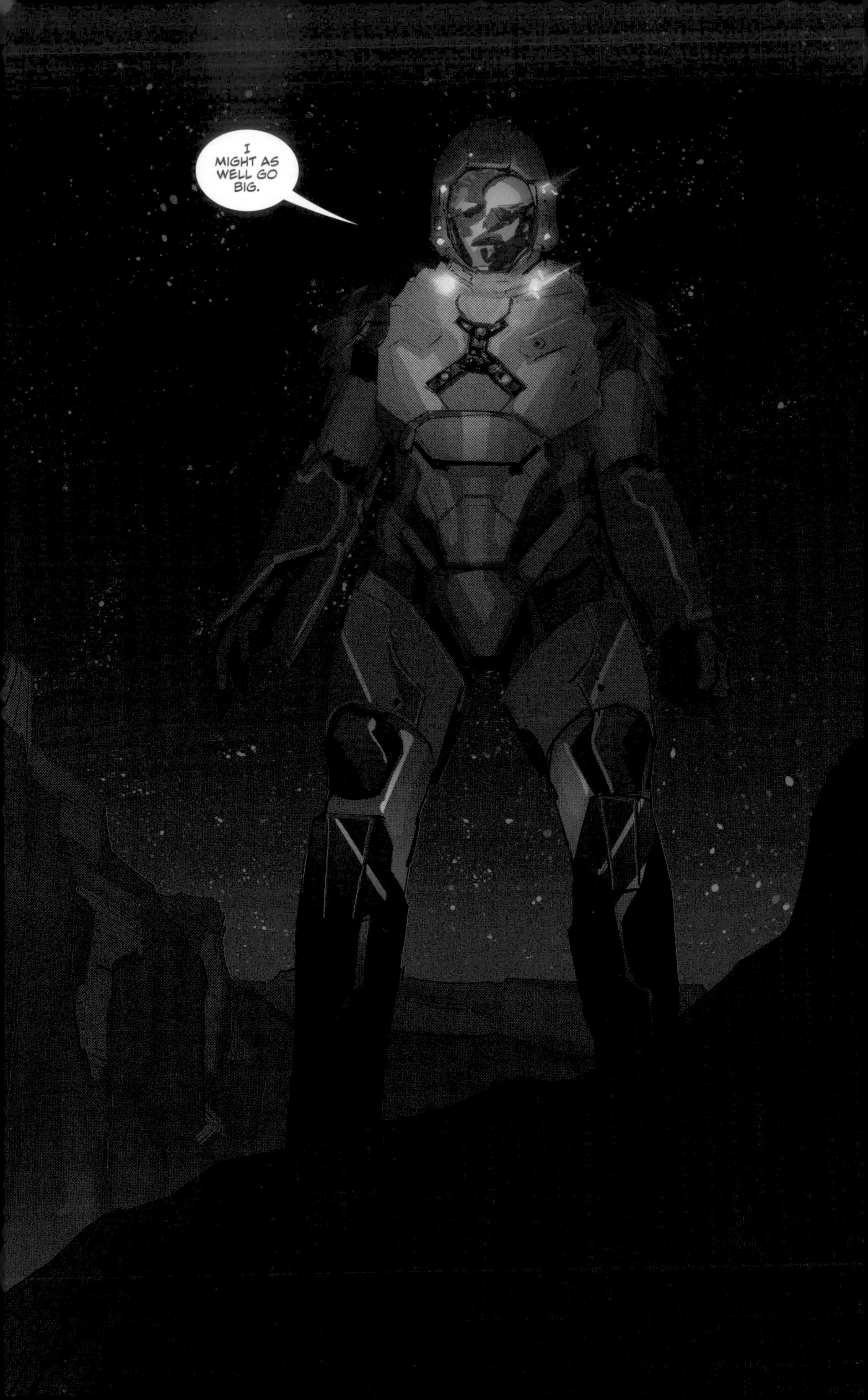
I MIGHT AS WELL GO BIG.

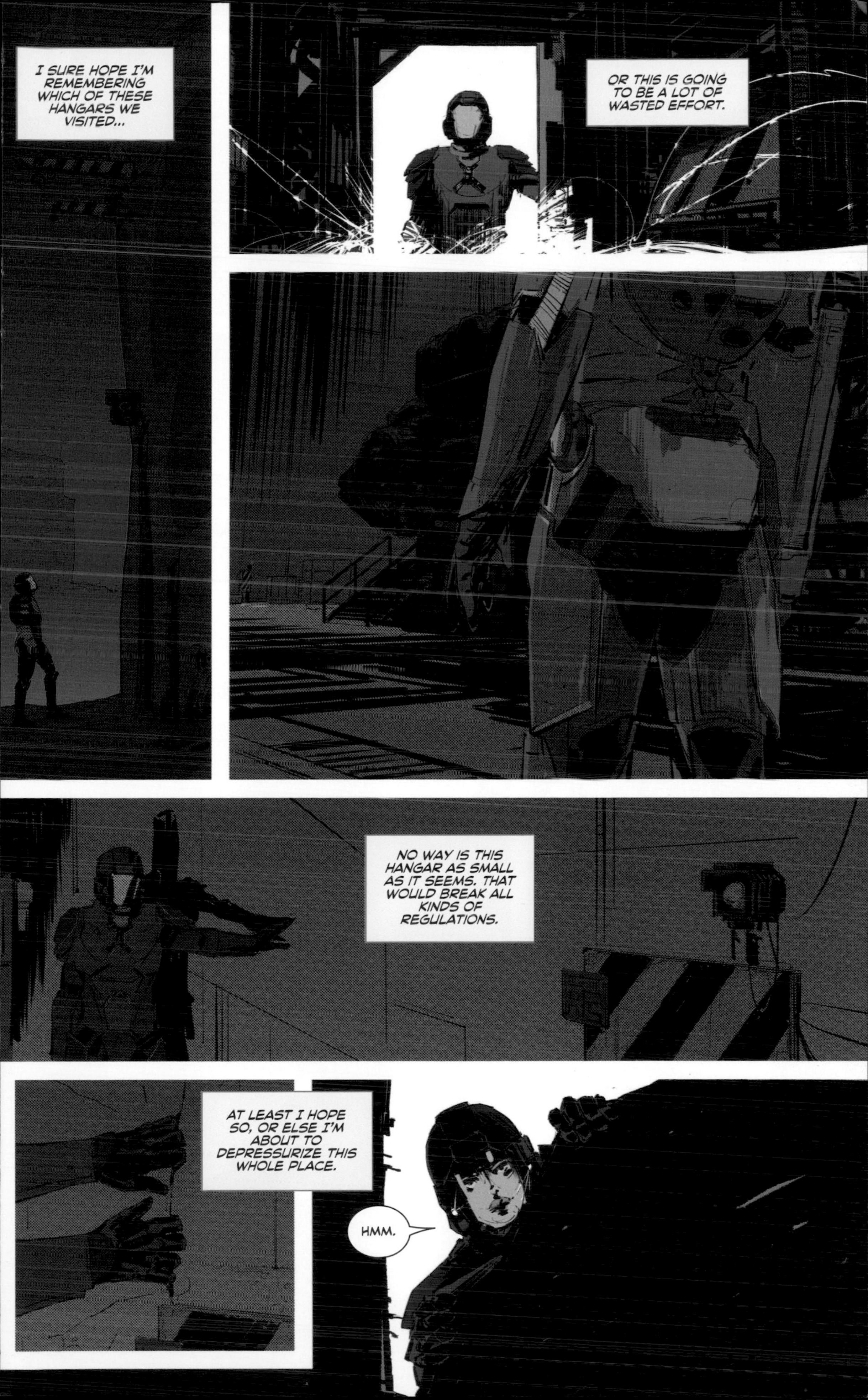
I SURE HOPE I'M REMEMBERING WHICH OF THESE HANGARS WE VISITED...
OR THIS IS GOING TO BE A LOT OF WASTED EFFORT.
NO WAY IS THIS HANGAR AS SMALL AS IT SEEMS. THAT WOULD BREAK ALL KINDS OF REGULATIONS.
AT LEAST I HOPE SO, OR ELSE I'M ABOUT TO DEPRESSURIZE THIS WHOLE PLACE.
HMM.

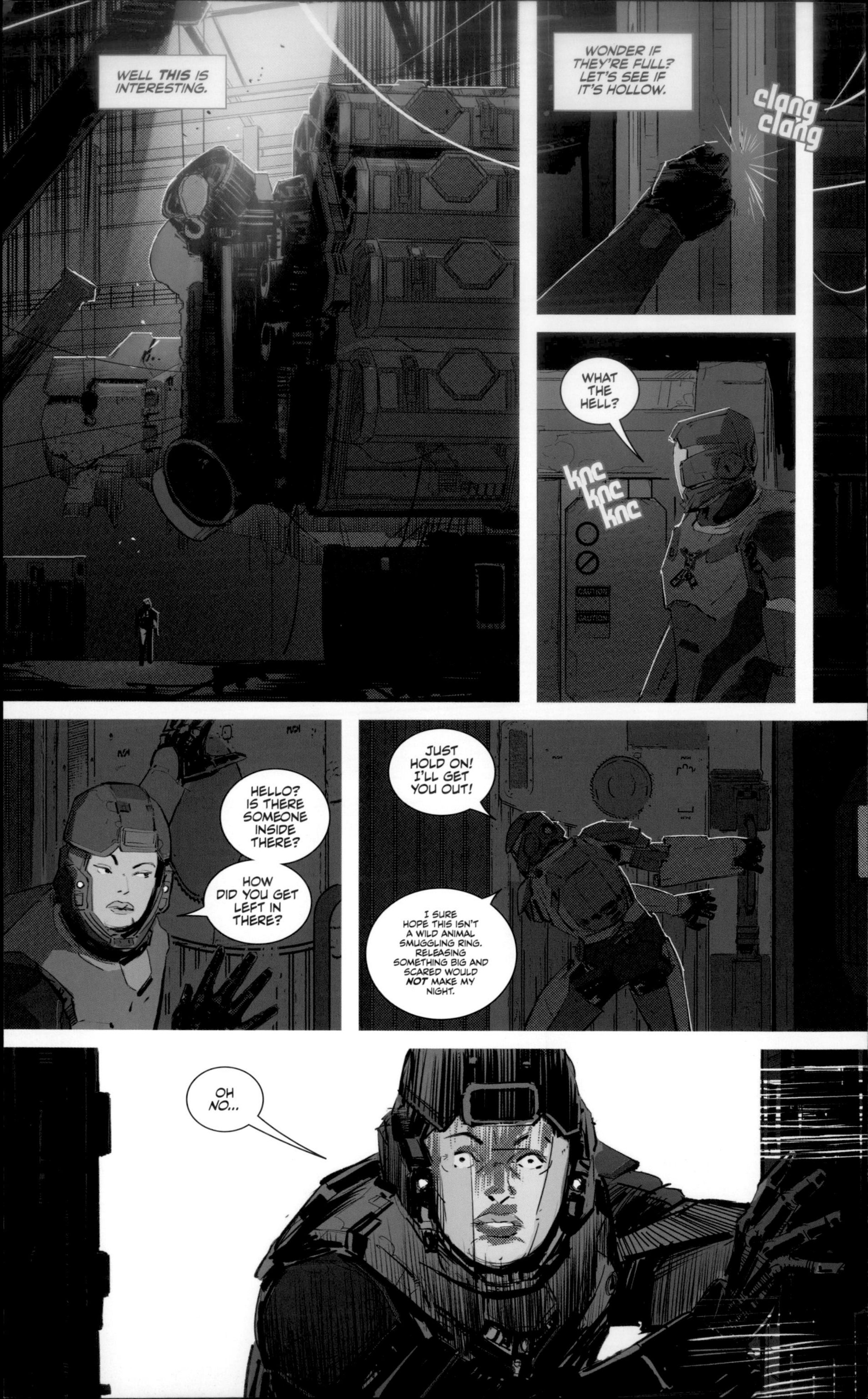
WELL THIS IS INTERESTING.
WONDER IF THEY'RE FULL? LET'S SEE IF IT'S HOLLOW.
clang clang
WHAT THE HELL?
knc knc knc
HELLO? IS THERE SOMEONE INSIDE THERE?
HOW DID YOU GET LEFT IN THERE?
JUST HOLD ON! I'LL GET YOU OUT!
I SURE HOPE THIS ISN'T A WILD ANIMAL SMUGGLING RING. RELEASING SOMETHING BIG AND SCARED WOULD NOT MAKE MY NIGHT.
OH NO...

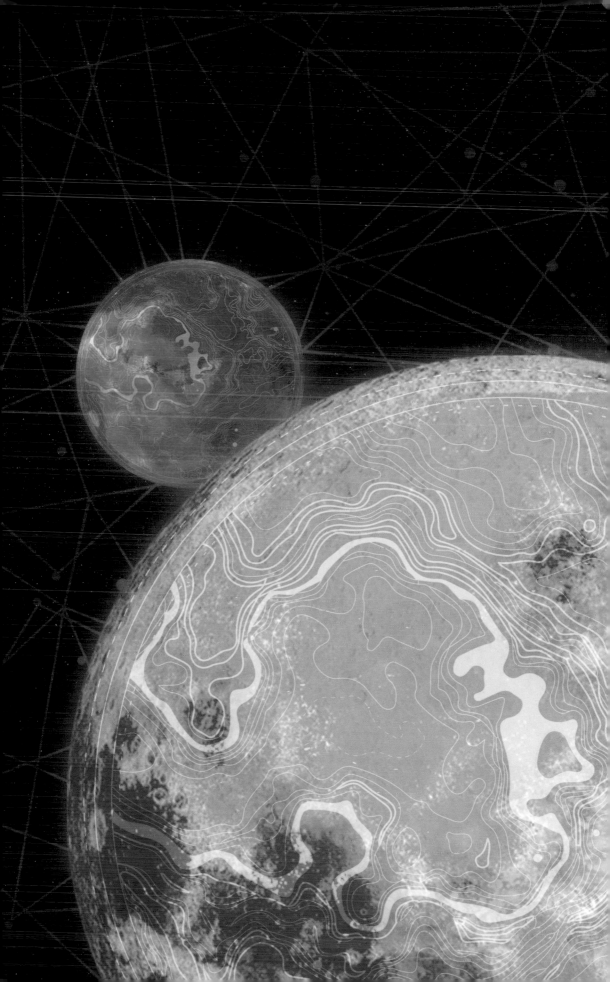

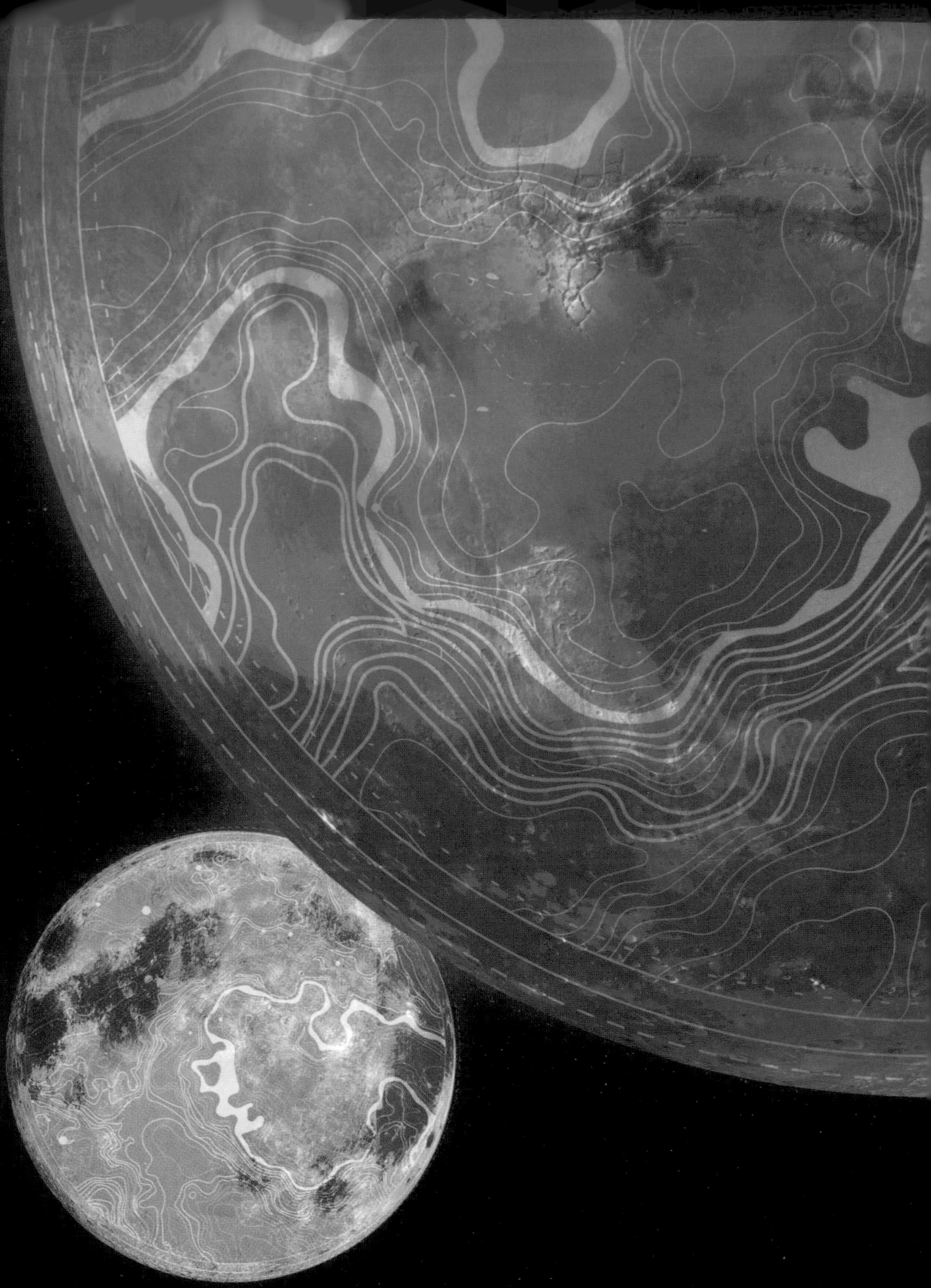

CHAPTER
FOUR

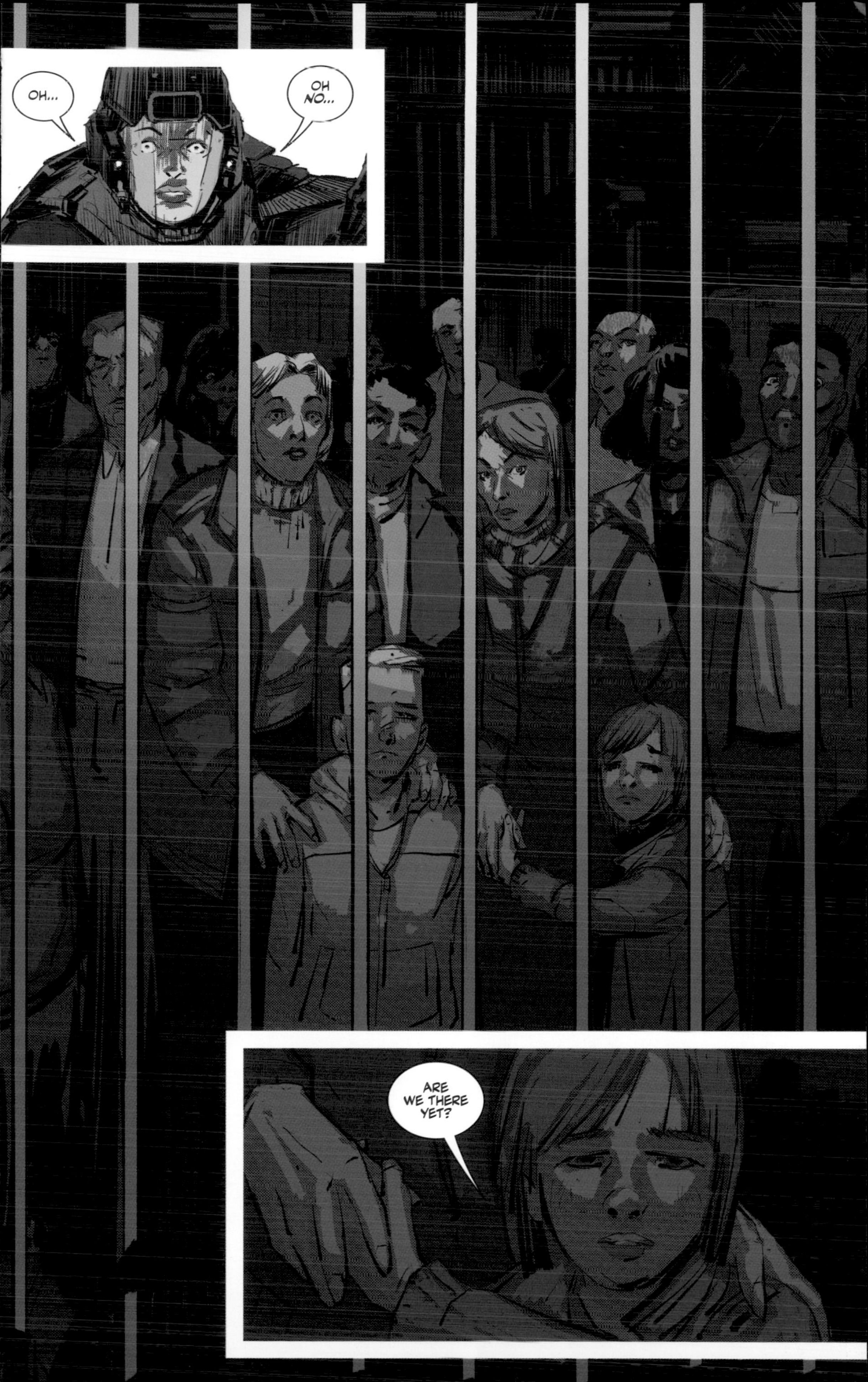
OH...
OH NO...
ARE WE THERE YET?

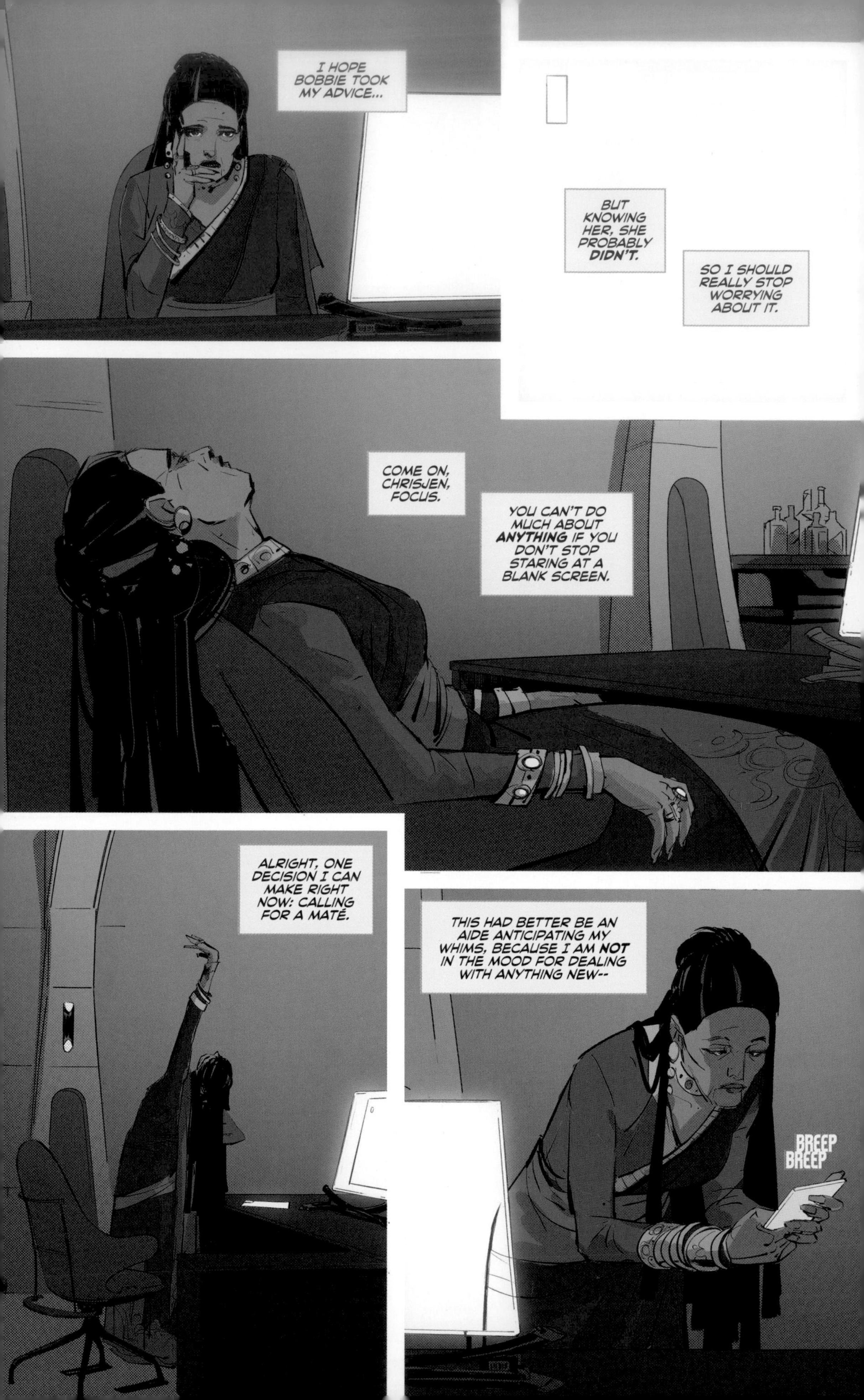
I HOPE BOBBIE TOOK MY ADVICE...
BUT KNOWING HER, SHE PROBABLY **DIDN'T.**
SO I SHOULD REALLY STOP WORRYING ABOUT IT.
COME ON, CHRISJEN, FOCUS.
YOU CAN'T DO MUCH ABOUT **ANYTHING** IF YOU DON'T STOP STARING AT A BLANK SCREEN.
ALRIGHT, ONE DECISION I CAN MAKE RIGHT NOW: CALLING FOR A MATÉ.
THIS HAD BETTER BE AN AIDE ANTICIPATING MY WHIMS, BECAUSE I AM **NOT** IN THE MOOD FOR DEALING WITH ANYTHING NEW--
BREEP BREEP

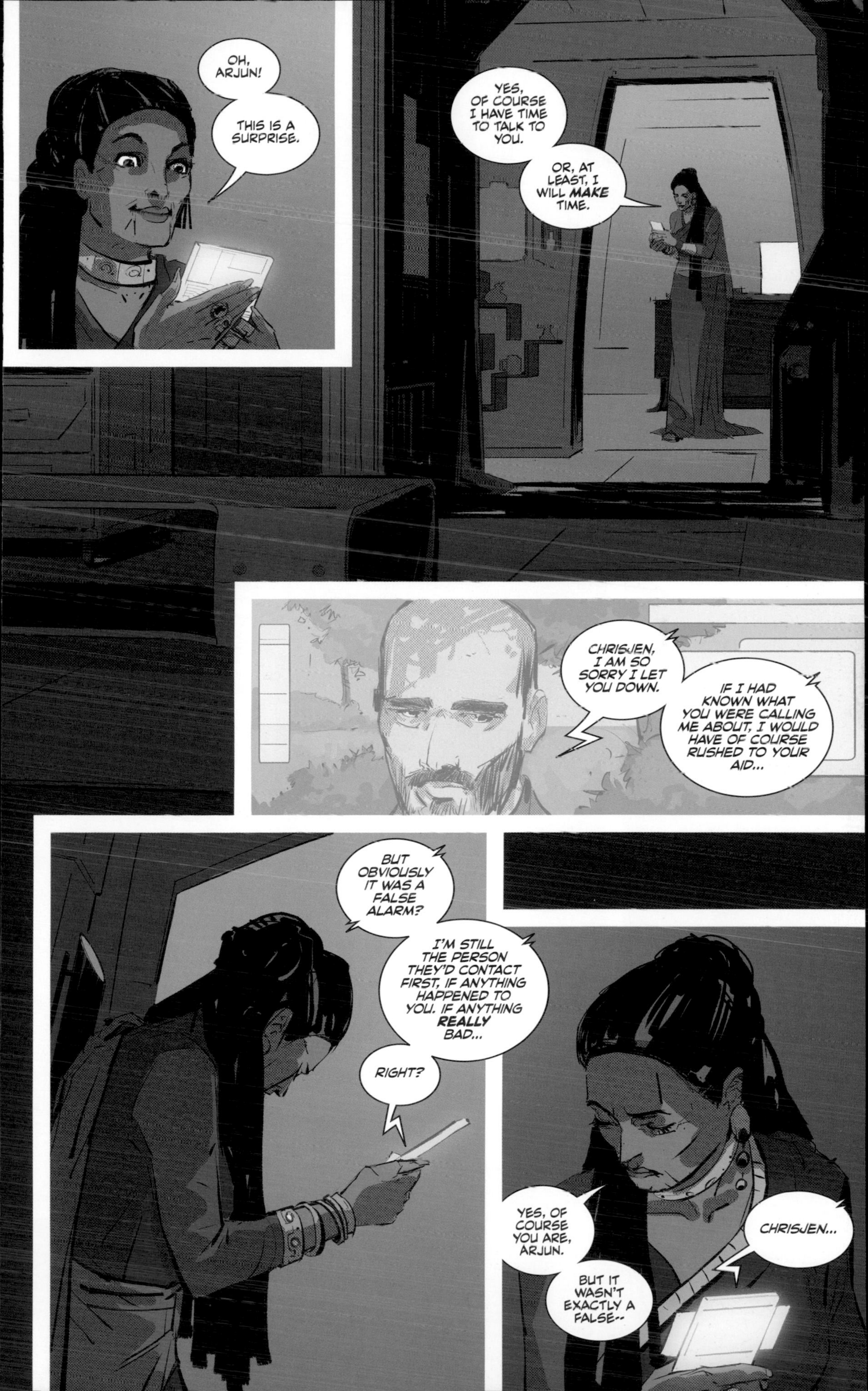
OH, ARJUN!
THIS IS A SURPRISE.
YES, OF COURSE I HAVE TIME TO TALK TO YOU.
OR, AT LEAST, I WILL MAKE TIME.
CHRISJEN, I AM SO SORRY I LET YOU DOWN.
IF I HAD KNOWN WHAT YOU WERE CALLING ME ABOUT, I WOULD HAVE OF COURSE RUSHED TO YOUR AID...
BUT OBVIOUSLY IT WAS A FALSE ALARM?
I'M STILL THE PERSON THEY'D CONTACT FIRST, IF ANYTHING HAPPENED TO YOU. IF ANYTHING REALLY BAD...
RIGHT?
YES, OF COURSE YOU ARE, ARJUN.
BUT IT WASN'T EXACTLY A FALSE--
CHRISJEN...

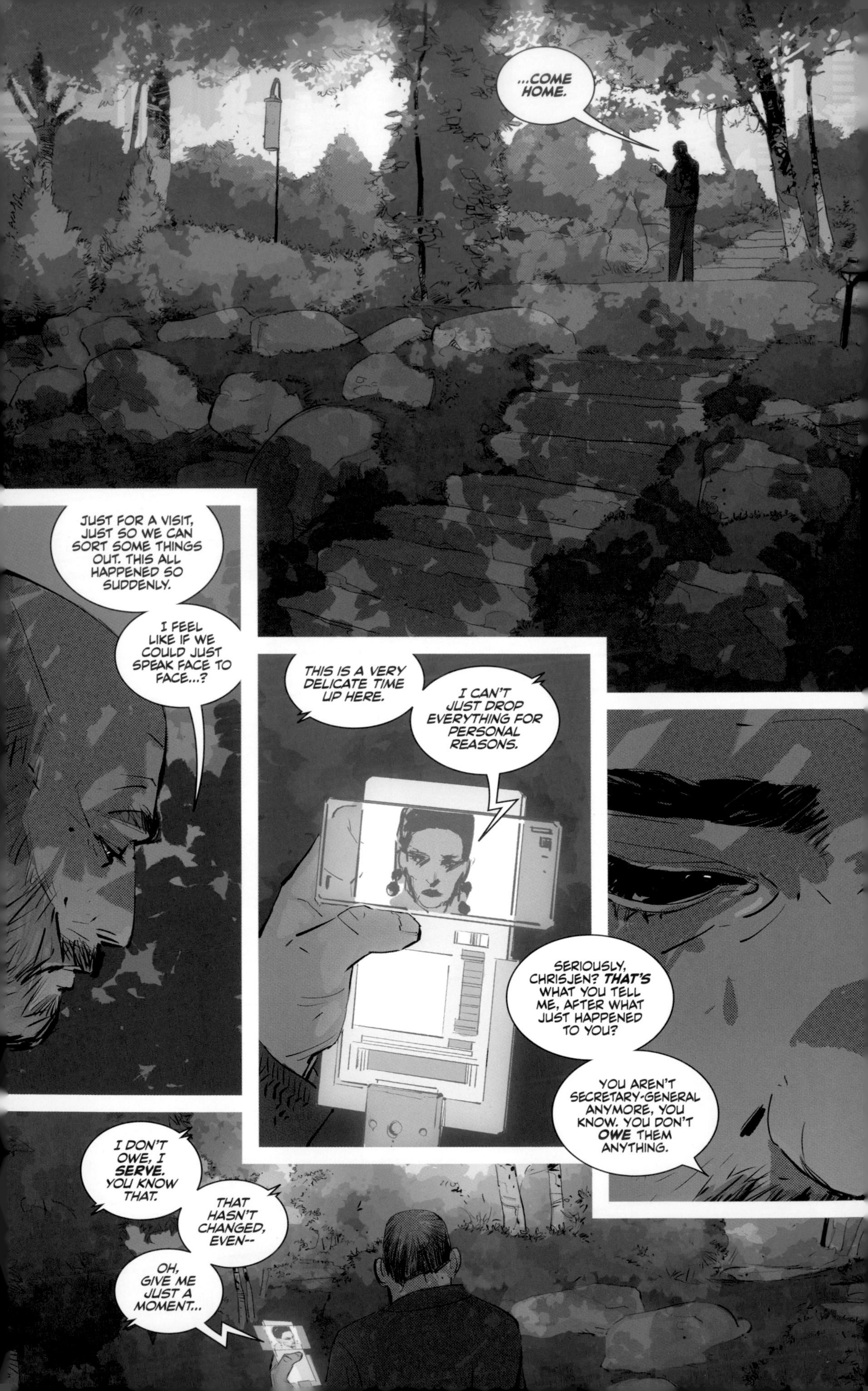
...COME HOME.
JUST FOR A VISIT, JUST SO WE CAN SORT SOME THINGS OUT. THIS ALL HAPPENED SO SUDDENLY.
I FEEL LIKE IF WE COULD JUST SPEAK FACE TO FACE...?
THIS IS A VERY DELICATE TIME UP HERE.
I CAN'T JUST DROP EVERYTHING FOR PERSONAL REASONS.
SERIOUSLY, CHRISJEN? THAT'S WHAT YOU TELL ME, AFTER WHAT JUST HAPPENED TO YOU?
YOU AREN'T SECRETARY-GENERAL ANYMORE, YOU KNOW. YOU DON'T OWE THEM ANYTHING.
I DON'T OWE, I SERVE. YOU KNOW THAT.
THAT HASN'T CHANGED, EVEN--
OH, GIVE ME JUST A MOMENT...

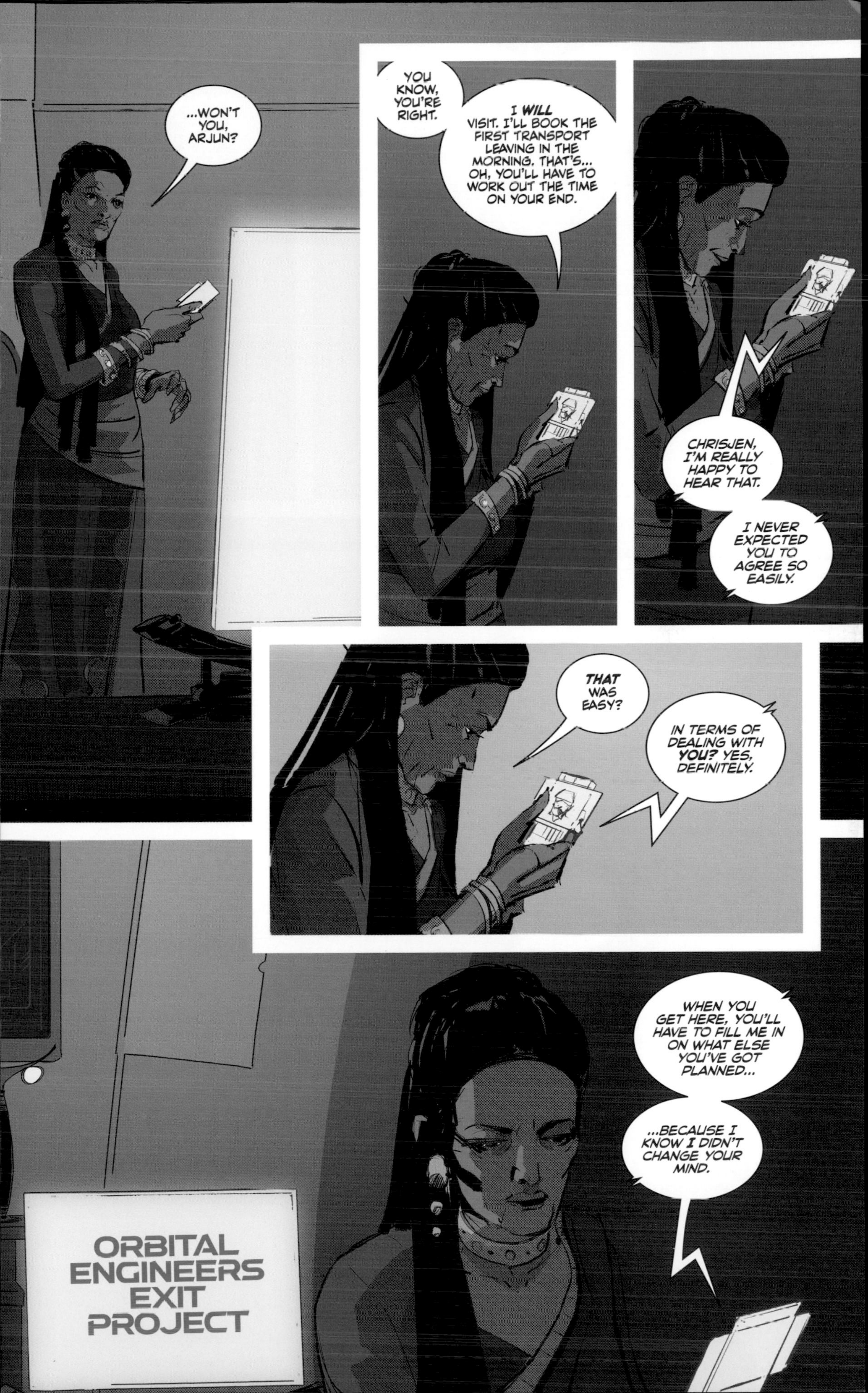
...WON'T YOU, ARJUN?
YOU KNOW, YOU'RE RIGHT.
I WILL VISIT. I'LL BOOK THE FIRST TRANSPORT LEAVING IN THE MORNING. THAT'S... OH, YOU'LL HAVE TO WORK OUT THE TIME ON YOUR END.
CHRISJEN, I'M REALLY HAPPY TO HEAR THAT.
I NEVER EXPECTED YOU TO AGREE SO EASILY.
THAT WAS EASY?
IN TERMS OF DEALING WITH YOU? YES, DEFINITELY.
WHEN YOU GET HERE, YOU'LL HAVE TO FILL ME IN ON WHAT ELSE YOU'VE GOT PLANNED...
...BECAUSE I KNOW I DIDN'T CHANGE YOUR MIND.
ORBITAL ENGINEERS EXIT PROJECT

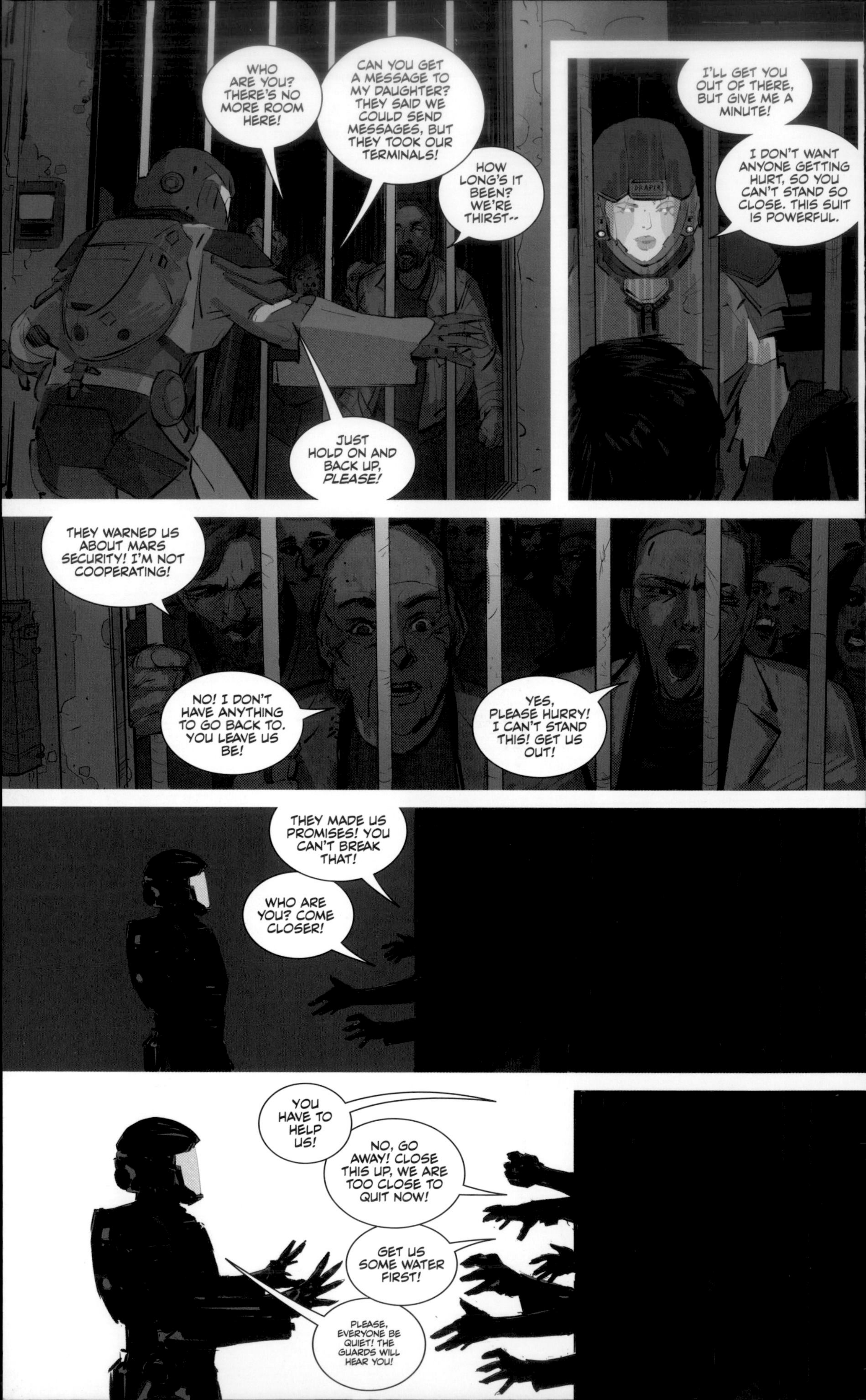
WHO ARE YOU? THERE'S NO MORE ROOM HERE!
CAN YOU GET A MESSAGE TO MY DAUGHTER? THEY SAID WE COULD SEND MESSAGES, BUT THEY TOOK OUR TERMINALS!
HOW LONG'S IT BEEN? WE'RE THIRST--
JUST HOLD ON AND BACK UP, *PLEASE!*
I'LL GET YOU OUT OF THERE, BUT GIVE ME A MINUTE!
I DON'T WANT ANYONE GETTING HURT, SO YOU CAN'T STAND SO CLOSE. THIS SUIT IS POWERFUL.
THEY WARNED US ABOUT MARS SECURITY! I'M NOT COOPERATING!
NO! I DON'T HAVE ANYTHING TO GO BACK TO. YOU LEAVE US BE!
YES, PLEASE HURRY! I CAN'T STAND THIS! GET US OUT!
THEY MADE US PROMISES! YOU CAN'T BREAK THAT!
WHO ARE YOU? COME CLOSER!
YOU HAVE TO HELP US!
NO, GO AWAY! CLOSE THIS UP, WE ARE TOO CLOSE TO QUIT NOW!
GET US SOME WATER FIRST!
PLEASE, EVERYONE BE QUIET! THE GUARDS WILL HEAR YOU!

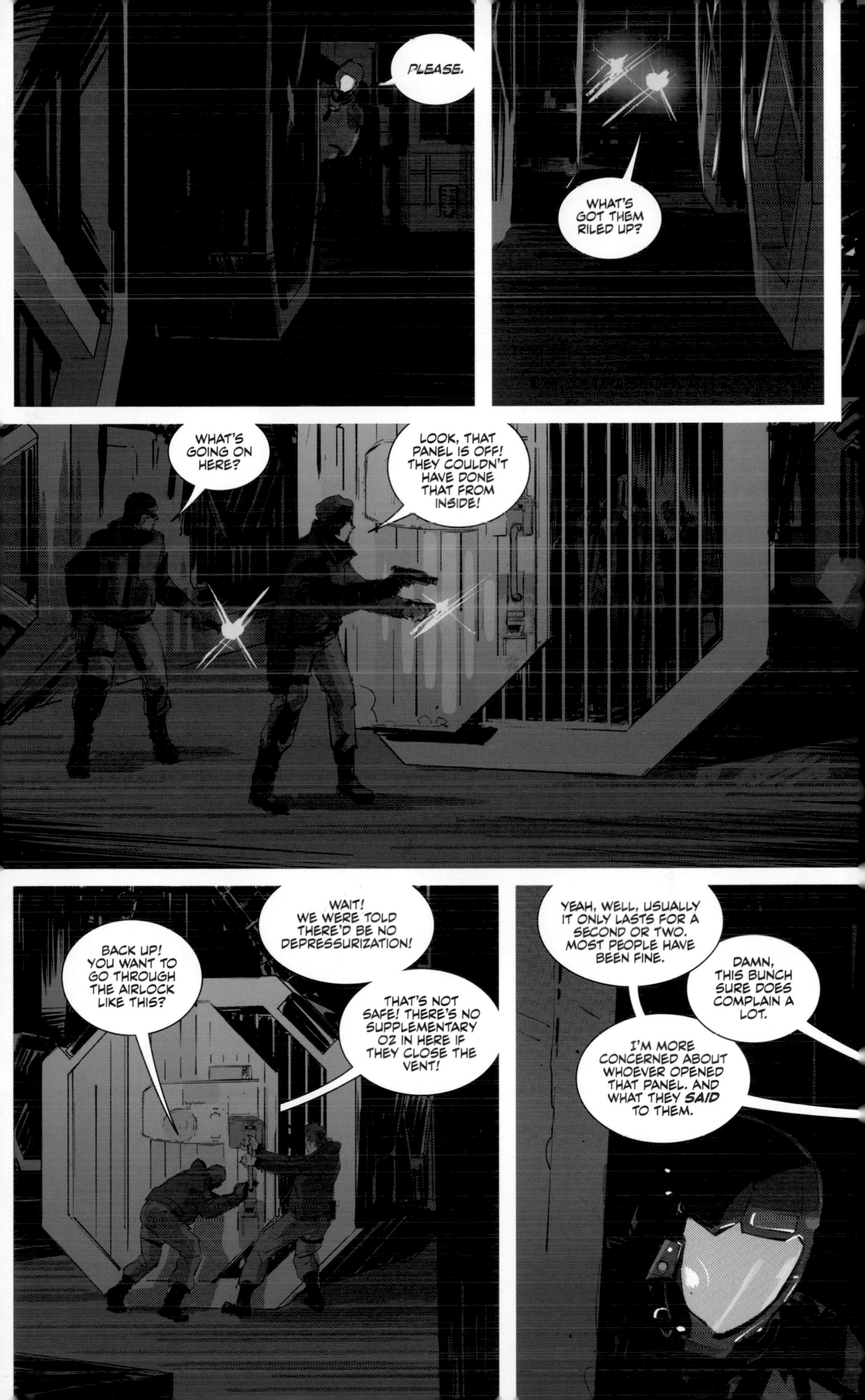
PLEASE.
WHAT'S GOT THEM RILED UP?
WHAT'S GOING ON HERE?
LOOK, THAT PANEL IS OFF! THEY COULDN'T HAVE DONE THAT FROM INSIDE!
BACK UP! YOU WANT TO GO THROUGH THE AIRLOCK LIKE THIS?
WAIT! WE WERE TOLD THERE'D BE NO DEPRESSURIZATION!
THAT'S NOT SAFE! THERE'S NO SUPPLEMENTARY O2 IN HERE IF THEY CLOSE THE VENT!
YEAH, WELL, USUALLY IT ONLY LASTS FOR A SECOND OR TWO. MOST PEOPLE HAVE BEEN FINE.
DAMN, THIS BUNCH SURE DOES COMPLAIN A LOT.
I'M MORE CONCERNED ABOUT WHOEVER OPENED THAT PANEL. AND WHAT THEY SAID TO THEM.

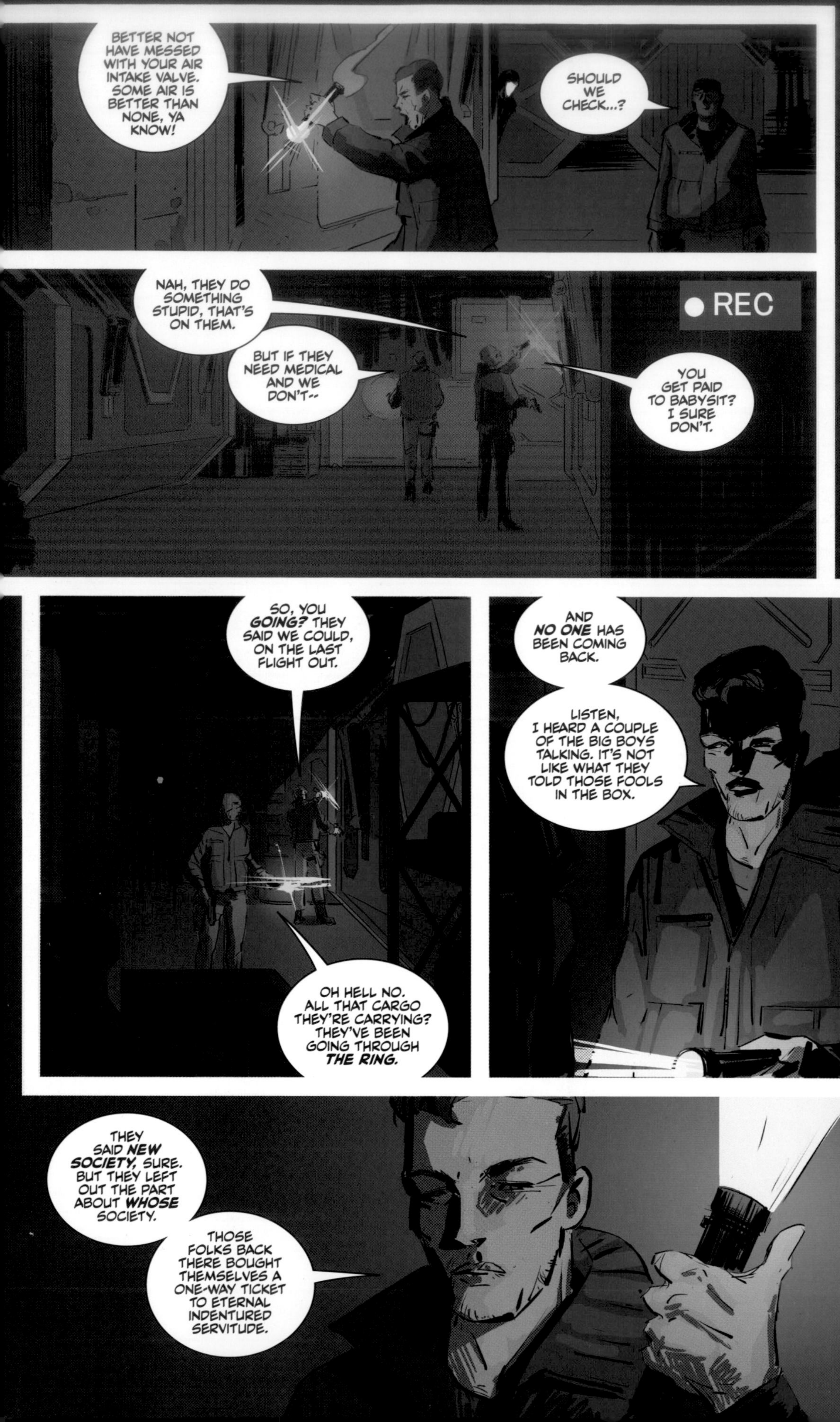
BETTER NOT HAVE MESSED WITH YOUR AIR INTAKE VALVE. SOME AIR IS BETTER THAN NONE, YA KNOW!
SHOULD WE CHECK...?
NAH, THEY DO SOMETHING STUPID, THAT'S ON THEM.
● REC
BUT IF THEY NEED MEDICAL AND WE DON'T--
YOU GET PAID TO BABYSIT? I SURE DON'T.
SO, YOU *GOING?* THEY SAID WE COULD, ON THE LAST FLIGHT OUT.
OH HELL NO. ALL THAT CARGO THEY'RE CARRYING? THEY'VE BEEN GOING THROUGH ***THE RING.***
AND ***NO ONE*** HAS BEEN COMING BACK.
LISTEN, I HEARD A COUPLE OF THE BIG BOYS TALKING. IT'S NOT LIKE WHAT THEY TOLD THOSE FOOLS IN THE BOX.
THEY SAID ***NEW SOCIETY,*** SURE. BUT THEY LEFT OUT THE PART ABOUT ***WHOSE*** SOCIETY.
THOSE FOLKS BACK THERE BOUGHT THEMSELVES A ONE-WAY TICKET TO ETERNAL INDENTURED SERVITUDE.

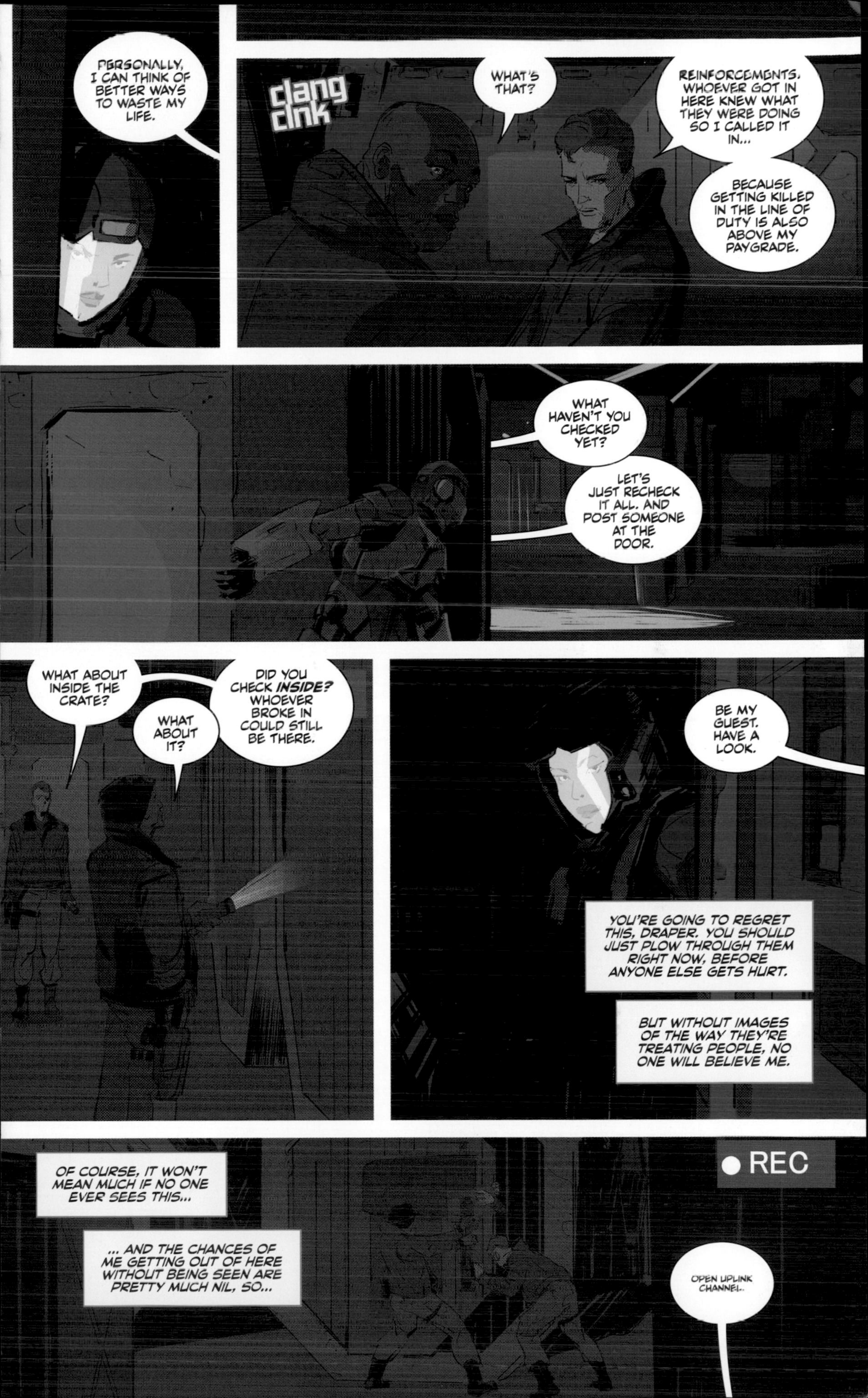
PERSONALLY, I CAN THINK OF BETTER WAYS TO WASTE MY LIFE.
clang clnk
WHAT'S THAT?
REINFORCEMENTS. WHOEVER GOT IN HERE KNEW WHAT THEY WERE DOING SO I CALLED IT IN...
BECAUSE GETTING KILLED IN THE LINE OF DUTY IS ALSO ABOVE MY PAYGRADE.
WHAT HAVEN'T YOU CHECKED YET?
LET'S JUST RECHECK IT ALL. AND POST SOMEONE AT THE DOOR.
WHAT ABOUT INSIDE THE CRATE?
WHAT ABOUT IT?
DID YOU CHECK *INSIDE?* WHOEVER BROKE IN COULD STILL BE THERE.
BE MY GUEST. HAVE A LOOK.
YOU'RE GOING TO REGRET THIS, DRAPER. YOU SHOULD JUST PLOW THROUGH THEM RIGHT NOW, BEFORE ANYONE ELSE GETS HURT.
BUT WITHOUT IMAGES OF THE WAY THEY'RE TREATING PEOPLE, NO ONE WILL BELIEVE ME.
REC
OF COURSE, IT WON'T MEAN MUCH IF NO ONE EVER SEES THIS...
... AND THE CHANCES OF ME GETTING OUT OF HERE WITHOUT BEING SEEN ARE PRETTY MUCH NIL, SO...
OPEN UPLINK CHANNEL.

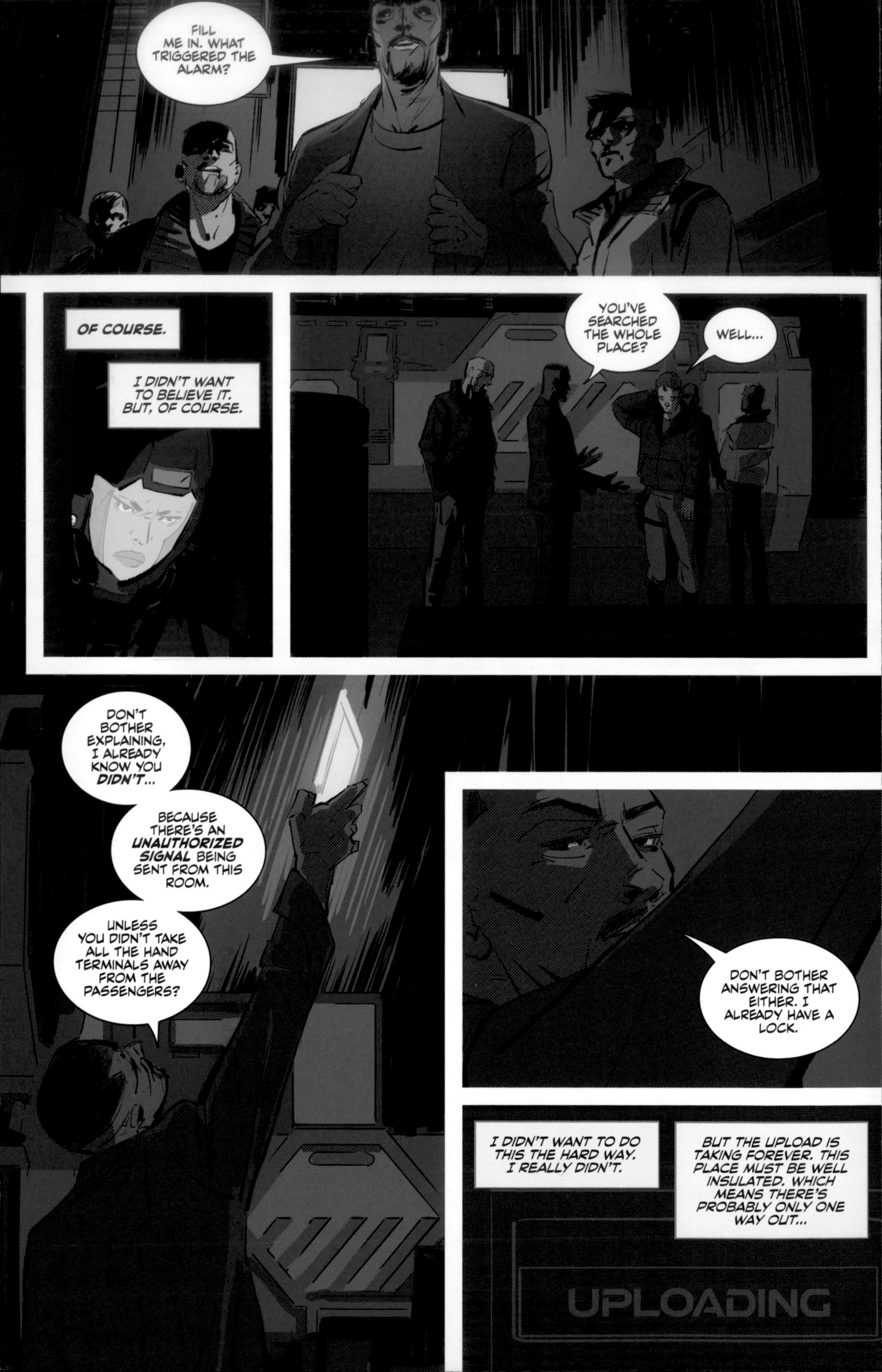
FILL ME IN. WHAT TRIGGERED THE ALARM?
OF COURSE.
I DIDN'T WANT TO BELIEVE IT. BUT, OF COURSE.
YOU'VE SEARCHED THE WHOLE PLACE?
WELL...
DON'T BOTHER EXPLAINING, I ALREADY KNOW YOU DIDN'T...
BECAUSE THERE'S AN UNAUTHORIZED SIGNAL BEING SENT FROM THIS ROOM.
UNLESS YOU DIDN'T TAKE ALL THE HAND TERMINALS AWAY FROM THE PASSENGERS?
DON'T BOTHER ANSWERING THAT EITHER. I ALREADY HAVE A LOCK.
I DIDN'T WANT TO DO THIS THE HARD WAY. I REALLY DIDN'T.
BUT THE UPLOAD IS TAKING FOREVER. THIS PLACE MUST BE WELL INSULATED. WHICH MEANS THERE'S PROBABLY ONLY ONE WAY OUT...
UPLOADING

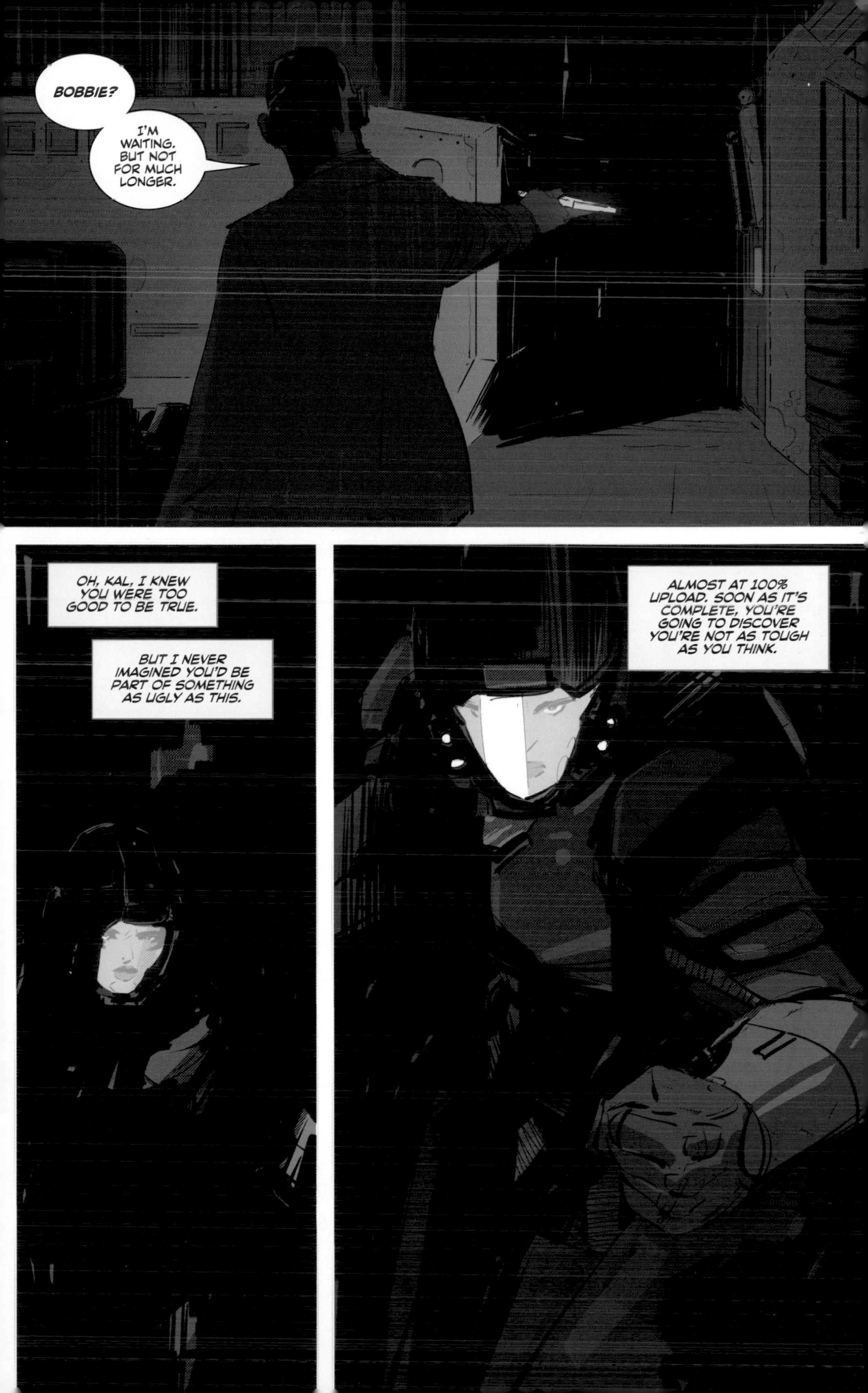
BOBBIE?
I'M WAITING. BUT NOT FOR MUCH LONGER.
OH, KAL, I KNEW YOU WERE TOO GOOD TO BE TRUE.
BUT I NEVER IMAGINED YOU'D BE PART OF SOMETHING AS UGLY AS THIS.
ALMOST AT 100% UPLOAD. SOON AS IT'S COMPLETE, YOU'RE GOING TO DISCOVER YOU'RE NOT AS TOUGH AS YOU THINK.

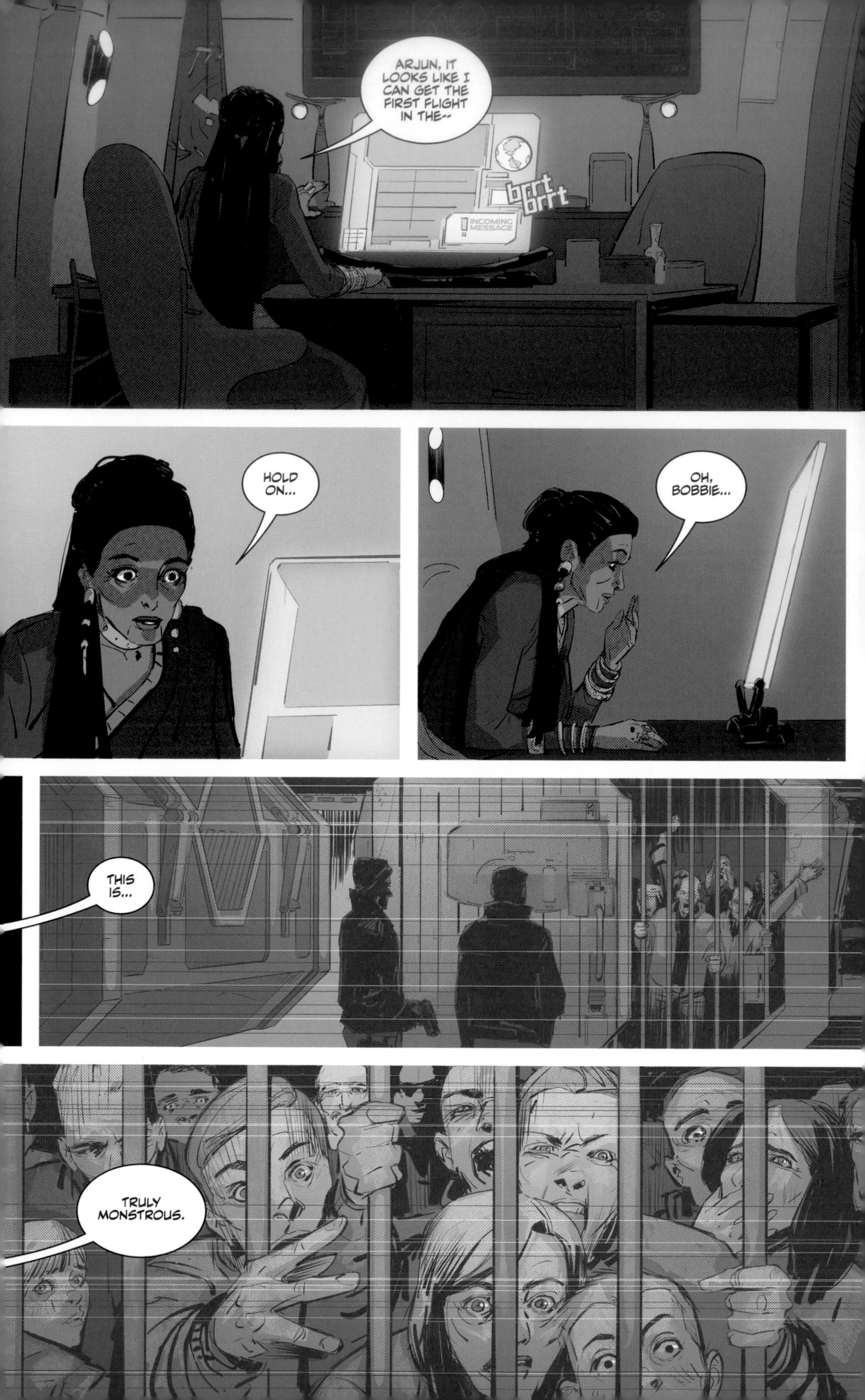
ARJUN, IT LOOKS LIKE I CAN GET THE FIRST FLIGHT IN THE--
brrt brrt
INCOMING MESSAGE
HOLD ON...
OH, BOBBIE...
THIS IS...
TRULY MONSTROUS.

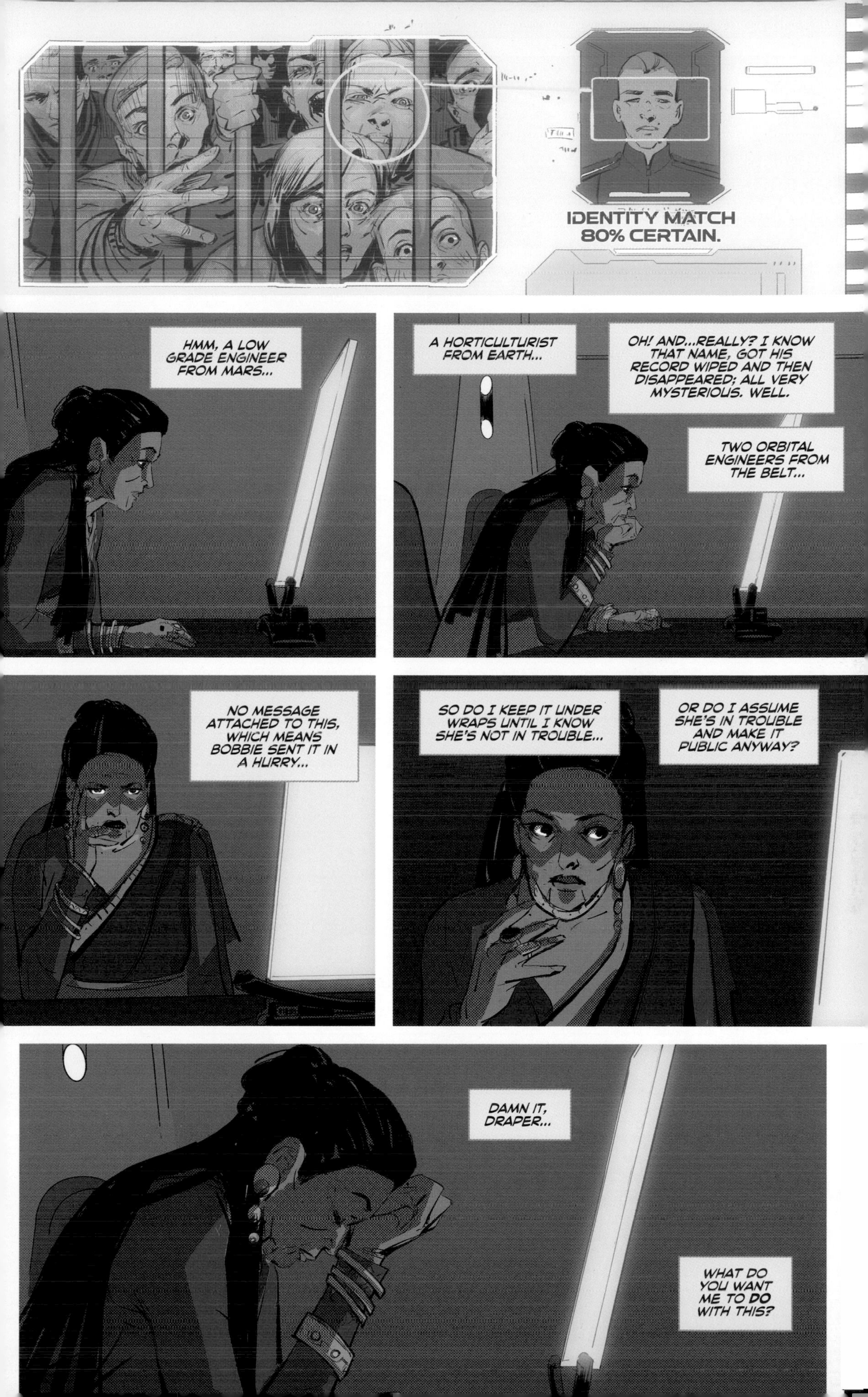
IDENTITY MATCH 80% CERTAIN.
HMM, A LOW GRADE ENGINEER FROM MARS...
A HORTICULTURIST FROM EARTH...
OH! AND...REALLY? I KNOW THAT NAME, GOT HIS RECORD WIPED AND THEN DISAPPEARED; ALL VERY MYSTERIOUS. WELL.
TWO ORBITAL ENGINEERS FROM THE BELT...
NO MESSAGE ATTACHED TO THIS, WHICH MEANS BOBBIE SENT IT IN A HURRY...
SO DO I KEEP IT UNDER WRAPS UNTIL I KNOW SHE'S NOT IN TROUBLE...
OR DO I ASSUME SHE'S IN TROUBLE AND MAKE IT PUBLIC ANYWAY?
DAMN IT, DRAPER...
WHAT DO YOU WANT ME TO DO WITH THIS?

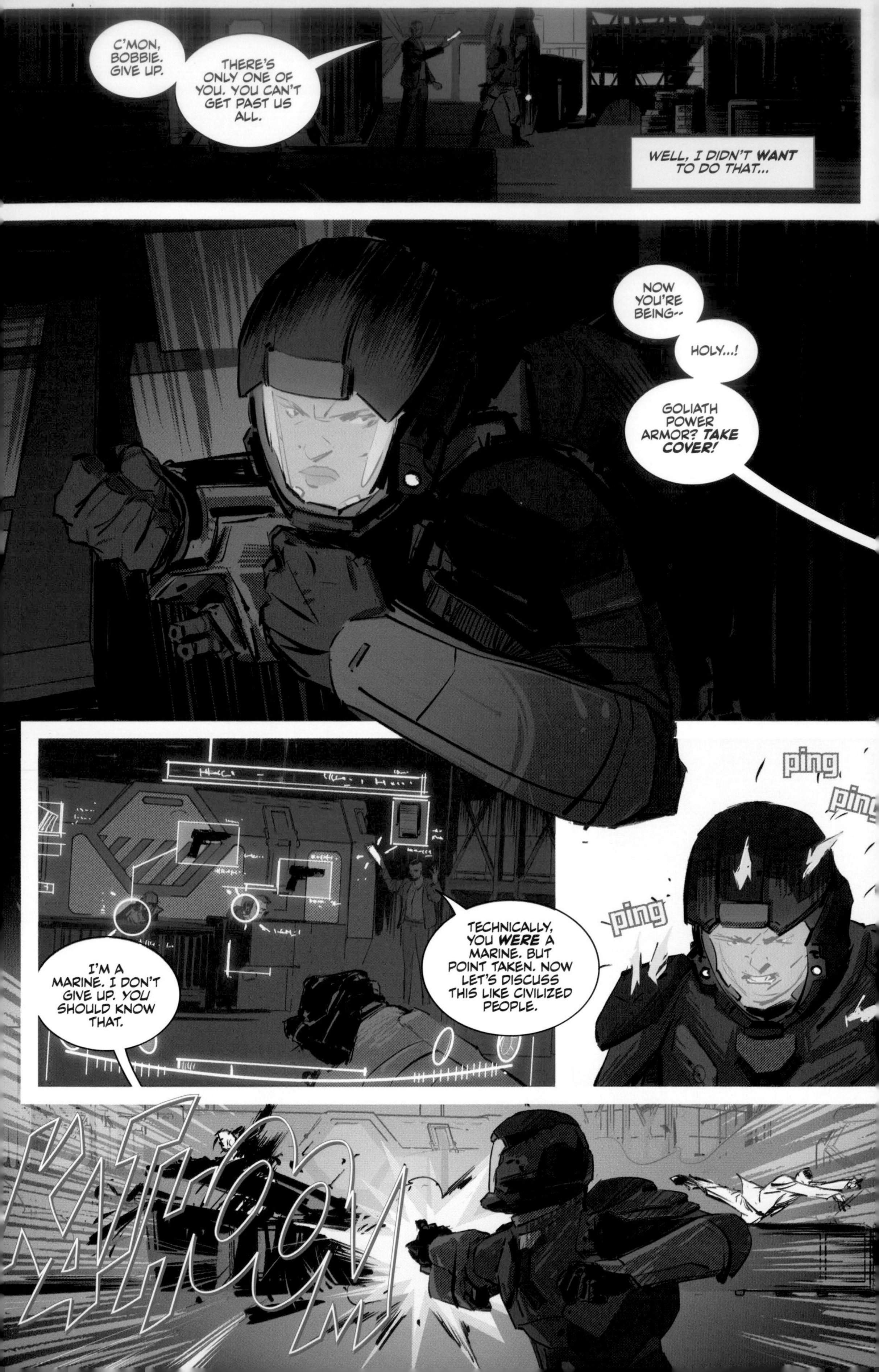
C'MON, BOBBIE. GIVE UP.
THERE'S ONLY ONE OF YOU. YOU CAN'T GET PAST US ALL.
WELL, I DIDN'T *WANT* TO DO THAT...
NOW YOU'RE BEING--
HOLY...!
GOLIATH POWER ARMOR? ***TAKE COVER!***
I'M A MARINE. I DON'T GIVE UP. *YOU* SHOULD KNOW THAT.
TECHNICALLY, YOU ***WERE*** A MARINE. BUT POINT TAKEN. NOW LET'S DISCUSS THIS LIKE CIVILIZED PEOPLE.
ping
ping
ping
KATHOOOM

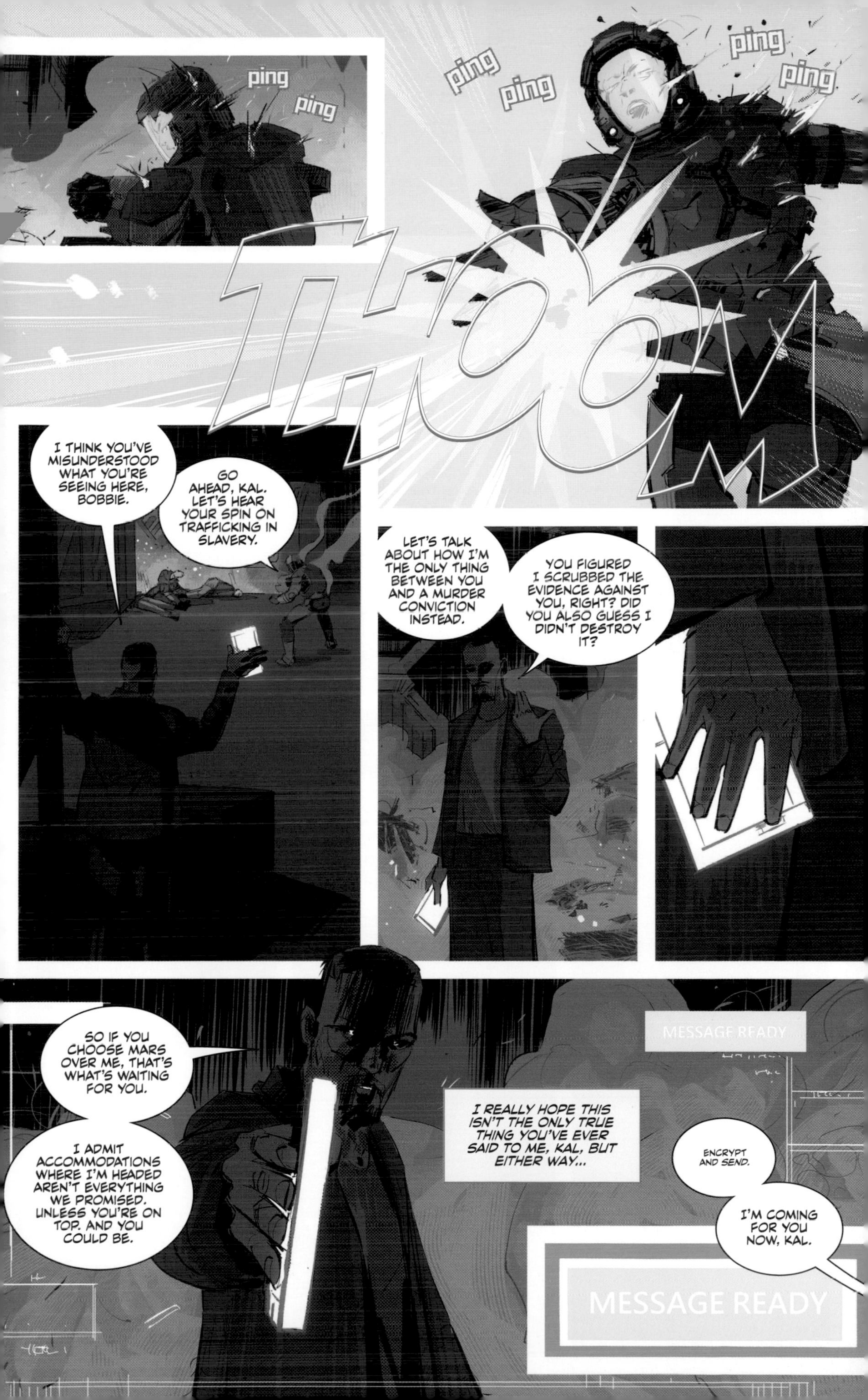
ping
ping
ping
ping
ping
ping
THOOM
I THINK YOU'VE MISUNDERSTOOD WHAT YOU'RE SEEING HERE, BOBBIE.
GO AHEAD, KAL. LET'S HEAR YOUR SPIN ON TRAFFICKING IN SLAVERY.
LET'S TALK ABOUT HOW I'M THE ONLY THING BETWEEN YOU AND A MURDER CONVICTION INSTEAD.
YOU FIGURED I SCRUBBED THE EVIDENCE AGAINST YOU, RIGHT? DID YOU ALSO GUESS I DIDN'T DESTROY IT?
SO IF YOU CHOOSE MARS OVER ME, THAT'S WHAT'S WAITING FOR YOU.
I ADMIT ACCOMMODATIONS WHERE I'M HEADED AREN'T EVERYTHING WE PROMISED. UNLESS YOU'RE ON TOP. AND YOU COULD BE.
MESSAGE READY
I REALLY HOPE THIS ISN'T THE ONLY TRUE THING YOU'VE EVER SAID TO ME, KAL, BUT EITHER WAY...
ENCRYPT AND SEND.
I'M COMING FOR YOU NOW, KAL.
MESSAGE READY

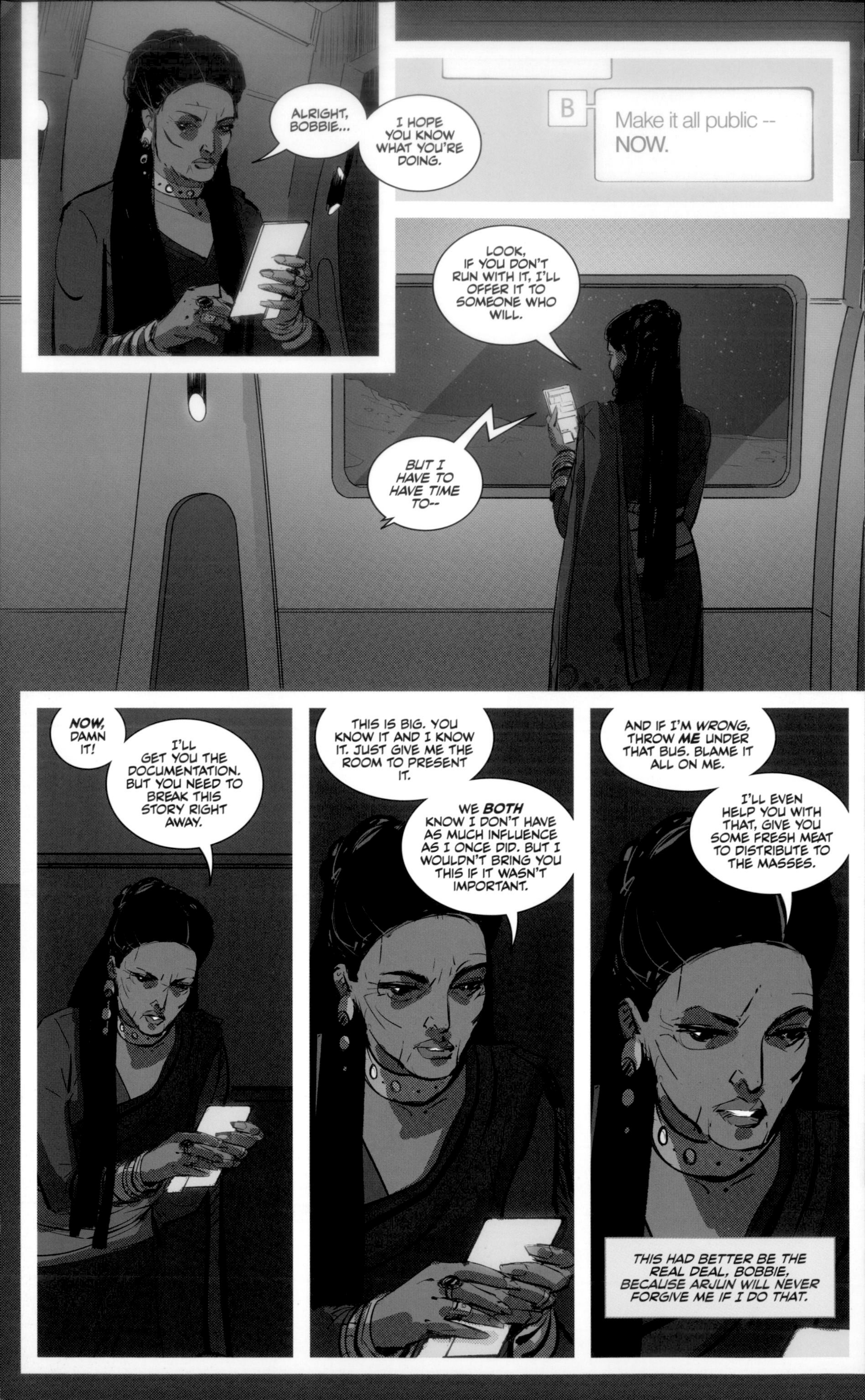

ALRIGHT, BOBBIE...
I HOPE YOU KNOW WHAT YOU'RE DOING.
B
Make it all public -- NOW.
LOOK, IF YOU DON'T RUN WITH IT, I'LL OFFER IT TO SOMEONE WHO WILL.
BUT I HAVE TO HAVE TIME TO--
NOW, DAMN IT!
I'LL GET YOU THE DOCUMENTATION. BUT YOU NEED TO BREAK THIS STORY RIGHT AWAY.
THIS IS BIG. YOU KNOW IT AND I KNOW IT. JUST GIVE ME THE ROOM TO PRESENT IT.
WE BOTH KNOW I DON'T HAVE AS MUCH INFLUENCE AS I ONCE DID. BUT I WOULDN'T BRING YOU THIS IF IT WASN'T IMPORTANT.
AND IF I'M WRONG, THROW ME UNDER THAT BUS. BLAME IT ALL ON ME.
I'LL EVEN HELP YOU WITH THAT, GIVE YOU SOME FRESH MEAT TO DISTRIBUTE TO THE MASSES.
THIS HAD BETTER BE THE REAL DEAL, BOBBIE, BECAUSE ARJUN WILL NEVER FORGIVE ME IF I DO THAT.

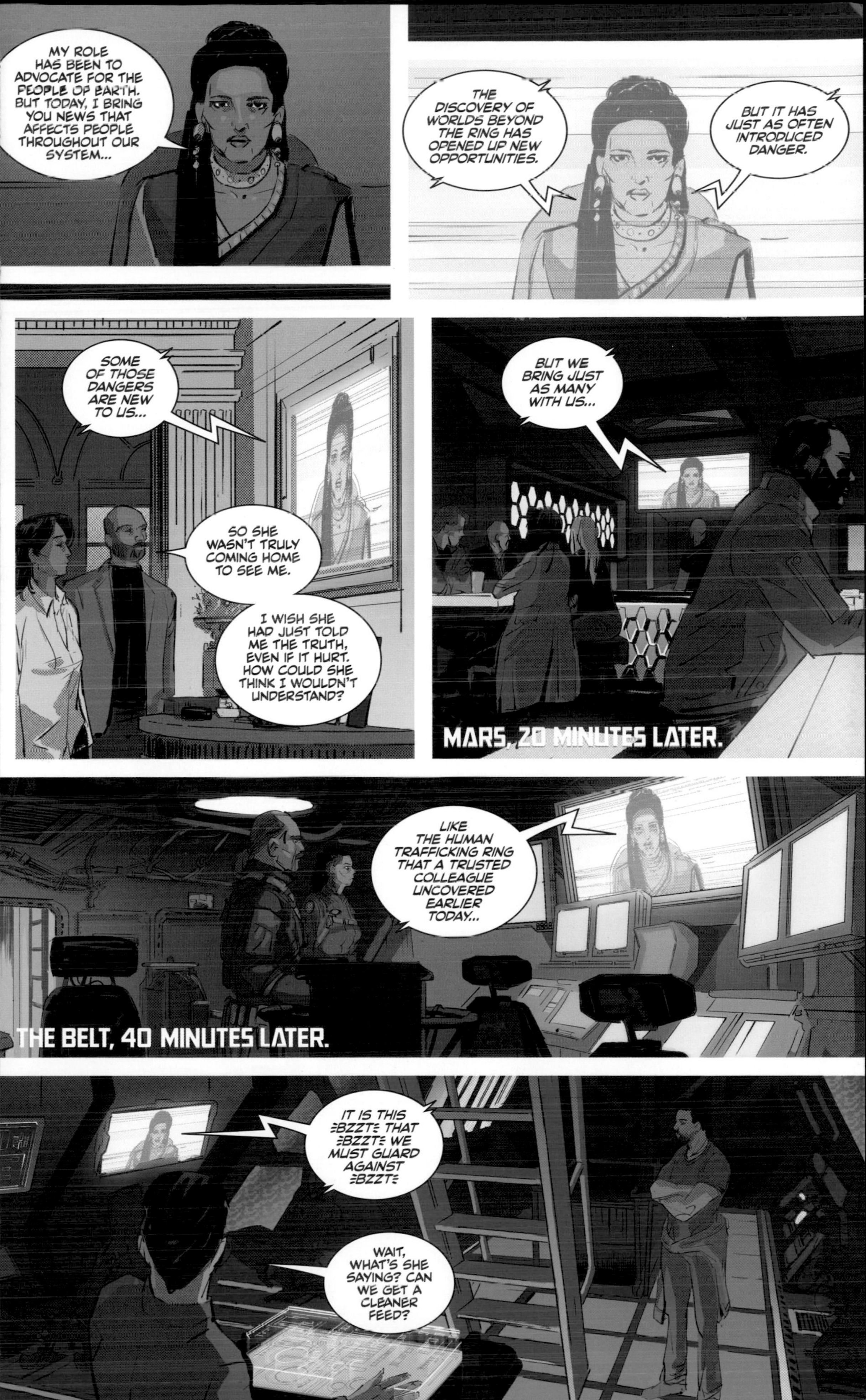

MY ROLE HAS BEEN TO ADVOCATE FOR THE PEOPLE OF EARTH. BUT TODAY, I BRING YOU NEWS THAT AFFECTS PEOPLE THROUGHOUT OUR SYSTEM...
THE DISCOVERY OF WORLDS BEYOND THE RING HAS OPENED UP NEW OPPORTUNITIES.
BUT IT HAS JUST AS OFTEN INTRODUCED DANGER.
SOME OF THOSE DANGERS ARE NEW TO US...
SO SHE WASN'T TRULY COMING HOME TO SEE ME.
I WISH SHE HAD JUST TOLD ME THE TRUTH, EVEN IF IT HURT. HOW COULD SHE THINK I WOULDN'T UNDERSTAND?
BUT WE BRING JUST AS MANY WITH US...
MARS, 20 MINUTES LATER.
LIKE THE HUMAN TRAFFICKING RING THAT A TRUSTED COLLEAGUE UNCOVERED EARLIER TODAY...
THE BELT, 40 MINUTES LATER.
IT IS THIS =BZZT= THAT =BZZT= WE MUST GUARD AGAINST =BZZT=
WAIT, WHAT'S SHE SAYING? CAN WE GET A CLEANER FEED?

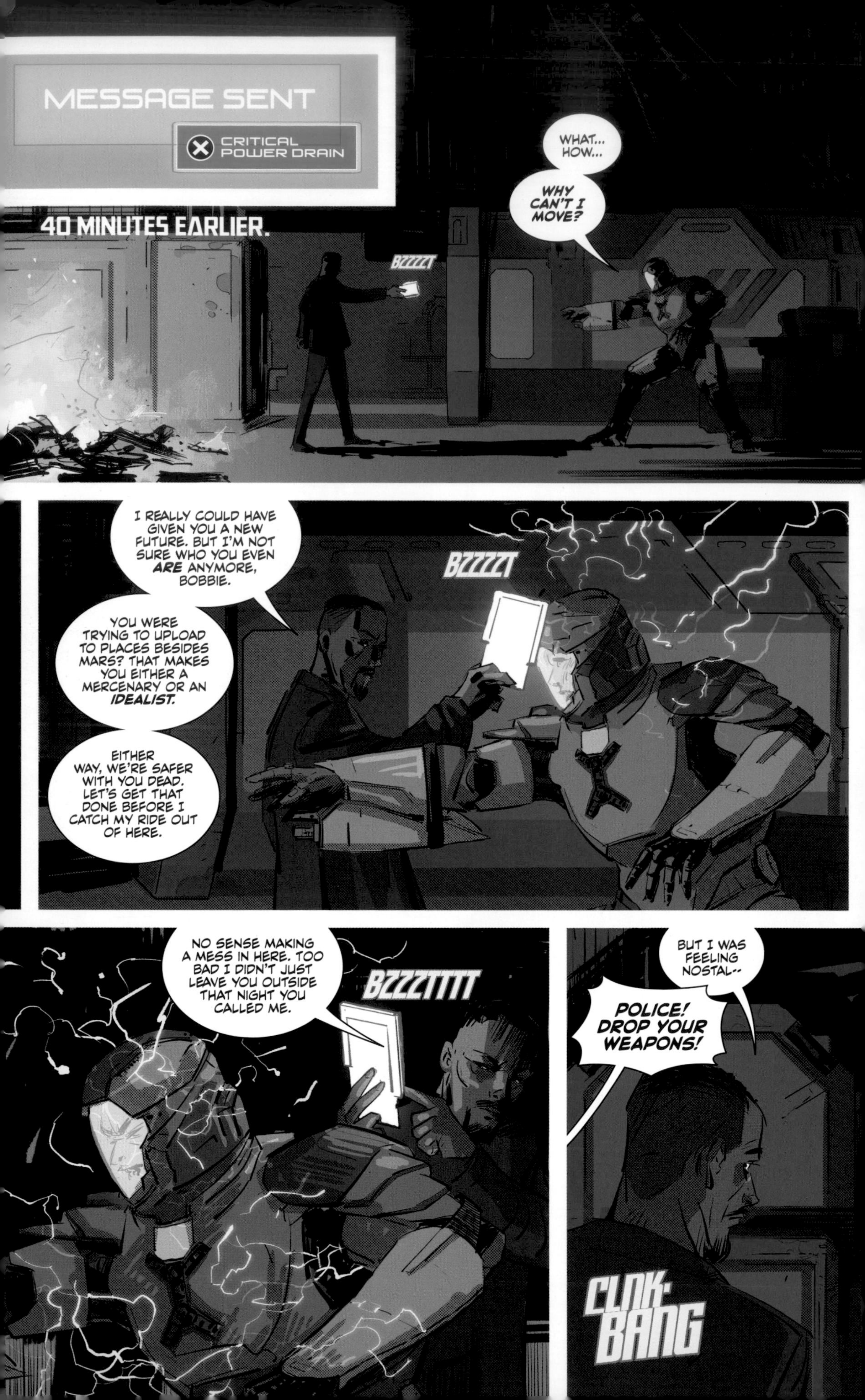

MESSAGE SENT
CRITICAL POWER DRAIN
40 MINUTES EARLIER.
WHAT... HOW...
WHY CAN'T I MOVE?
BZZZZT
I REALLY COULD HAVE GIVEN YOU A NEW FUTURE. BUT I'M NOT SURE WHO YOU EVEN ARE ANYMORE, BOBBIE.
BZZZZT
YOU WERE TRYING TO UPLOAD TO PLACES BESIDES MARS? THAT MAKES YOU EITHER A MERCENARY OR AN IDEALIST.
EITHER WAY, WE'RE SAFER WITH YOU DEAD. LET'S GET THAT DONE BEFORE I CATCH MY RIDE OUT OF HERE.
NO SENSE MAKING A MESS IN HERE. TOO BAD I DIDN'T JUST LEAVE YOU OUTSIDE THAT NIGHT YOU CALLED ME.
BZZZTTTT
BUT I WAS FEELING NOSTAL--
POLICE! DROP YOUR WEAPONS!
CLNK-BANG

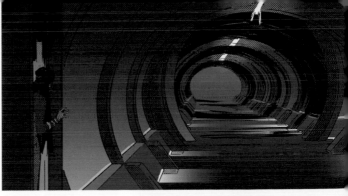

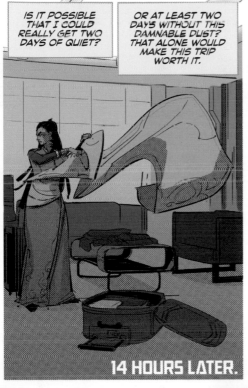

IS IT POSSIBLE THAT I COULD REALLY GET TWO DAYS OF QUIET?
OR AT LEAST TWO DAYS WITHOUT THIS DAMNABLE DUST? THAT ALONE WOULD MAKE THIS TRIP WORTH IT.
14 HOURS LATER.
I CAN'T KEEP BEING SO JUMPY. I DOUBT WE'VE CRIPPLED THEM TOO BADLY, BUT SURELY THEY'VE GONE TO GROUND.
AND THEY WOULDN'T DARE TRY ANYTHING WITH ME AGAIN.
MAYBE FULL GRAVITY WILL HELP. AND A BLUE SKY. I NEVER REALIZED HOW MUCH I'D MISS THAT.
WHAT'S GOING ON HERE?
ALL LUNAR TRAFFIC IS SUSPENDED UNTIL FULL IDENTITY VERIFICATIONS ARE RUN FOR EVERYONE ON THIS BASE.
BUT THAT COULD TAKE UNTIL TOMORROW, OR LONGER IF IT'S DONE IN PERSON.
Departures
Arrivals
Baggage
I'M EXPECTED ON EARTH TODAY. WHY WASN'T I TOLD ABOUT THIS?
GATE 6-F
SO SORRY, MADAM AVASARALA. I THOUGHT YOU'D BE AWARE THAT WE WOULD HAVE TO TAKE THIS STEP, AFTER YOUR NEWS YESTERDAY.
SO FAR WE'VE FOUND TWO UNAUTHORIZED PERSONS STAYING IN CREW QUARTERS. THERE MAY BE OTHERS. WE CAN'T RISK THEM LEAVING.
YES, OF COURSE. IF YOU ALREADY HAVE THEM DETAINED I WOULD LIKE A WORD WITH THEM MYSELF...
AFTER I MAKE A CALL.

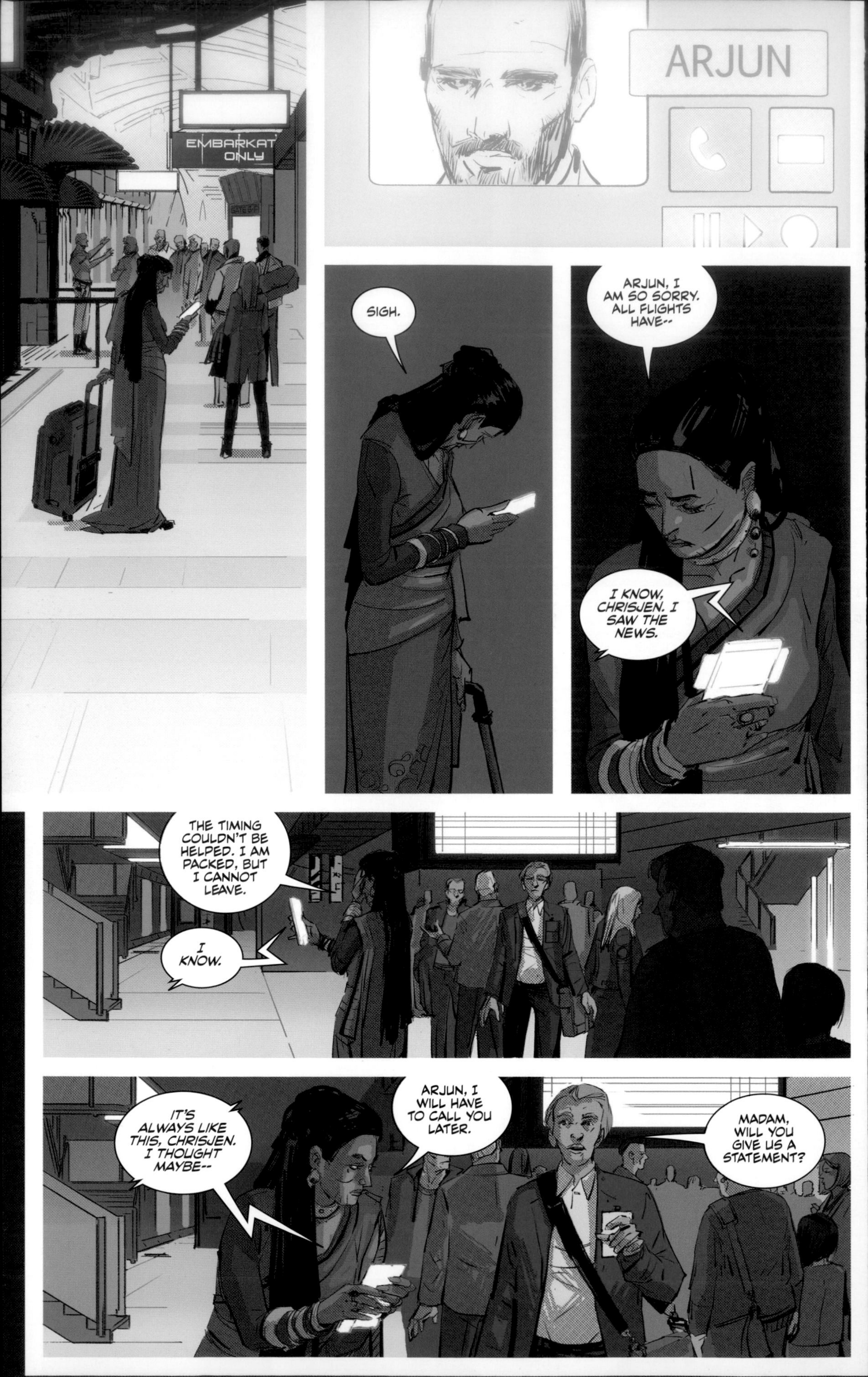
EMBARKAT
ONLY
GATE
ARJUN
SIGH.
ARJUN, I AM SO SORRY. ALL FLIGHTS HAVE--
I KNOW, CHRISJEN. I SAW THE NEWS.
THE TIMING COULDN'T BE HELPED. I AM PACKED, BUT I CANNOT LEAVE.
I KNOW.
IT'S ALWAYS LIKE THIS, CHRISJEN. I THOUGHT MAYBE--
ARJUN, I WILL HAVE TO CALL YOU LATER.
MADAM, WILL YOU GIVE US A STATEMENT?

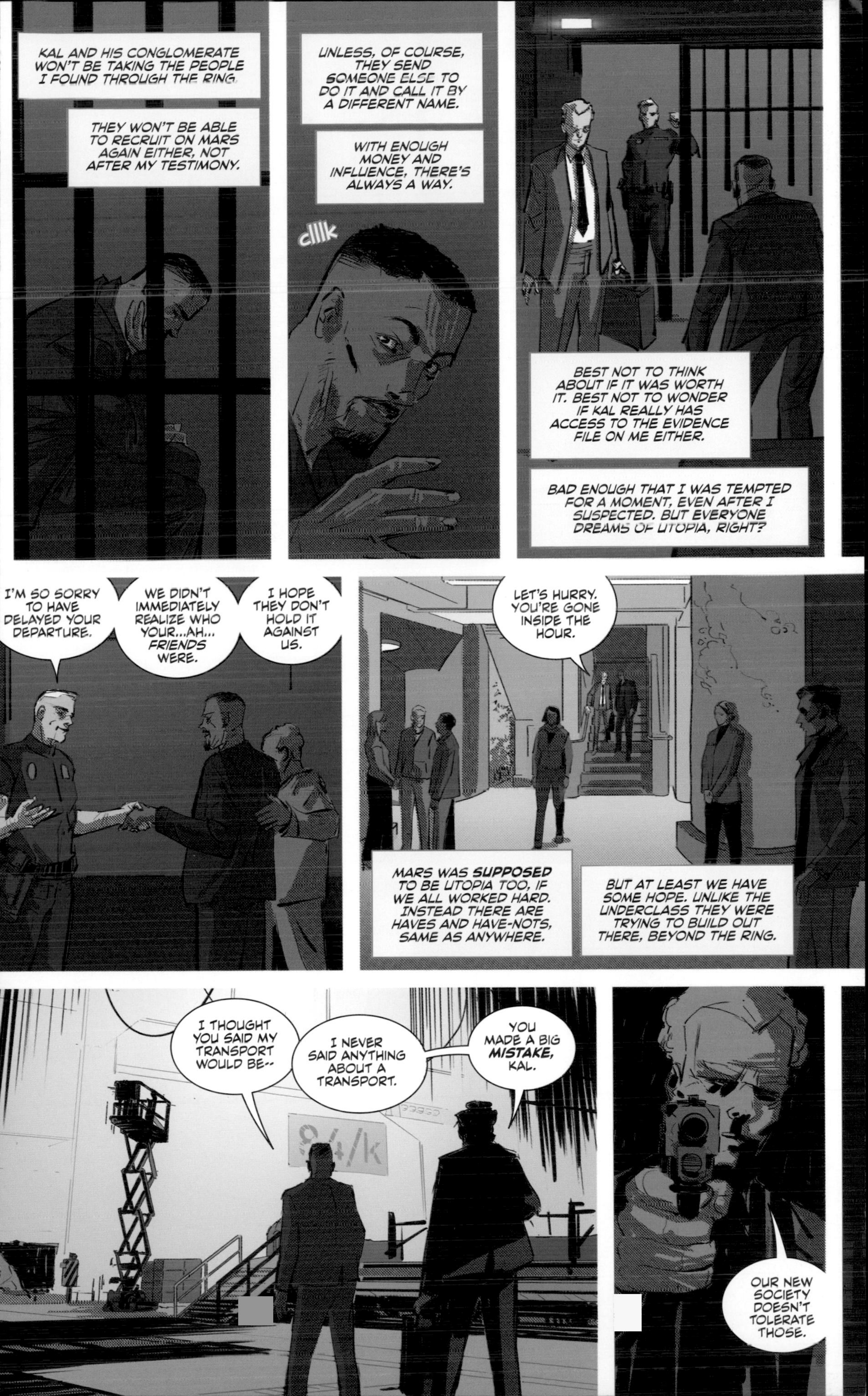
KAL AND HIS CONGLOMERATE WON'T BE TAKING THE PEOPLE I FOUND THROUGH THE RING.
THEY WON'T BE ABLE TO RECRUIT ON MARS AGAIN EITHER, NOT AFTER MY TESTIMONY.
UNLESS, OF COURSE, THEY SEND SOMEONE ELSE TO DO IT AND CALL IT BY A DIFFERENT NAME.
WITH ENOUGH MONEY AND INFLUENCE, THERE'S ALWAYS A WAY.
cllk
BEST NOT TO THINK ABOUT IF IT WAS WORTH IT. BEST NOT TO WONDER IF KAL REALLY HAS ACCESS TO THE EVIDENCE FILE ON ME EITHER.
BAD ENOUGH THAT I WAS TEMPTED FOR A MOMENT, EVEN AFTER I SUSPECTED. BUT EVERYONE DREAMS OF UTOPIA, RIGHT?
I'M SO SORRY TO HAVE DELAYED YOUR DEPARTURE.
WE DIDN'T IMMEDIATELY REALIZE WHO YOUR...AH... FRIENDS WERE.
I HOPE THEY DON'T HOLD IT AGAINST US.
LET'S HURRY. YOU'RE GONE INSIDE THE HOUR.
MARS WAS SUPPOSED TO BE UTOPIA TOO, IF WE ALL WORKED HARD. INSTEAD THERE ARE HAVES AND HAVE-NOTS, SAME AS ANYWHERE.
BUT AT LEAST WE HAVE SOME HOPE. UNLIKE THE UNDERCLASS THEY WERE TRYING TO BUILD OUT THERE, BEYOND THE RING.
I THOUGHT YOU SAID MY TRANSPORT WOULD BE--
I NEVER SAID ANYTHING ABOUT A TRANSPORT.
YOU MADE A BIG MISTAKE, KAL.
OUR NEW SOCIETY DOESN'T TOLERATE THOSE.

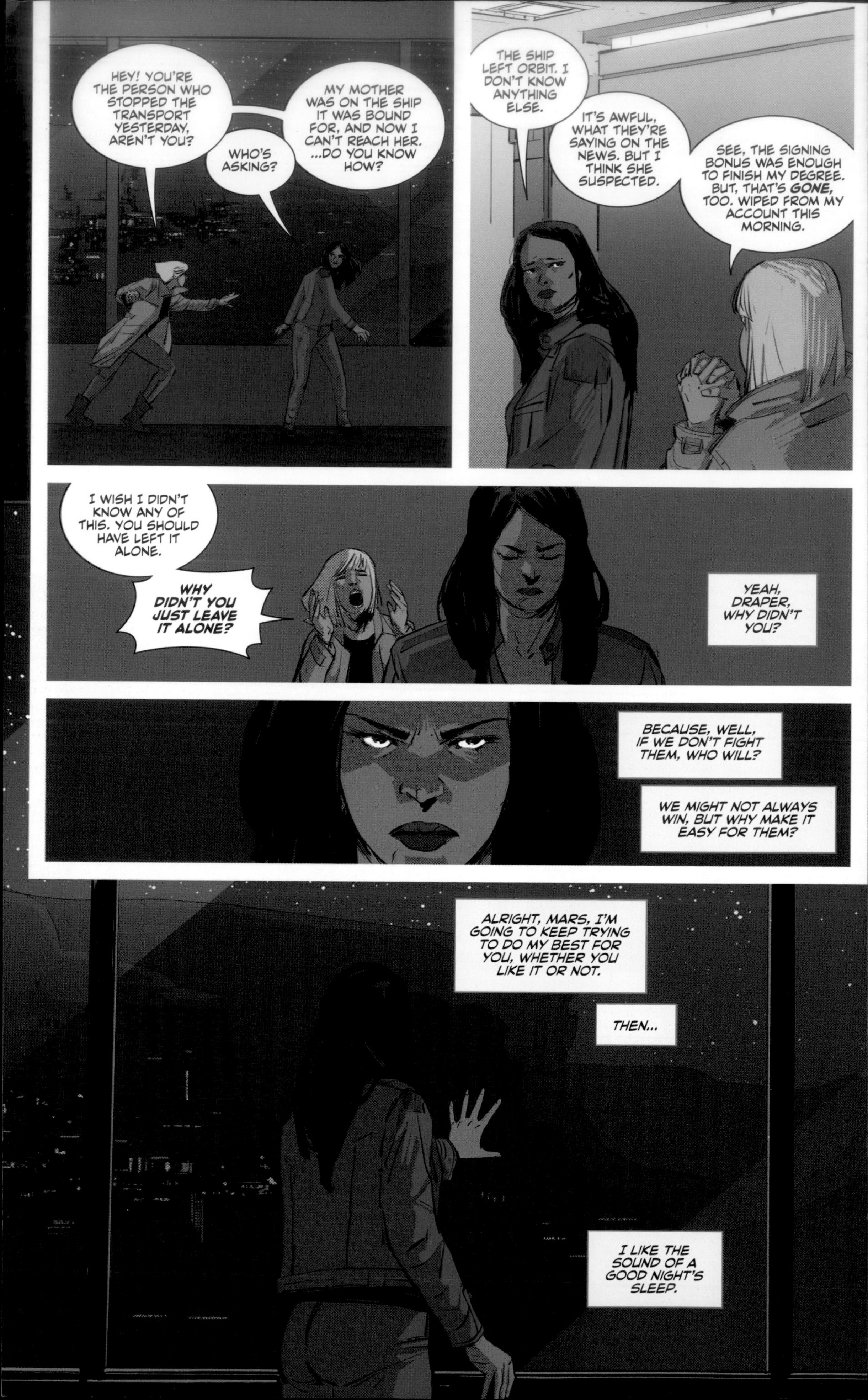
HEY! YOU'RE THE PERSON WHO STOPPED THE TRANSPORT YESTERDAY, AREN'T YOU?
WHO'S ASKING?
MY MOTHER WAS ON THE SHIP IT WAS BOUND FOR, AND NOW I CAN'T REACH HER. ...DO YOU KNOW HOW?
THE SHIP LEFT ORBIT. I DON'T KNOW ANYTHING ELSE.
IT'S AWFUL, WHAT THEY'RE SAYING ON THE NEWS. BUT I THINK SHE SUSPECTED.
SEE, THE SIGNING BONUS WAS ENOUGH TO FINISH MY DEGREE. BUT, THAT'S GONE, TOO. WIPED FROM MY ACCOUNT THIS MORNING.
I WISH I DIDN'T KNOW ANY OF THIS. YOU SHOULD HAVE LEFT IT ALONE.
WHY DIDN'T YOU JUST LEAVE IT ALONE?
YEAH, DRAPER, WHY DIDN'T YOU?
BECAUSE, WELL, IF WE DON'T FIGHT THEM, WHO WILL?
WE MIGHT NOT ALWAYS WIN, BUT WHY MAKE IT EASY FOR THEM?
ALRIGHT, MARS, I'M GOING TO KEEP TRYING TO DO MY BEST FOR YOU, WHETHER YOU LIKE IT OR NOT.
THEN...
I LIKE THE SOUND OF A GOOD NIGHT'S SLEEP.

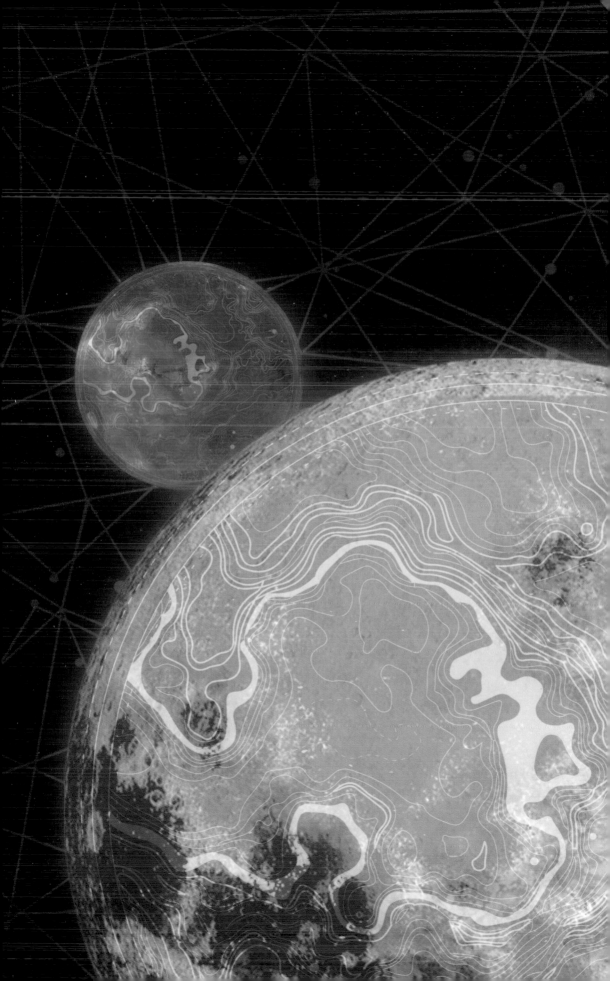

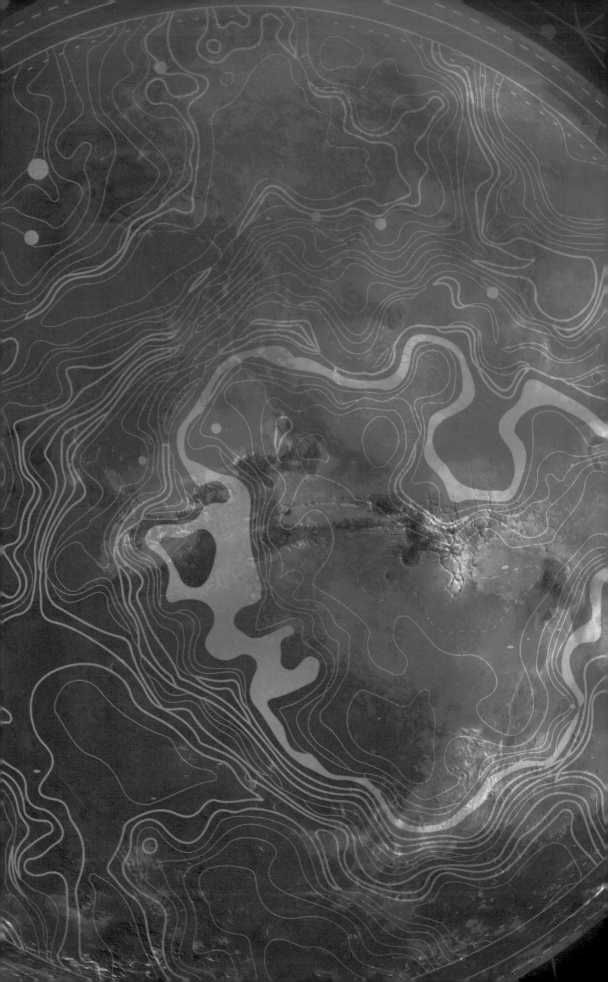

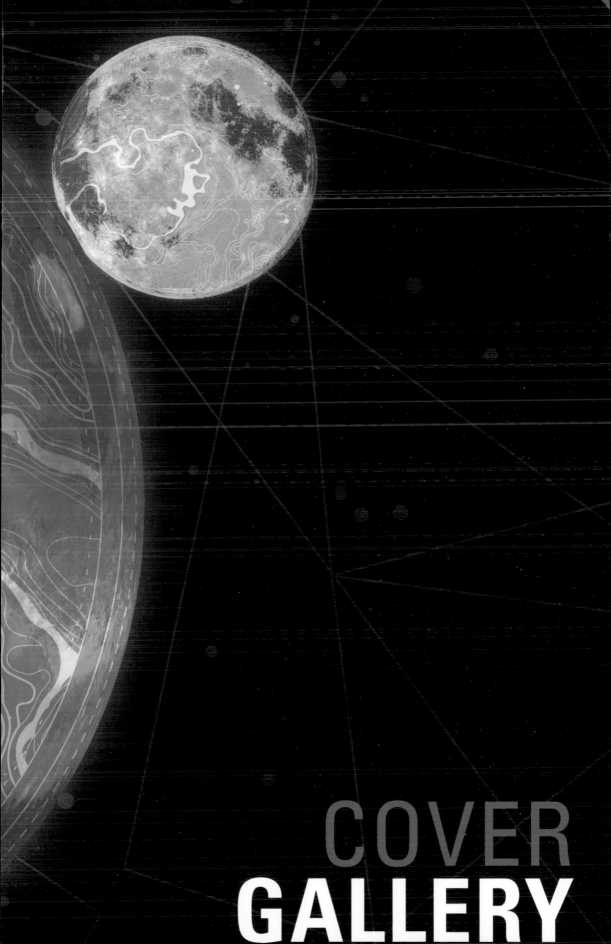

COVER
GALLERY

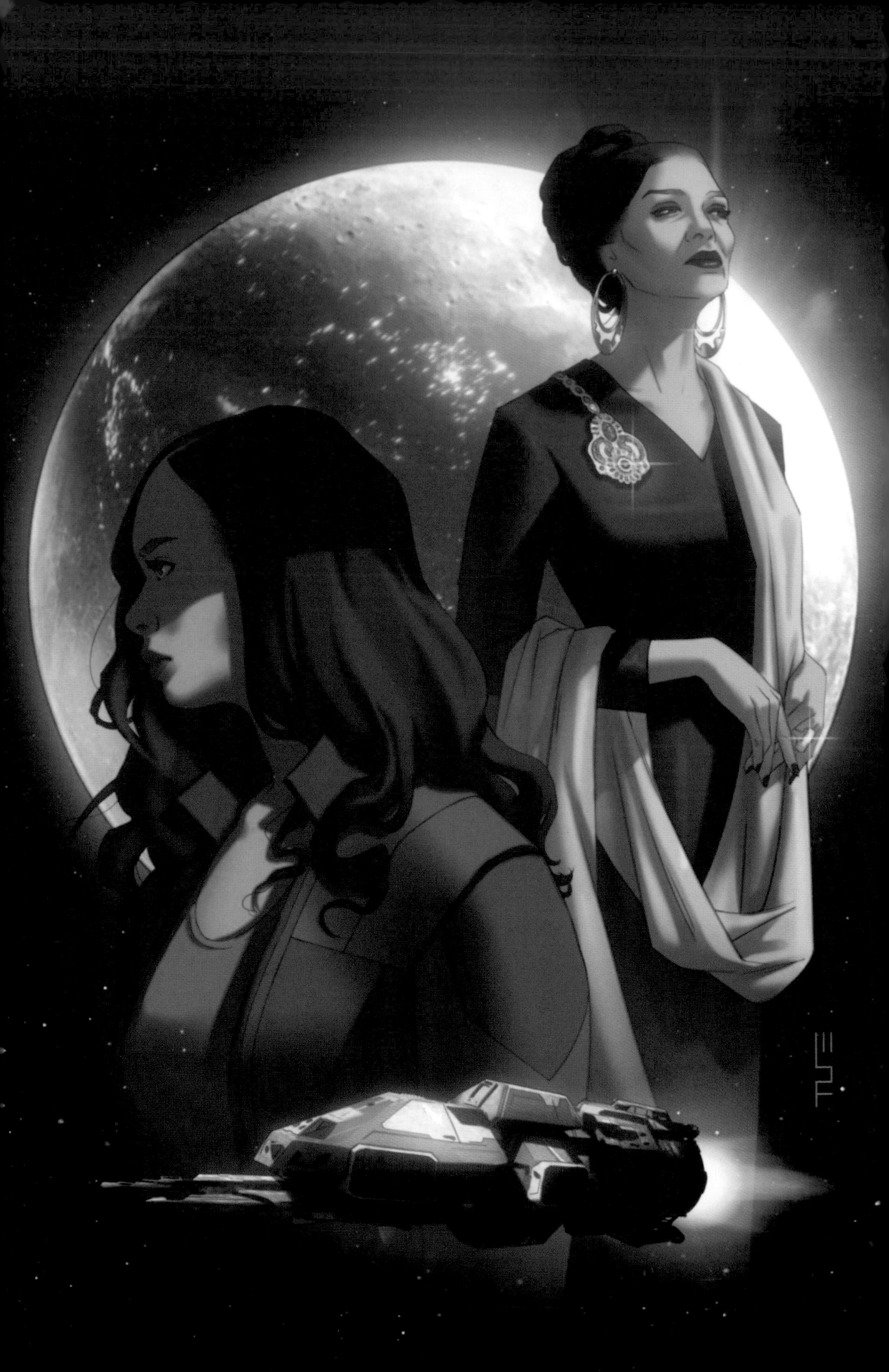

ISSUE ONE MAIN COVER BY **W. SCOTT FORBES**

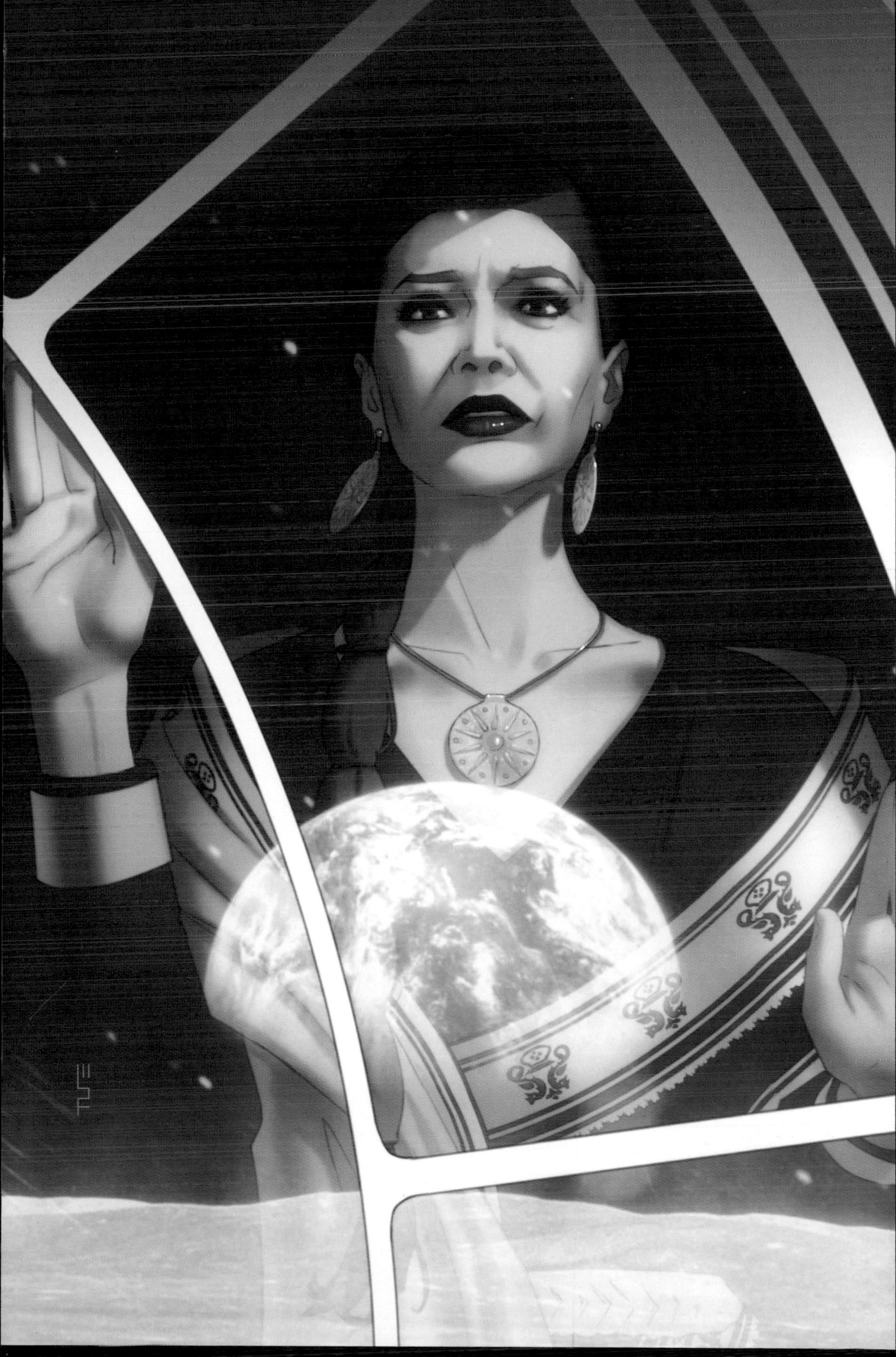

ISSUE TWO MAIN COVER BY **W. SCOTT FORBES**

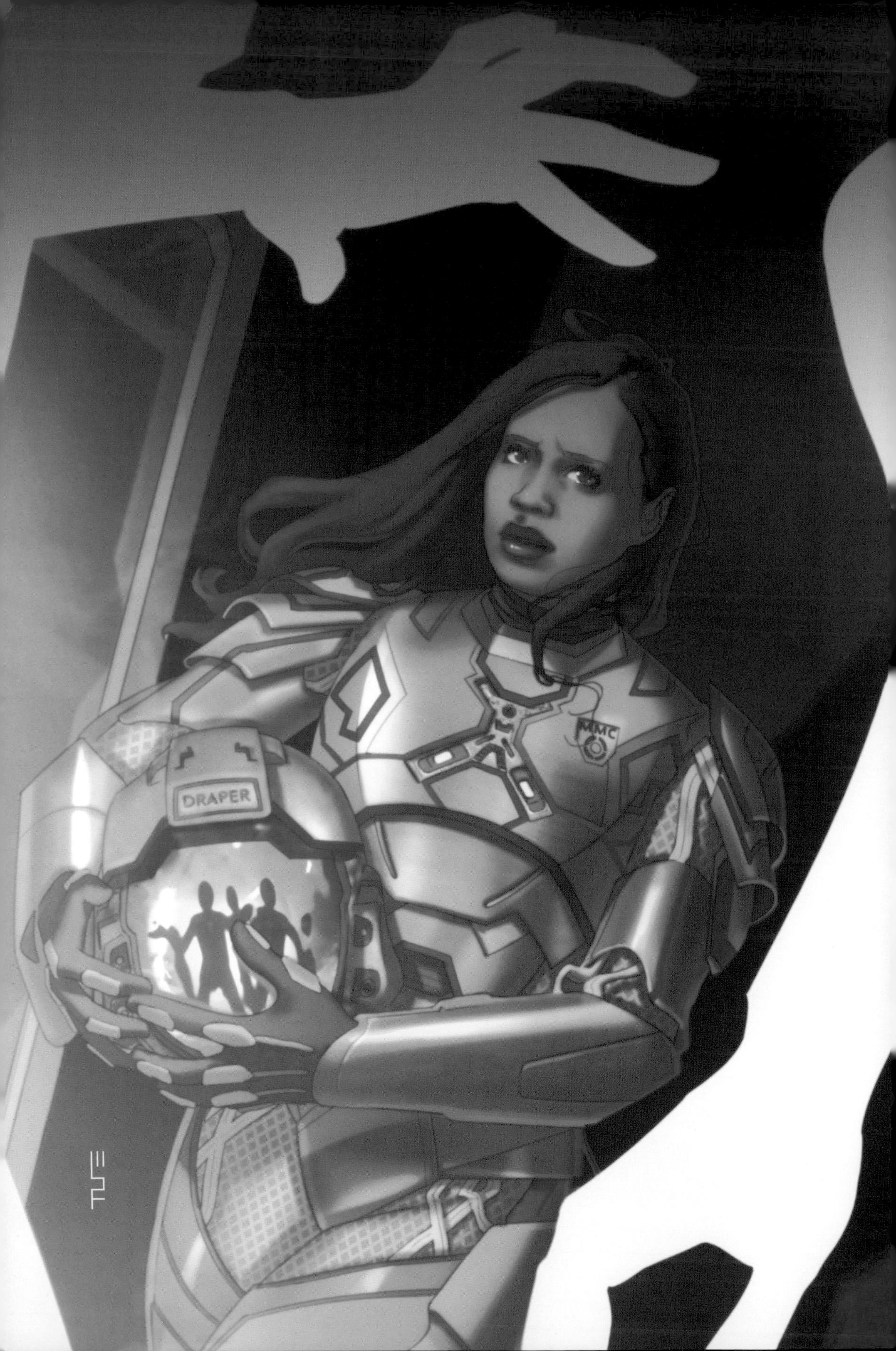
DRAPER
MMC

ISSUE THREE MAIN COVER BY **W. SCOTT FORBES**

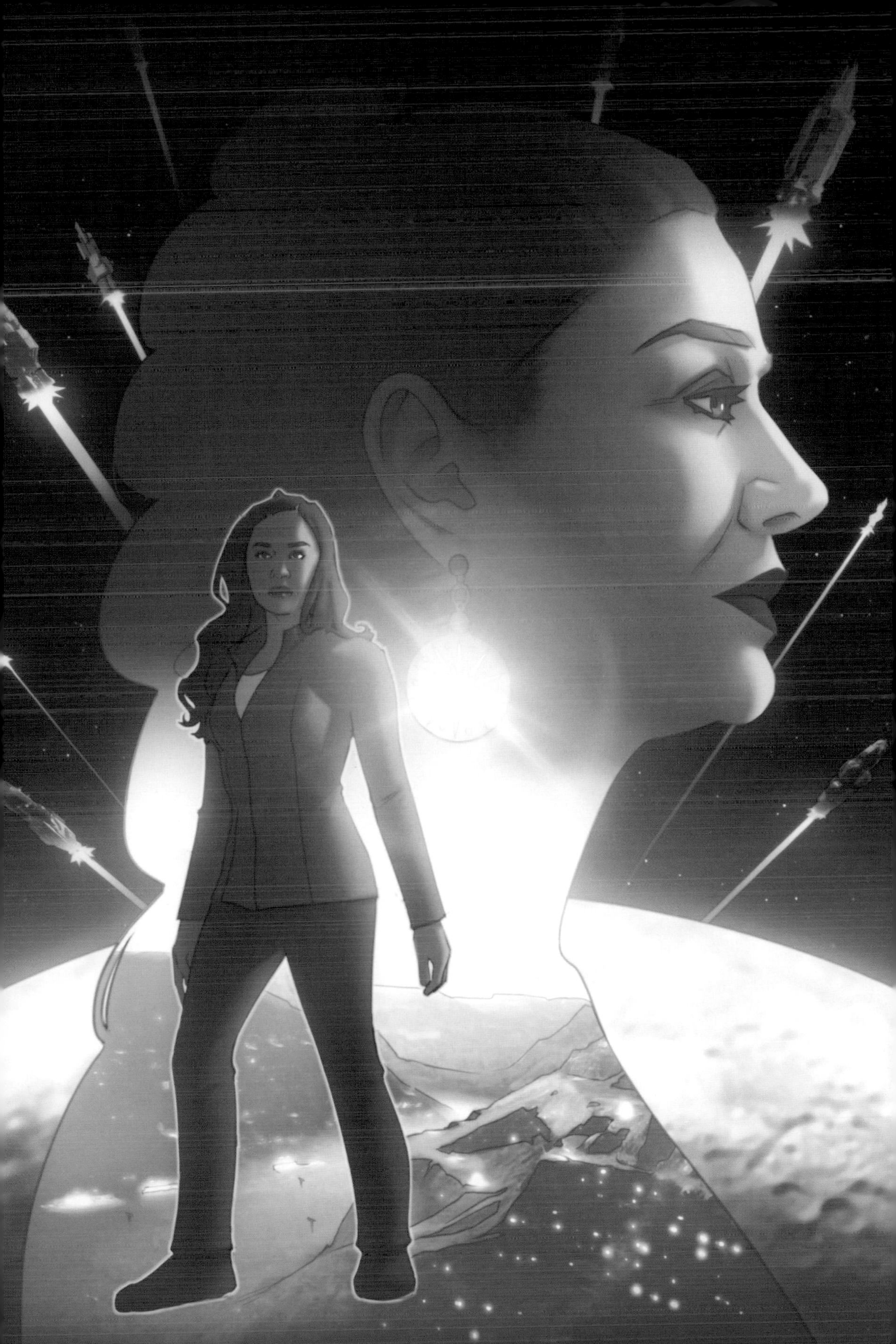

ISSUE FOUR MAIN COVER BY **W. SCOTT FORBES**

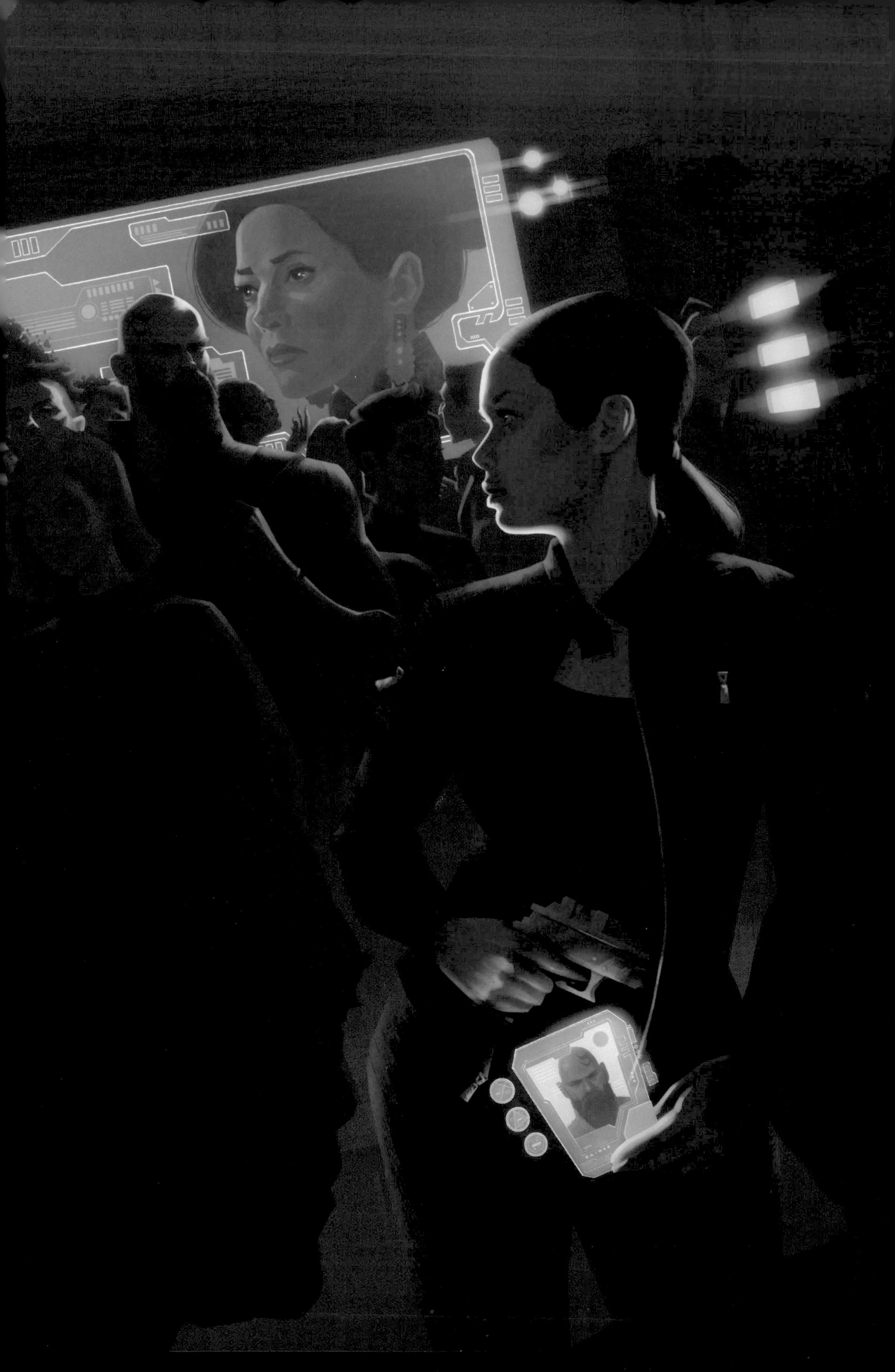

ISSUE ONE VARIANT COVER BY **TIGH WALKER**

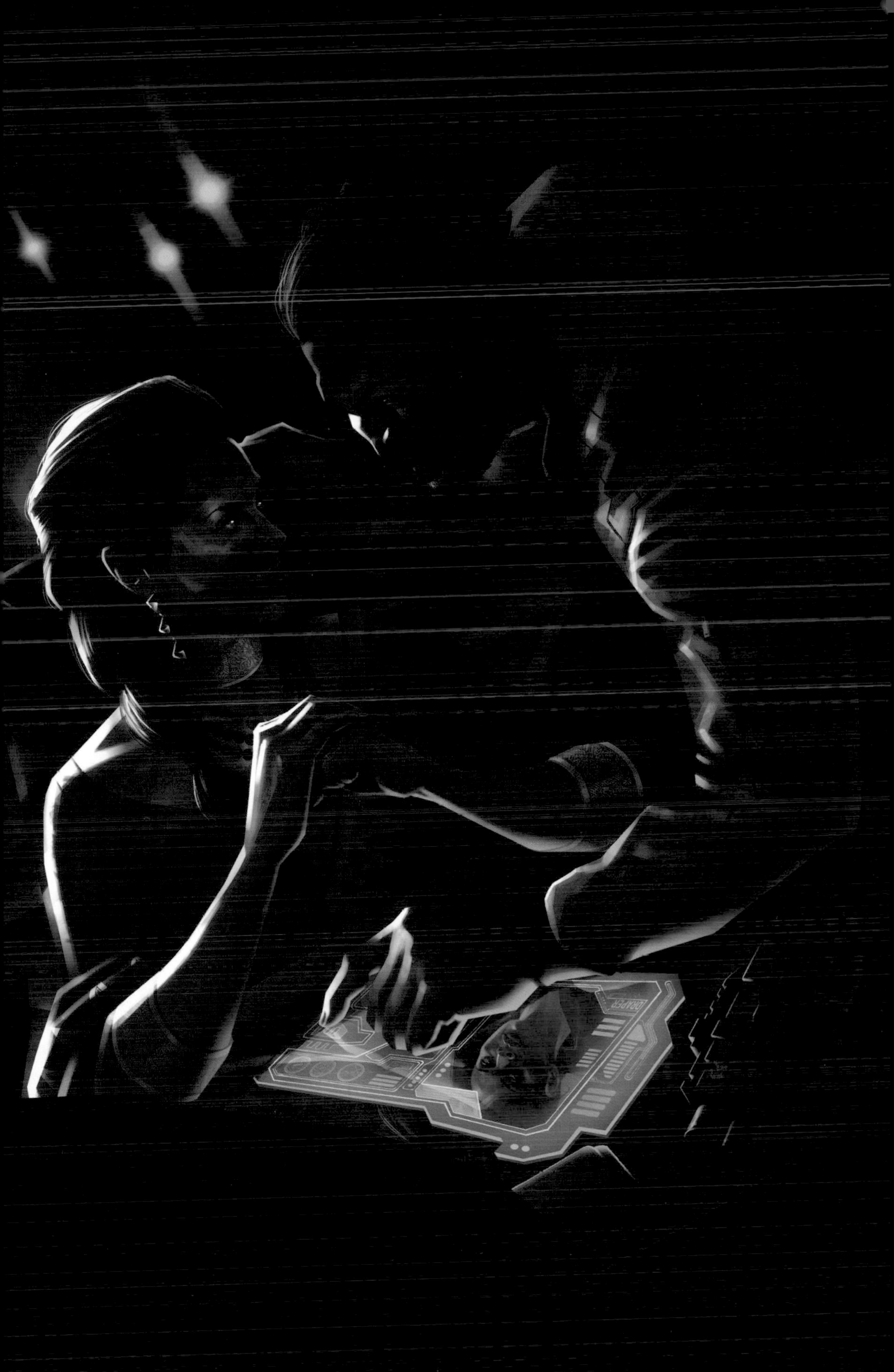

ISSUE TWO VARIANT COVER BY **TIGH WALKER**

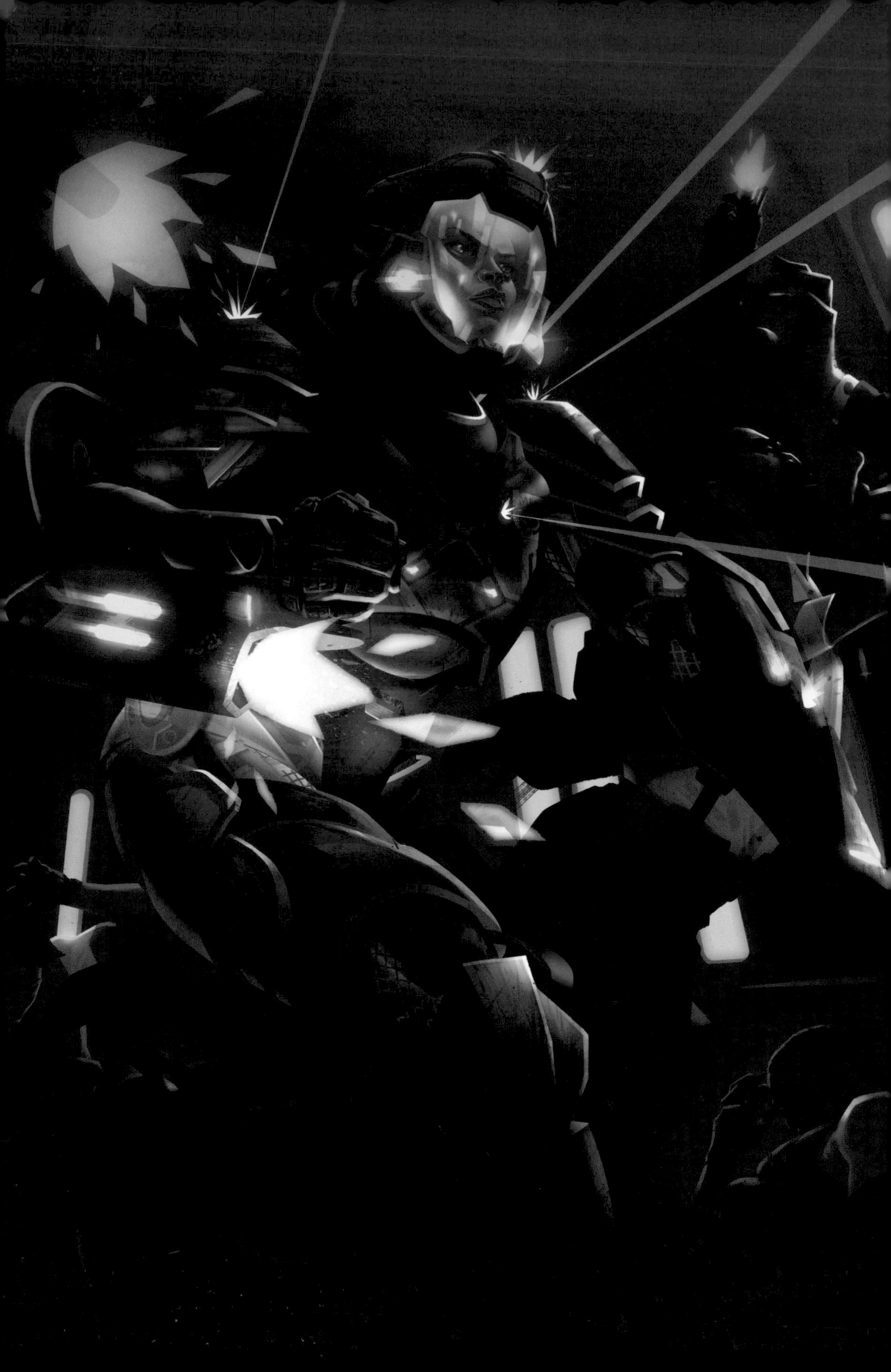

ISSUE THREE VARIANT COVER BY **TIGH WALKER**

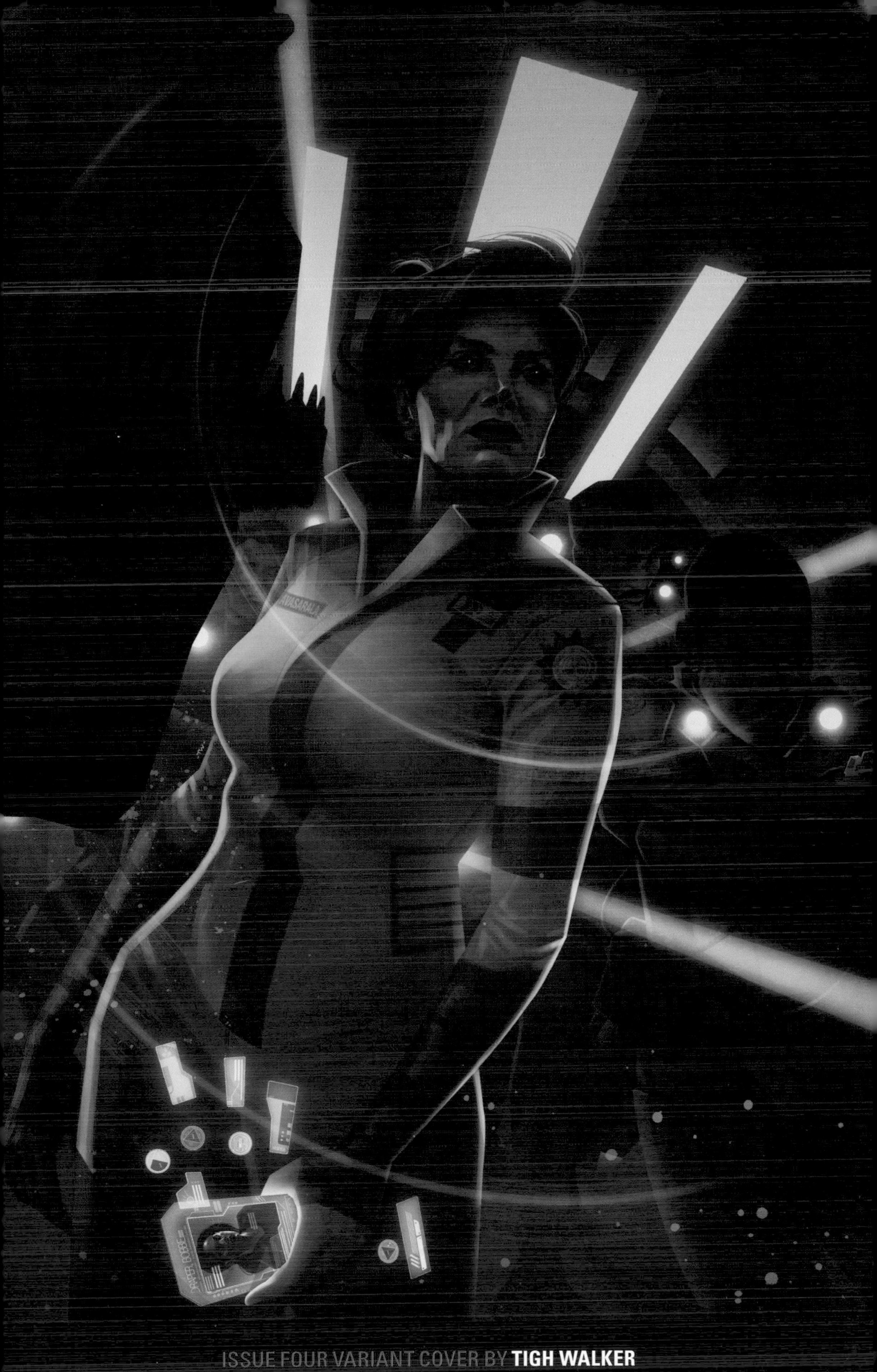
AVASARALA
DRAPER, BOBBIE

ISSUE FOUR VARIANT COVER BY **TIGH WALKER**

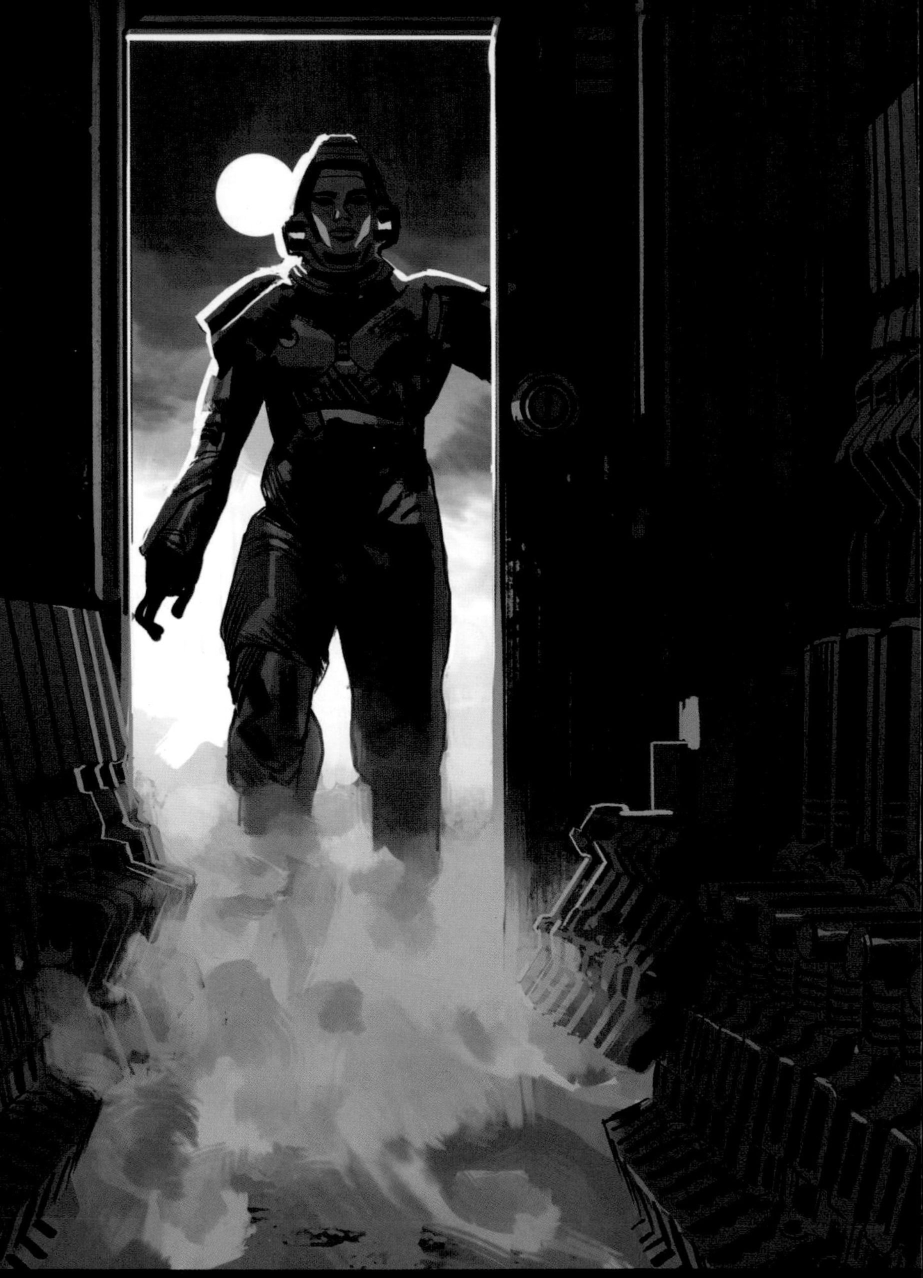

ISSUE ONE VARIANT COVER BY **LORENZO DE FELICI**

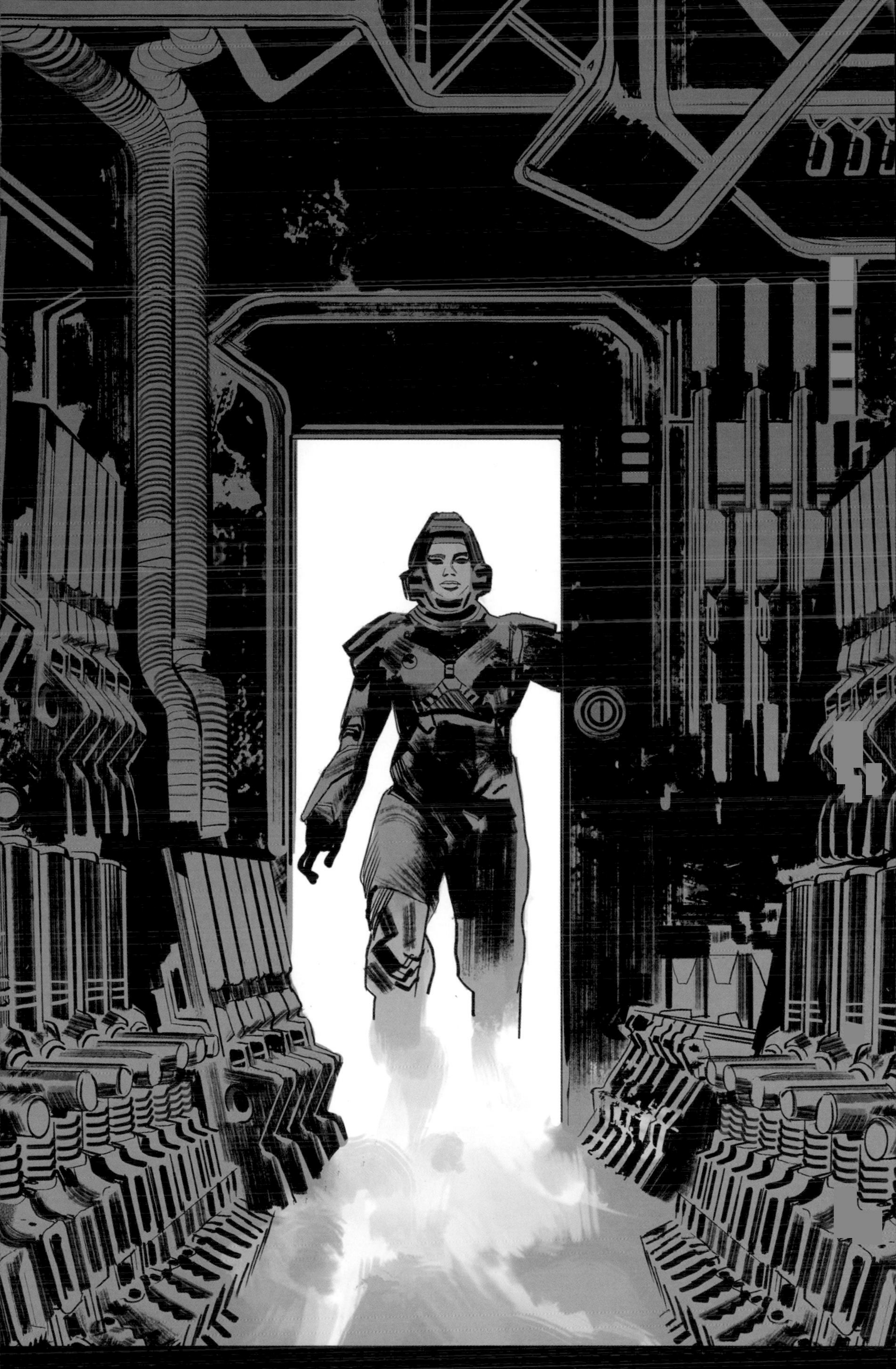

ISSUE ONE VARIANT COVER BY **LORENZO DE FELICI**

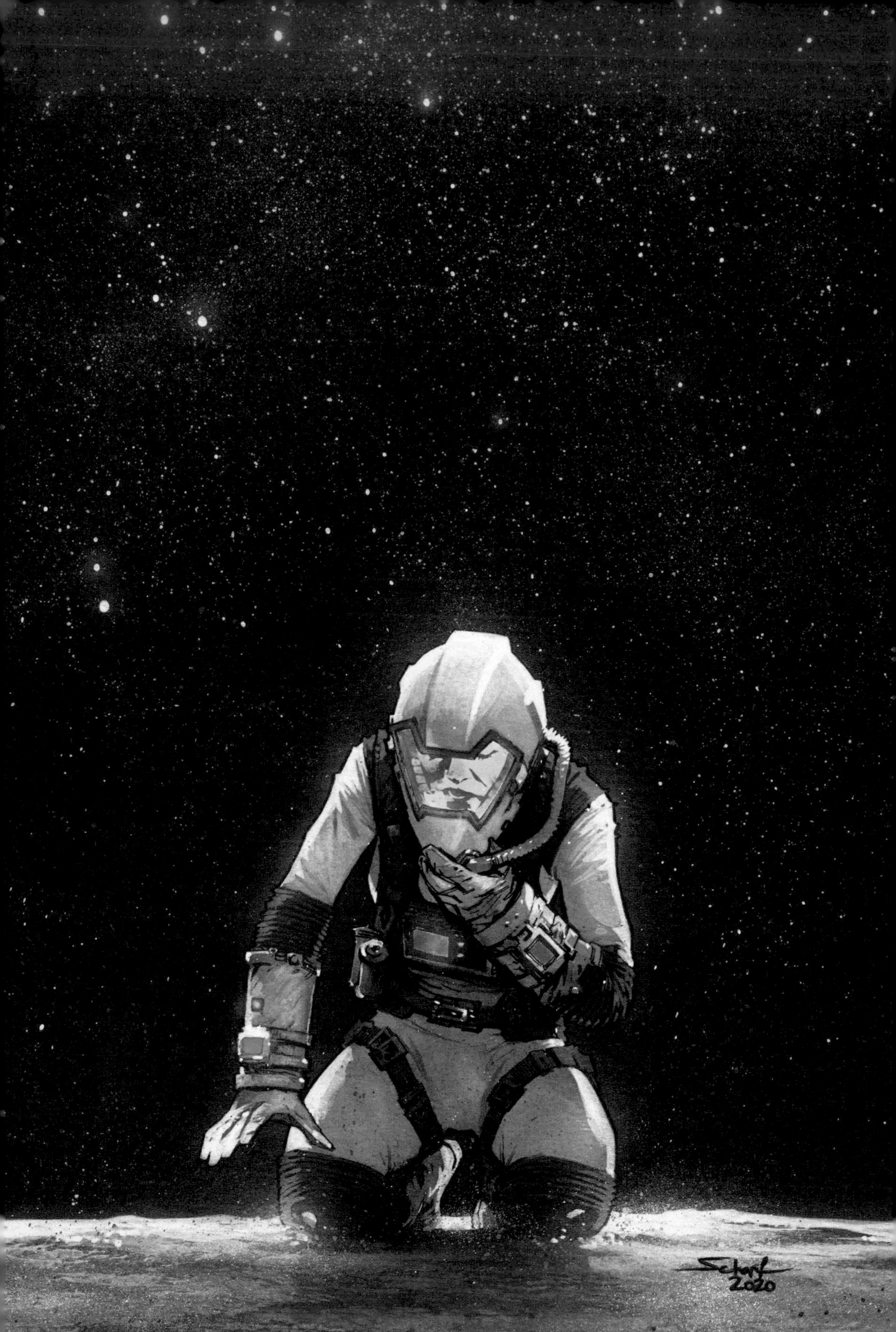
Scharf
2020

ISSUE TWO VARIANT COVER BY **JONAS SCHARF**

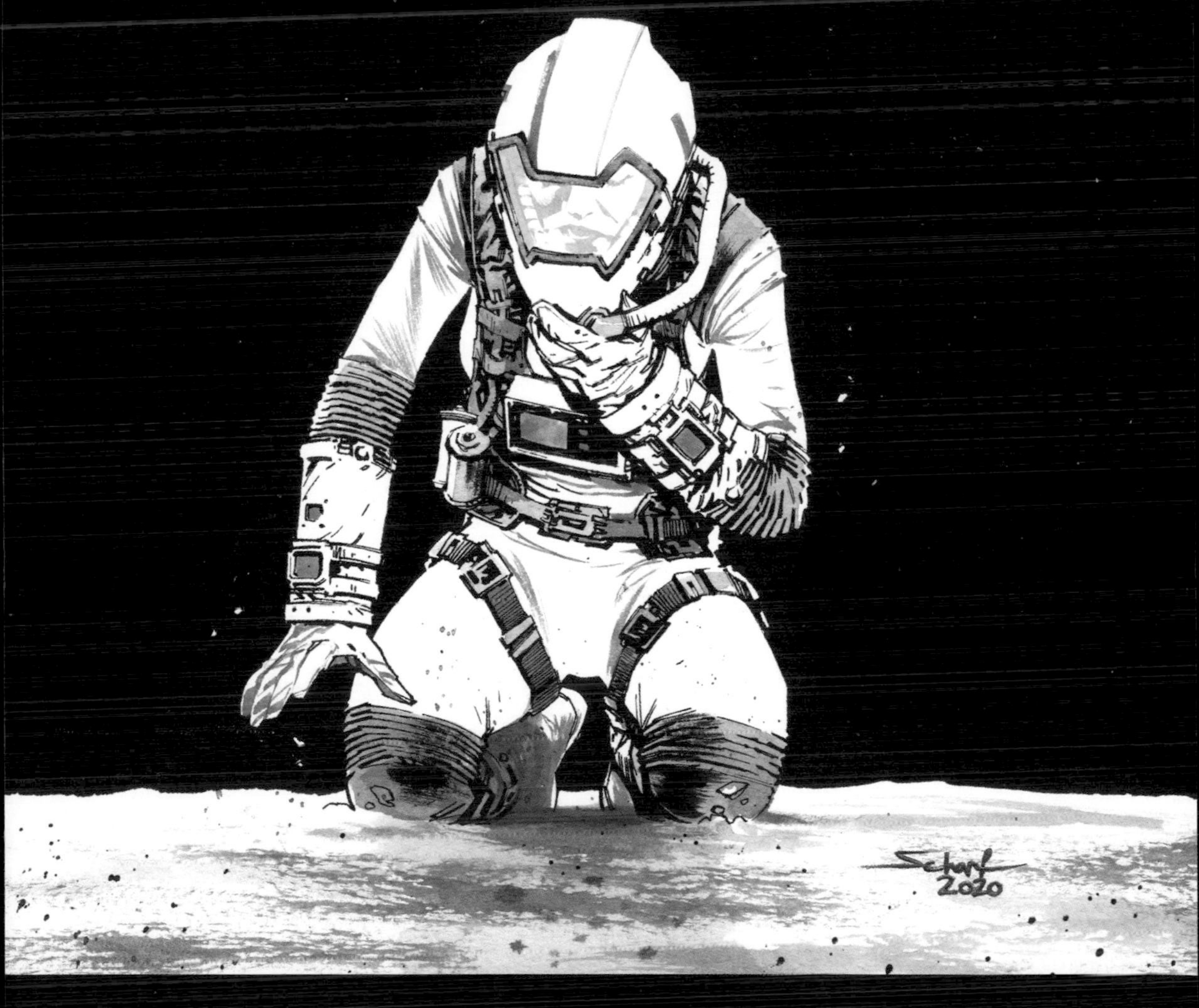
Scharf
2020

ISSUE TWO VARIANT COVER BY **JONAS SCHARF**

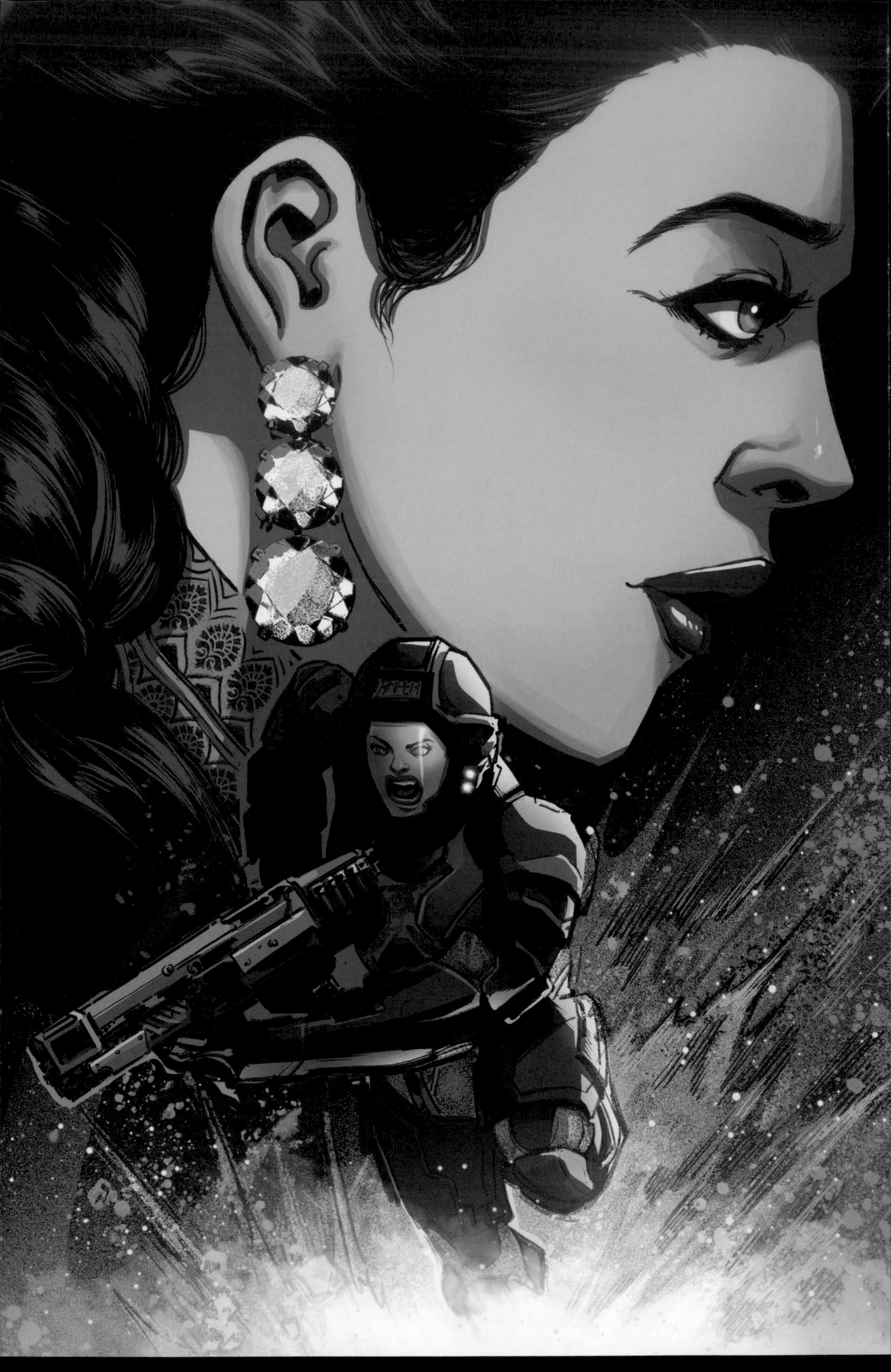

ISSUE THREE VARIANT COVER BY **PRISCILLA PETRAITES** WITH COLORS BY **MARCO LESKO**

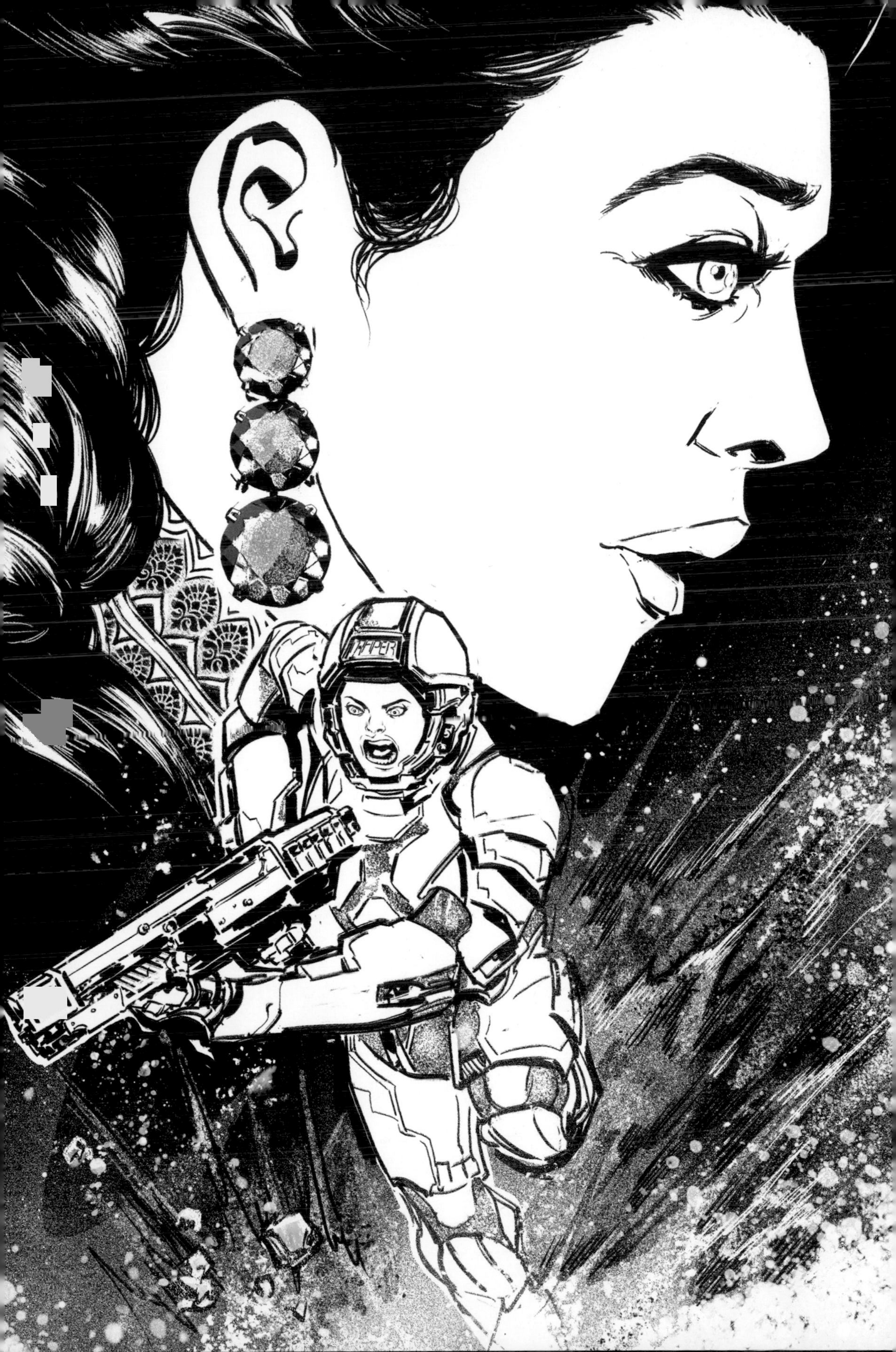

ISSUE THREE VARIANT COVER BY **PRISCILLA PETRAITES**

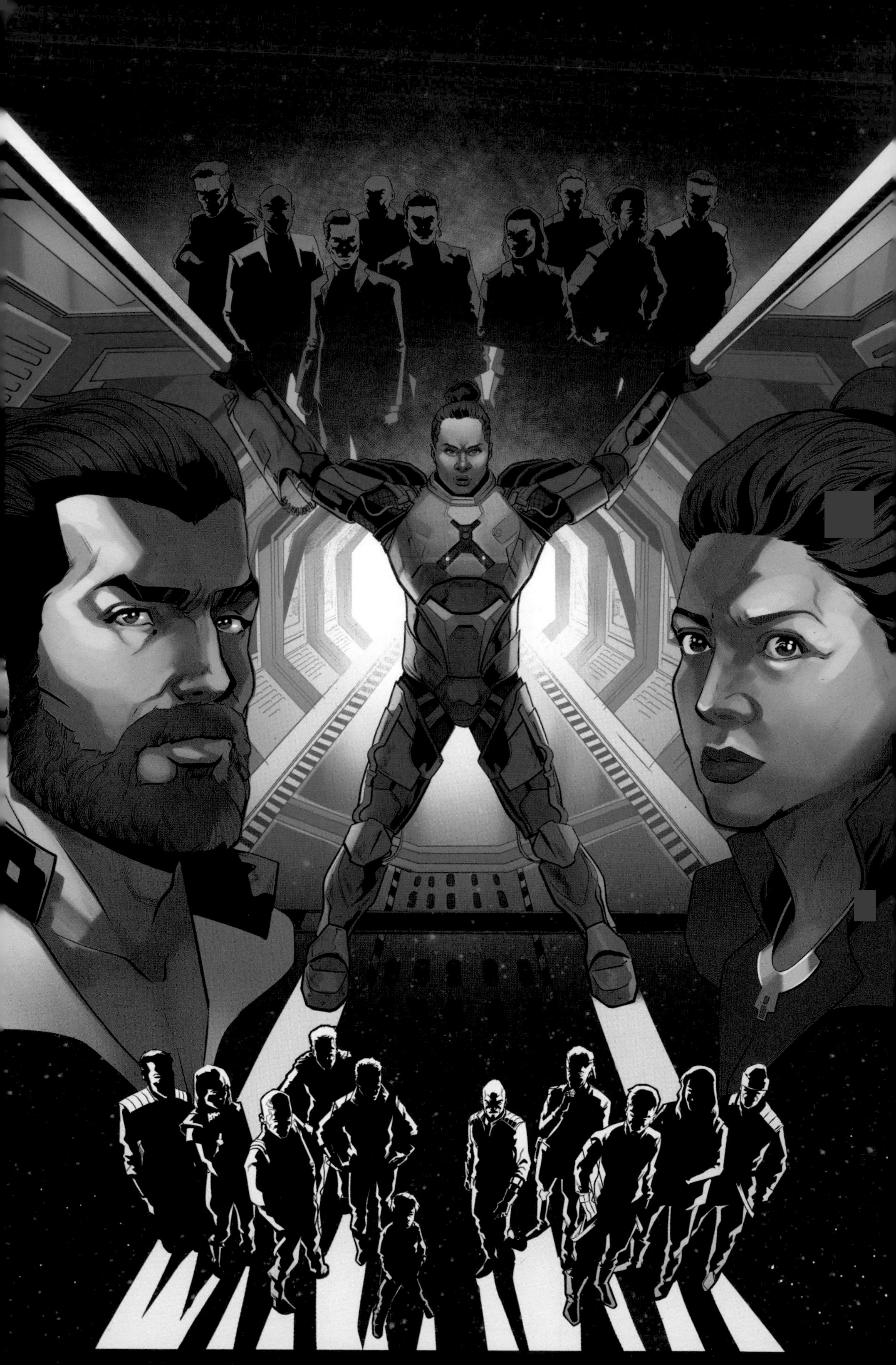

ISSUE FOUR VARIANT COVER BY **WILL SLINEY** WITH COLORS BY **TRIONA O'FARRELL**

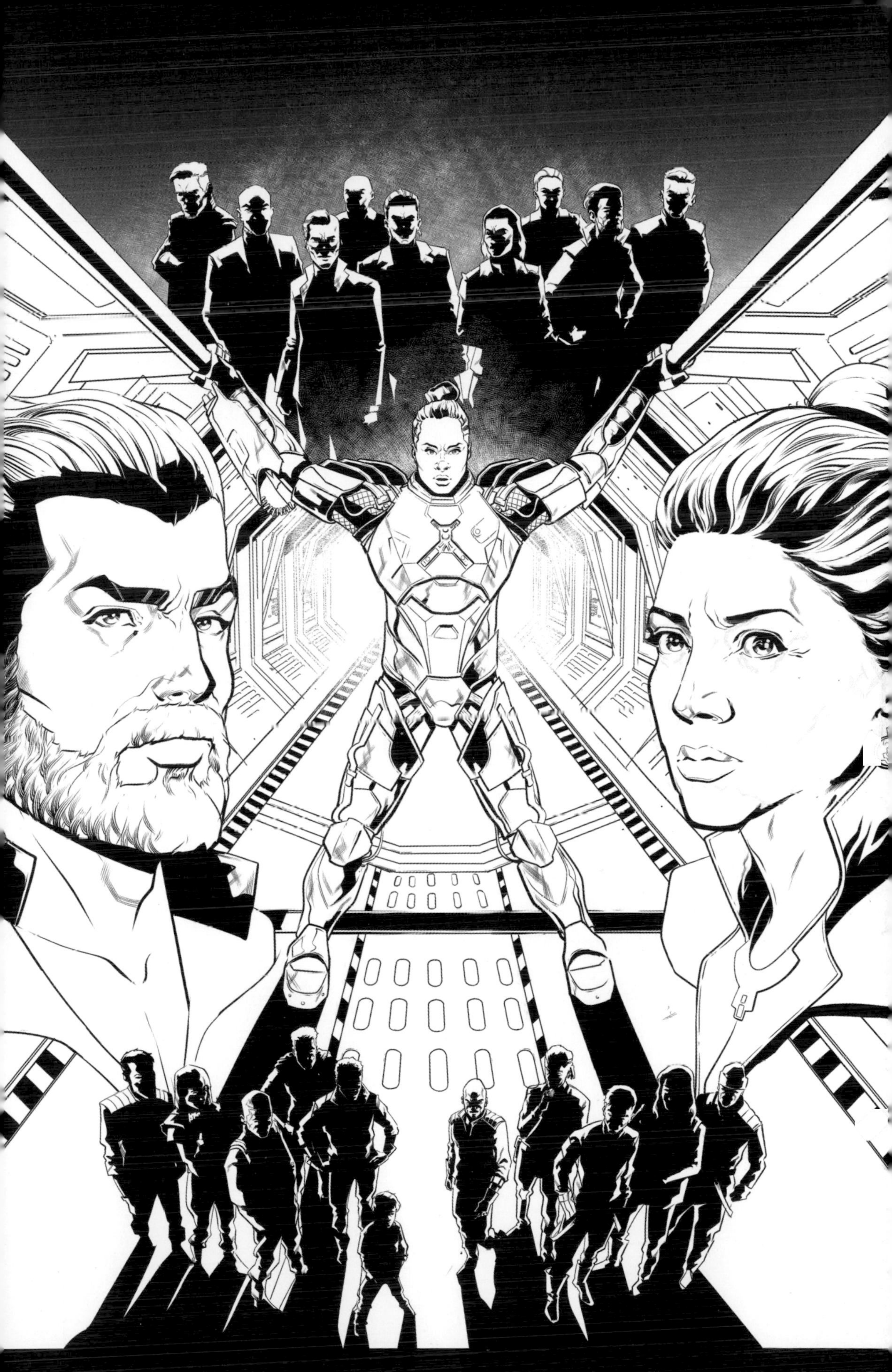

ISSUE FOUR VARIANT COVER BY **WILL SLINEY**

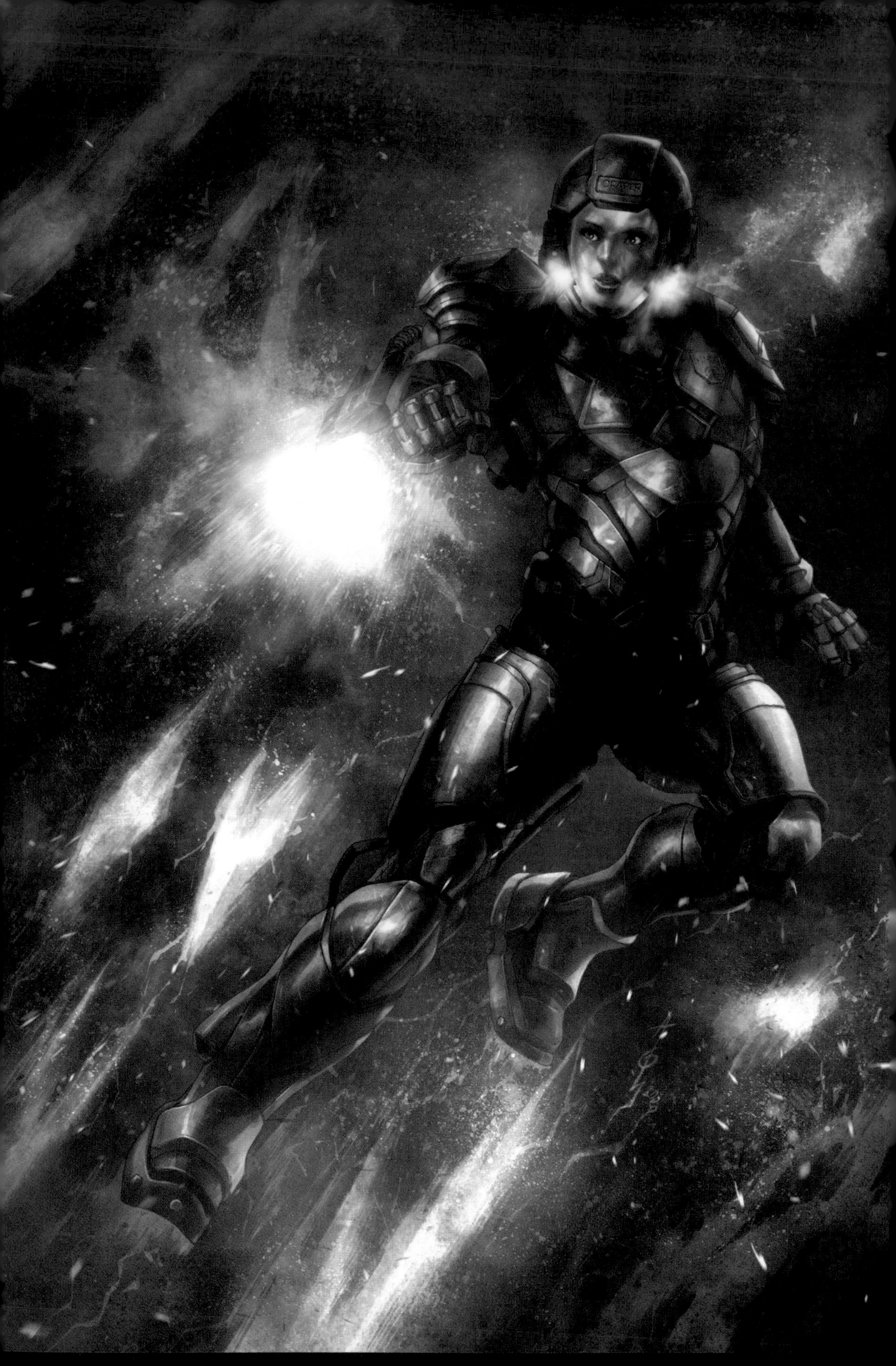

ISSUE ONE WICKED GATOR COMICS EXCLUSIVE VARIANT COVER BY **ALAN QUAH**

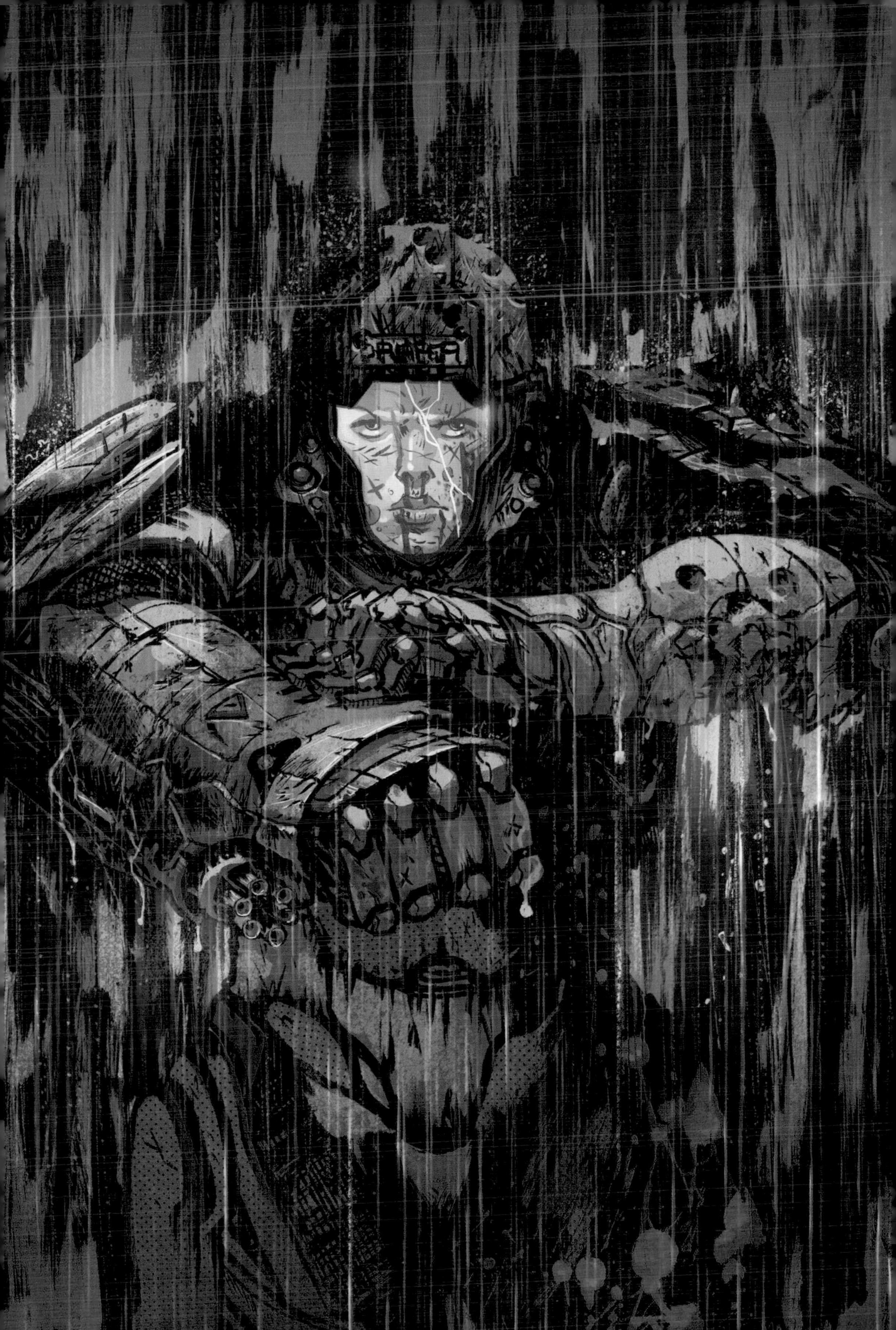

ISSUE ONE COVER ALPHA EXCLUSIVE VARIANT COVER BY
DANIEL WARREN JOHNSON WITH COLORS BY **MIKE SPICER**

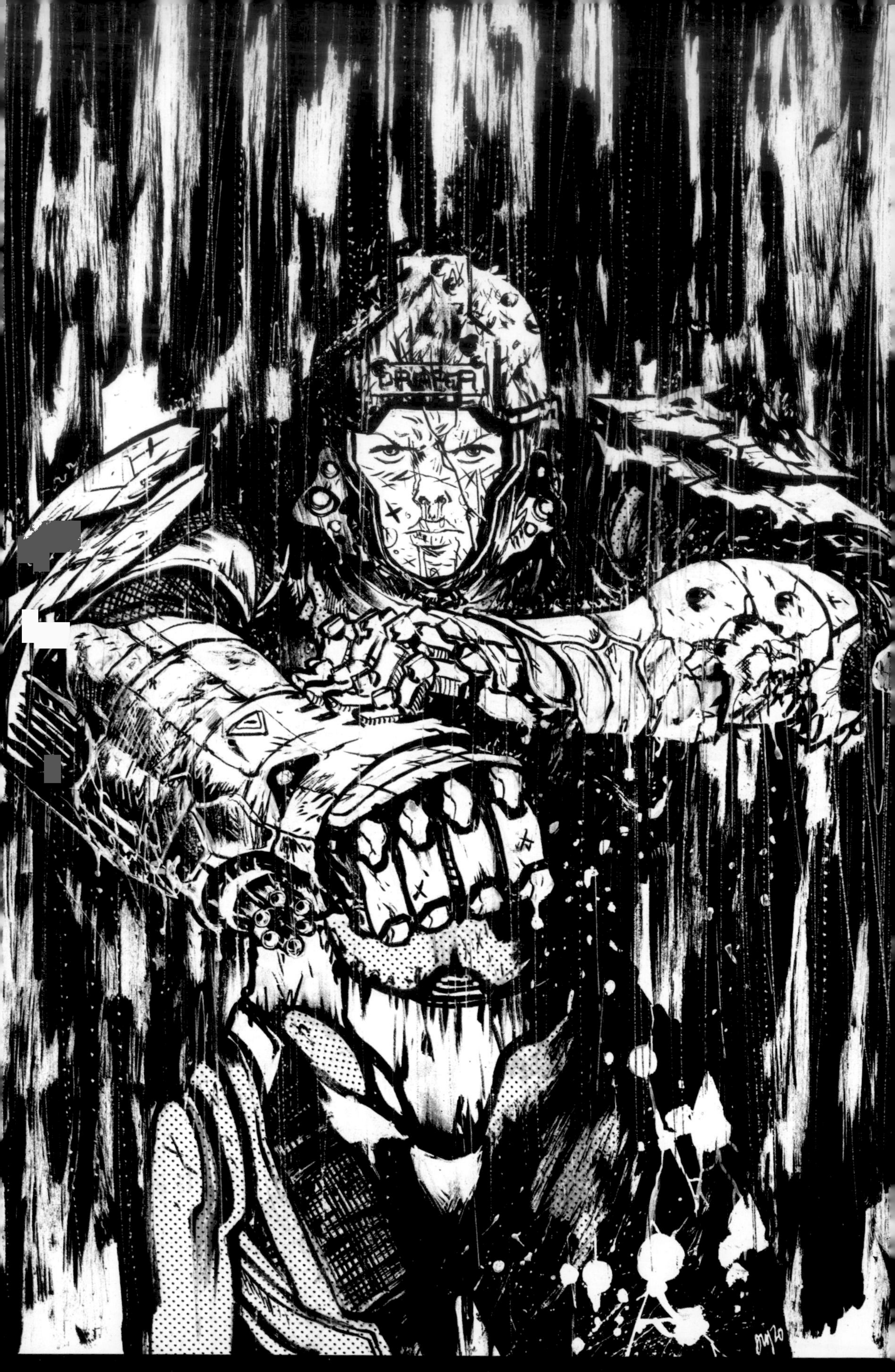

ISSUE ONE COVER ALPHA EXCLUSIVE VARIANT COVER BY **DANIEL WARREN JOHNSON**

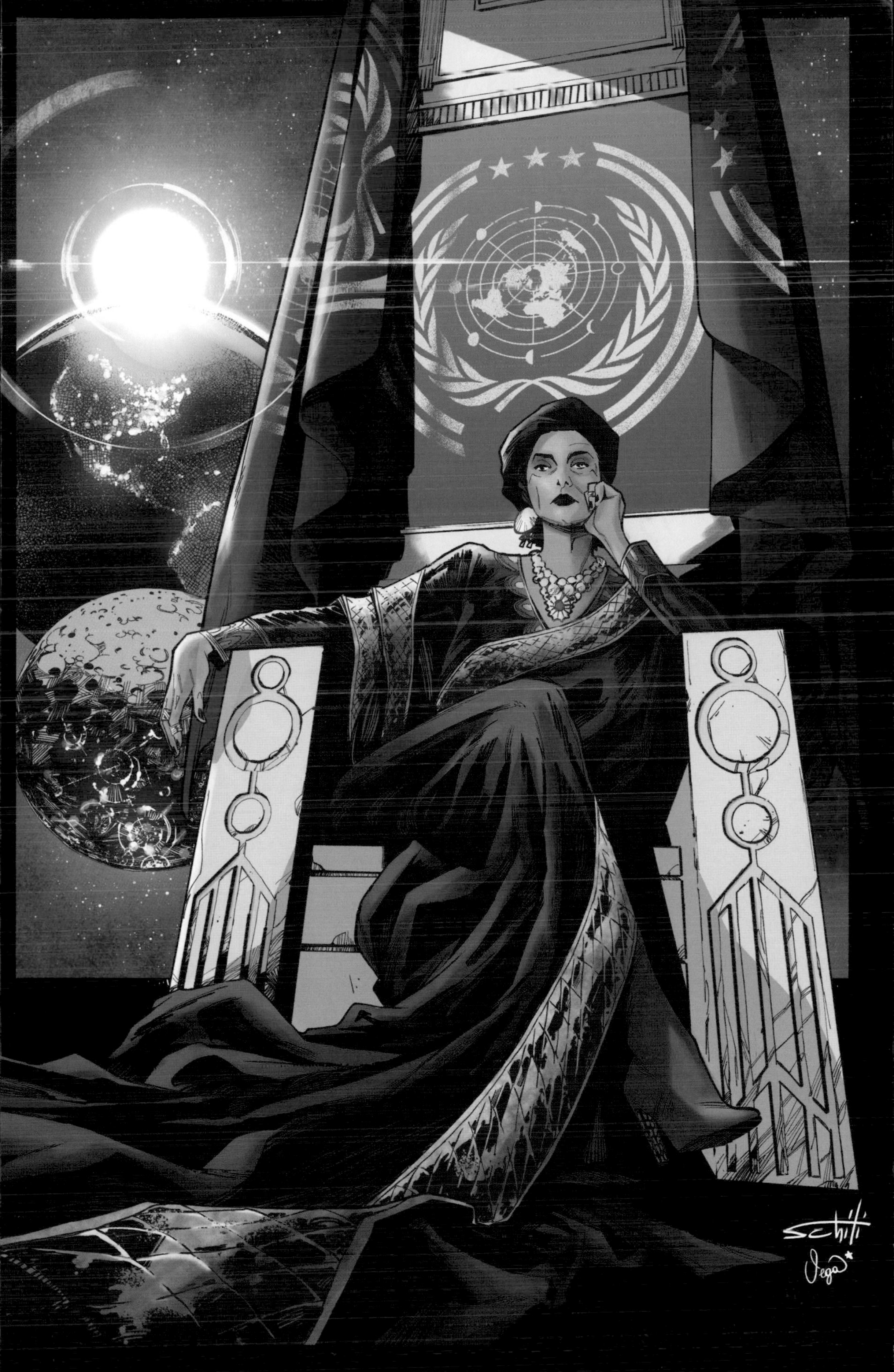
schiti
Vega

VARIANT COVER BY **VALERIO SCHITI** WITH COLORS BY **VEGA GUERRIERI**

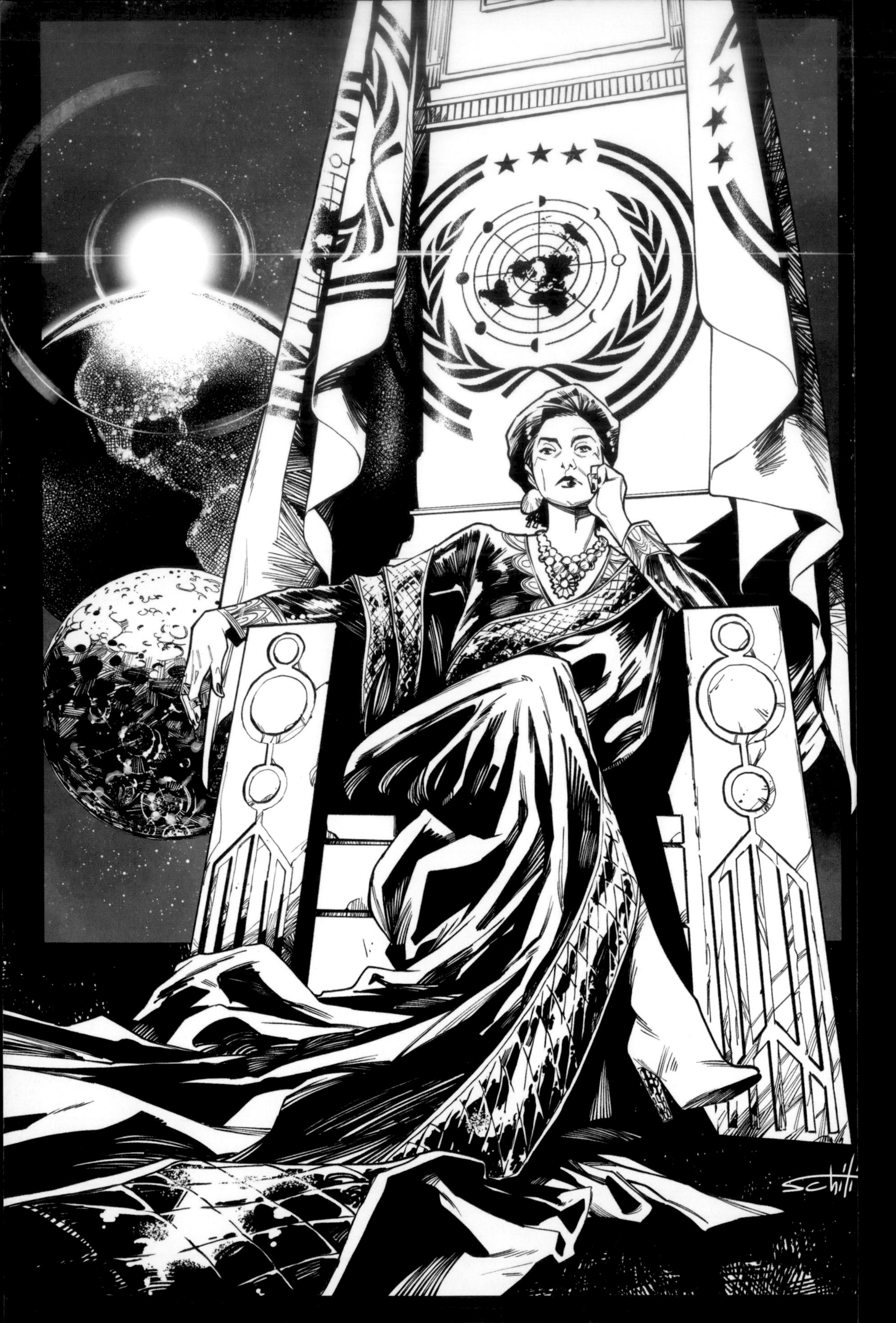
SCHITI

VARIANT COVER BY **VALERIO SCHITI**

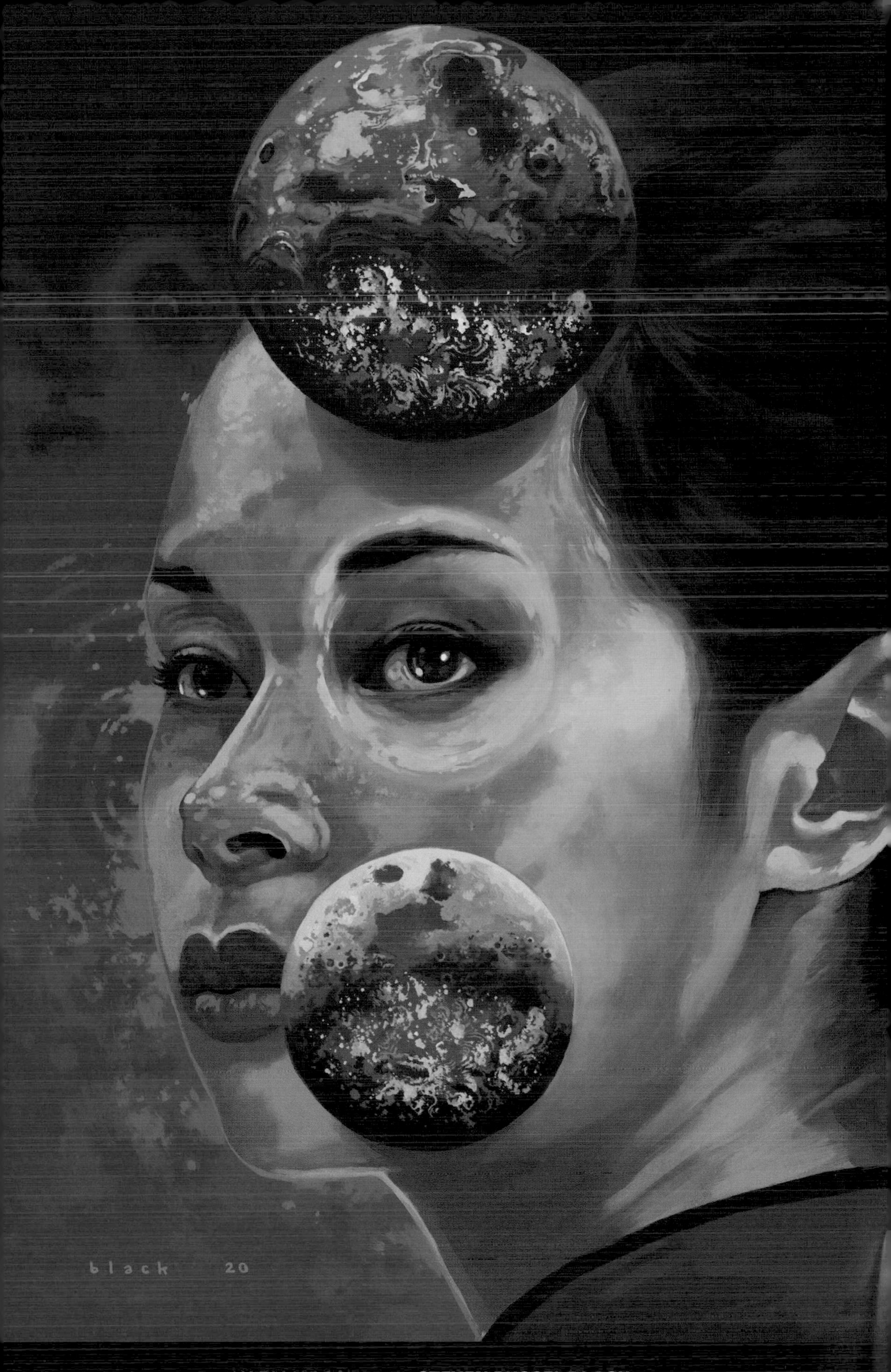
black 20

VARIANT COVER BY **STEVEN RUSSEL BLACK**

SCRIPT TO PAGE: ISSUE 3, PAGE 13

PANEL 1: Bobbie and Kal are entering a large hangar now, where a gleaming ship sits with workers swarming over it. It does indeed look very sleek and state-of-the-art. This is not a huge ship, just big enough to carry some cargo and a few passengers. Fewer than you would think, really.

        KAL: This is just a small transport ship, to get people and supplies to the much bigger ship we have in orbit.

        KAL: We've been making runs all week, getting ready. You wouldn't believe the logistics. Especially since we're recruiting all over the system.

PANEL 2: Closer on Kal and Bobbie now. Kal has become serious.

        KAL: You could be on the next run, if you wanted. It leaves day after tomorrow.

        KAL: Or, and I don't say this lightly, you could leave with me, after the contracts are all signed.

        KAL: There are certain advantages to traveling with someone who has my connections.

PANEL 3: Kal leads Bobbie deeper into the hanger now, so that we see more of the ship. The space is a bit truncated, with the ship sitting very close to the front but still almost touching the wall at the back, nearly filling the space front to back but not side to side.

ISSUE 3, PAGE 13

PANEL 3: There's a tall window cut into one wall of the hangar, letting in natural light and showing a very industrial section of Mars, but we're not focused on this right now. Instead Kal is pointing to the ship.

> KAL: But, let me show you around!
>
> BOBBIE: This is a strange space. Most of the hangars in this section are larger. I've never seen one this size. Is this the biggest ship you have?
>
> KAL: Not even close. But even deep pockets have to be cost-conscious about some things these days. Why rent space you don't need?

PANEL 4: Kal and Bobbie stand at the window now, looking out. Kal gestures to the landscape. If appropriate, maybe we can include one of the terraforming complexes in the distance, lying fallow.

> KAL: Face it, Bobbie. Mars had its day.
>
> KAL: Humanity just isn't built for this kind of life. It's exhausting to work so hard just so your great-grand-children might have a better life.

PANEL 5: Kal turns to face Bobbie now, earnest as possible, but Bobbie is looking down at her hand terminal. She is rapidly moves away from him, her body between him and what she's looking at in her hand.

> KAL: Don't you want a better life right now, Bobbie?
>
> BOBBIE: Hold that thought, Kal.
>
> BOBBIE: I've got to listen to this.

DISCOVER
VISIONARY CREATORS

Once & Future
Kieron Gillen, Dan Mora
Volume 1
ISBN: 978-1-68415-491-3 | $16.99 US

Something is Killing the Children
James Tynion IV, Werther Dell'Edera
Volume 1
ISBN: 978-1-68415-558-3 | $14.99 US

Faithless
Brian Azzarello, Maria Llovet
ISBN: 978-1-68415-432-6 | $17.99 US

Klaus
Grant Morrison, Dan Mora
Klaus: How Santa Claus Began SC
ISBN: 978-1-68415-393-0 | $15.99 US
Klaus: The New Adventures of Santa Claus HC
ISBN: 978-1-68415-666-5 | $17.99 US

Coda
Simon Spurrier, Matias Bergara
Volume 1
ISBN: 978-1-68415-321-3 | $14.99 US
Volume 2
ISBN: 978-1-68415-369-5 | $14.99 US
Volume 3
ISBN: 978-1-68415-429-6 | $14.99 US

Grass Kings
Matt Kindt, Tyler Jenkins
Volume 1
ISBN: 978-1-64144-362-3 | $17.99 US
Volume 2
ISBN: 978-1-64144-557-3 | $17.99 US
Volume 3
ISBN: 978-1-64144-650-1 | $17.99 US

Bone Parish
Cullen Bunn, Jonas Scharf
Volume 1
ISBN: 978-1-64144-337-1 | $14.99 US
Volume 2
ISBN: 978-1-64144-542-9 | $14.99 US
Volume 3
ISBN: 978-1-64144-543-6 | $14.99 US

Ronin Island
Greg Pak, Giannis Milonogiannis
Volume 1
ISBN: 978-1-64144-576-4 | $14.99 US
Volume 2
ISBN: 978-1-64144-723-2 | $14.99 US
Volume 3
ISBN: 978-1-64668-035-1 | $14.99 US

Victor LaValle's Destroyer
Victor LaValle, Dietrich Smith
ISBN: 978-1-61398-732-2 | $19.99 US